Praise for *Doing the Best I Can*

"This book smashes the stereotype of poor dads as the 'hit and run' or 'deadbeat' men who care only about casual sex and have no interest in the resulting kids. It is also unflinchingly honest about the sometimes egregious behavior of the men. Its poignant narratives and astute analysis make it *the* book to read on poor fathers."
—Paula England, New York University

"I am confident that this book will instantly become the leading source of information on the nature of unwed fatherhood today. It shows a new path of intimate life for unwed young men, suggesting that marriage is no longer central in low-income young adults' intimate partnerships. It is an eye-opener, a detailed portrait we have not seen before."
—Andrew Cherlin, Johns Hopkins University

DOING THE BEST I CAN

# DOING THE BEST I CAN

## FATHERHOOD IN THE INNER CITY

KATHRYN EDIN AND
TIMOTHY J. NELSON

**UNIVERSITY OF CALIFORNIA PRESS**

BERKELEY   LOS ANGELES   LONDON

University of California Press, one of the most
distinguished university presses in the United States,
enriches lives around the world by advancing
scholarship in the humanities, social sciences, and
natural sciences. Its activities are supported by the
UC Press Foundation and by philanthropic contributions
from individuals and institutions. For more information,
visit www.ucpress.edu.

University of California Press
Berkeley and Los Angeles, California

University of California Press, Ltd.
London, England

Portions of chapter 3 were first published in Kathryn
Edin, Timothy Nelson, and Joanna Miranda Reed,
"Daddy, Baby; Momma Maybe: Low-Income Urban
Fathers and the 'Package Deal' of Family Life," in *Social
Class and Changing Families in an Unequal America,* edited by
Paula England and Marcia Carlson (Palo Alto: Stanford
University Press, 2011), 85–107.

Library of Congress Cataloging-in-Publication Data

Edin, Kathryn, 1962–
  Doing the best I can : fatherhood in the inner city /
Kathryn Edin and Timothy J. Nelson.
       p.  cm.
  Includes bibliographical references and index.
  ISBN 978-0-520-27406-8 (cloth : alk. paper)
    1. Unmarried fathers—United States.   2. Single
fathers—United States.   3. Fatherhood—United
States.   4. Poor children—United States.   I. Nelson,
Timothy Jon.   II. Title.
  HV700.7.E35  2013
  362.82'940973—dc23                    2012030147

Manufactured in the United States of America

21  20  19  18  17  16  15  14  13
10  9  8  7  6  5  4  3  2  1

The paper used in this publication meets the
minimum requirements of ANSI/NISO Z39.48–1992 (R 2002)
(*Permanence of Paper*).

TO LAURA LEIN AND LINDA MELLGREN,
WHO INSPIRED THIS WORK, AND TO THE
110 MEN WHO SHARED THEIR STORIES

# CONTENTS

# ACKNOWLEDGMENTS

*Doing the Best I Can* is a deeply collaborative work; though the authors' names appear in alphabetical order, Edin and Nelson contributed equally to the project. After the years of data collection in Camden and Philadelphia, we spent hundreds of hours discussing the research and our findings, trading chapters and paragraphs so frequently that it is now impossible to determine who wrote what sentence of the book. Favorite writing venues included Peet's Coffee in Evanston, Infusion in Philadelphia, Lord Tyler's House and the Fells Grind in Baltimore, and especially the coffee shops along Second Minjiang Road, Qingdao, China.

This research was funded by the William T. Grant Foundation, which not only covered the research costs but also paid the rent on a small apartment in the Rosedale section of Camden, NJ, so we could live there part-time. Additional funding came from the Institute for Policy Research at Northwestern University.

Andrew Cherlin, Stefanie DeLuca, and Paula England read multiple drafts of this manuscript and offered many valuable suggestions and insights. Monica Bell, Matthew Desmond, Jamie Fader, Sarah Halpern-Meekin, Barbara Kiviat, James Quane, Laura Tach, Kristin Turney, Julie Wilson, Holly Wood, and an anonymous reviewer also offered comments, pointed out errors, and sharpened our thinking. Early versions of this work benefited from the feedback from members of the MacArthur Network on the Family and the Economy: Jeanne Brooks-Gunn, Lindsay Chase-Lansdale, Cecilia Contrad, Paula England, Nancy Folbre, Irwin Garfinkel, Sara McLanahan, Ronald Mincy, Robert Pollak, Timothy Smeeding, and Robert Willis. Lisa Adams, our agent, and Naomi Schneider, our editor, offered vital assistance and a wealth of practical advice. Responsibility for errors and oversights, however, is our own.

Amy Abraham, Antwi Akom, Susan Clampet-Lundquist, Rebecca Kissane, David Mitchell, Jennifer Morgan, Shelley Shannon, Eric Shaw, and Kimberly Torres assisted in data collection. Jennifer Augustine, Steve Augustine, Susan Clampet-Lundquist, Heidi Hiemstra, Kathryn Linnenberg, Rechelle Paranel, and Verity Sandell coded the data.

In Camden Sam Apple, Jodina Hicks, Bruce Main, Mary Ann Merion, Jay Rosen, and Shelley Shannon helped us to learn about the city and its history. Shelley and Jay were also our landlords, providing the small apartment on the first floor of their Camden home.

Drew and Leah Hood spent several weeks photographing the fathers and children who appear on the cover and insert photos. Due to confidentiality concerns, those portrayed in the photographs are not in the study, though all live in neighborhoods where we conducted our fieldwork.

# Introduction

"It is unmarried fathers who are missing in record numbers, who impregnate women and selfishly flee," raged conservative former U.S. secretary of education William Bennett in his 2001 book, *The Broken Hearth*. "And it is these absent men, above all, who deserve our censure and disesteem. Abandoning alike those who they have taken as sexual partners, and whose lives they have created, they strike at the heart of the marital ideal, traduce generations yet to come, and disgrace their very manhood."[1] "No longer is a boy considered an embarrassment if he tries to run away from being the father of the unmarried child," Bill Cosby declared in 2004 at the NAACP's gala commemorating the fiftieth anniversary of *Brown versus Board of Education,* as he publicly indicted unwed fathers for merely "inserting the sperm cell" while blithely eschewing the responsibilities of fatherhood.[2] Then, in 2007, two days before Father's Day, presidential candidate Barack Obama admonished the congregants of Mount Moriah Baptist Church in Spartanburg, South Carolina, saying, "There are a lot of men out there who need to stop acting like boys, who need to realize that responsibility does not end at conception, who need to know that what makes you a man is not the ability to have a child but the courage to raise one."[3]

Across the political spectrum, from Bennett to Obama, unwed fatherhood is denounced as one of the leading social problems of our day. These men are irresponsible, so the story goes. They hit and then run—run away, selfishly flee, act like boys rather than men. According to these portrayals, such men are interested in sex, not fatherhood. When their female conquests come up pregnant, they quickly flee the scene, leaving the expectant mother holding the diaper bag. Unwed fathers, you see, simply don't care.[4]

About a decade before we began our exploration of the topic, the archetype of this "hit and run" unwed father made a dramatic media debut straight from the devastated streets of Newark, New Jersey, in a 1986 CBS Special Report, *The Vanishing Family: Crisis in Black America*. The program's host, Great Society liberal Bill Moyers, promised viewers a vivid glimpse into the lives of the real people behind the ever-mounting statistics chronicling family breakdown.

But by far the most sensational aspect of the documentary—the segment referenced by almost every review, editorial, and commentary following the broadcast—was the footage of Timothy McSeed. As the camera zooms in on McSeed and Moyers on a Newark street corner, the voiceover reveals that McSeed has fathered six children by four different women. "I got strong sperm," he says, grinning into the camera. When Moyers asks why he doesn't use condoms, he scoffs, "Girls don't like them things." Yet Timothy says he doesn't worry about any pregnancies that might result. "If a girl, you know, she's having a baby, carryin' a baby, that's on her, you know? I'm not going to stop my pleasures." Moyers then takes us back several weeks to the moment when Alice Johnson delivers Timothy's sixth child. McSeed dances around the delivery room with glee, fists raised in the air like a victorious prizefighter. "I'm the king!" he shouts repeatedly. Later, Timothy blithely admits to Moyers that he doesn't support any of his children. When pressed on this point, he shrugs, grins, and offers up the show's most quoted line: "Well, the majority of the mothers are on welfare, [so] what I'm not doing the government does."

The impact of *The Vanishing Family* was immediate and powerful, creating an almost instantaneous buzz in the editorial columns of leading newspapers.[5] In the week after the broadcast, CBS News received hundreds of requests for tapes of the show, including three from U.S. senators. The California public schools created a logjam when they tried to order a copy for each of the 7,500 schools in their system. "It is the largest demand for a CBS News product we've ever had," marveled senior vice president David Fuchs.[6]

The response to Timothy McSeed was particularly intense and visceral. An editorialist in the *Washington Post* could barely contain his outrage, writing, "One man Moyers talked to had six children by four different women. He recited his accomplishments with a grin you wanted to smash a fist into."[7] William Raspberry's brother-in-law wrote the noted columnist that the day after viewing the program, he drove past a young black couple and found himself reacting with violent emotion. "I was looking at a problem, a threat, a catastrophe, a disease. Suspicion, disgust and contempt welled up within me."[8] But it was George Will who reached the heights of outraged rhetoric in his syndicated column, declaring that "the Timothies are more of a menace to black progress than the Bull Connors ever were."[9]

*The Vanishing Family* went on to win every major award in journalism.[10] Those commenting publicly on the broadcast were nearly unanimous in their ready acceptance of Timothy as the archetype of unmarried fatherhood. Congressional action soon followed: in May 1986 Senator Bill Bradley proposed the famous Bradley Amendment, the first of several of "deadbeat dad" laws aimed at tightening the screws on unwed fathers who fell behind on their child support, even if nonpayment was due to unemployment or incarceration. Only a lone correspondent from Canada's *Globe and Mail* offered a rebuttal, fuming that Timothy "could have been cast by the Ku Klux Klan: you couldn't find a black American more perfectly calculated to arouse loathing, contempt and fear."[11]

Bill Moyers's interest in the black family was not new. In 1965, two decades before *The Vanishing Family* was first broadcast, Daniel Patrick

Moynihan, then assistant secretary of labor for President Lyndon Johnson, penned the now-infamous report titled *The Negro Family: The Case for National Action*. Moynihan claimed that due to the sharp increase in out-of-wedlock childbearing—a condition affecting only a small fraction of white children but one in five African Americans at the time—the black family, particularly in America's inner cities, was nearing what he called "complete breakdown."[12] Moynihan was labeled a racist for his views, and Moyers, then an assistant press secretary to the president, helped manage the controversy.

Moynihan drew his data from the early 1960s, when America stood on the threshold of seismic social change. At the dawn of that decade, in February, four young African Americans refused to leave a segregated lunch counter in Greensboro, North Carolina, an action soon emulated across the South. In March the Eisenhower administration announced that 3,500 U.S. troops would be sent to a country called Vietnam. In May the public approved the first oral contraceptive for use. And in November an Irish Catholic was narrowly elected to the White House. Yet across the nation as a whole, nine in ten American children still went to bed each night in the same household as their biological father; black children were the outliers, as one in four lived without benefit of their father's presence at home.[13]

Now, a half century after the Moynihan report was written, and two-and-a-half decades since Moyer's award-winning broadcast, nearly three in ten American children live apart from their fathers. Divorce played a significant role in boosting these rates in the 1960s and 1970s, but by the mid-1980s, when Timothy McSeed shocked the nation, the change was being driven solely by increases in unwed parenthood. About four in every ten (41 percent) American children in 2008 were born outside of marriage, and, like Timothy's six children, they are disproportionately minority and poor. A higher portion of white fathers give birth outside of marriage (29 percent) than black fathers did in Moynihan's time, but rates among blacks and Hispanics have also grown dramatically—to 56 and 73 percent respectively.[14] And the gap between unskilled Americans and the educated elite is especially wide. Here, the statistics are stunning: only about 6 percent of college-educated mothers' births are nonmarital versus 60 percent of those of high school dropouts.[15]

In the wake of this dramatic increase in so-called fatherless families, public outrage has grown and policy makers have responded. In the 1960s and 1970s liberals worked to help supplement the incomes of single mothers, who were disproportionately poor, while conservatives balked, believing this would only reward those who put motherhood before marriage and would thus lead to more such families. Meanwhile, surly taxpayers increasingly demanded answers as to why their hard-earned dollars were going to support what many saw as an immoral lifestyle choice and not an unavoidable hardship. This taxpayer sentiment fueled Ronald Reagan's efforts to sharply curtail welfare benefits in the 1980s and prompted Bill Clinton's promise to "end welfare as we know it," which he fulfilled in 1996.

Meanwhile, scholars have responded to the trend by devoting a huge amount of attention to studying single-parent families, detailing the struggles of the parents and documenting the deleterious effects on the children. These studies have offered the American public a wealth of knowledge about the lives of the mothers and their progeny, yet they have told us next to nothing about the fathers of these children.[16] Part of the problem is that most surveys have provided very little systematic information from which to draw any kind of representative picture.[17] Unwed fathers' often-tenuous connections to households make them hard to find, and many refuse to admit to survey researchers that they have fathered children. Thus, vast numbers have been invisible to even the largest, most carefully conducted studies.[18]

The conventional wisdom spun by pundits and public intellectuals across the political spectrum blames the significant difficulties that so many children born to unwed parents face—poor performance in school, teen pregnancy and low school-completion rates, criminal behavior, and difficulty securing a steady job—on their fathers' failure to care. The question that first prompted our multiyear exploration into the lives of inner-city, unmarried fathers is whether this is, in fact, the case.

## CAMDEN AND THE PHILADELPHIA METROPOLITAN AREA

In the following chapters we go beyond the stereotyped portrayals of men like Timothy McSeed and delve deep into the lives of 110 white and black inner-city fathers. Each of the fathers whose stories we tell also hails from the urban core—in our case, Camden, New Jersey, and its sister city across the Delaware River, Philadelphia. Like McSeed's Newark, these cities have some of the highest rates of nonmarital childbearing in the country. Roughly six in ten children in Philadelphia and an even greater percentage in Camden—nearly three out of four—are now born outside of marriage.

We argue that to truly comprehend unmarried fatherhood, it is not sufficient to focus on the men alone. Understanding their environments—the neighborhood contexts and the histories of the urban areas they are embedded in—is also essential. The streets of Camden and Philadelphia are such a critical part of the story, so we begin with a description of the neighborhoods we lived and worked in to gather the stories of the fathers whose lives we chronicle. At the outset of our study, we loaded a Ryder truck and moved into the Rosedale neighborhood of East Camden.[19] We were to take up part-time residence in a tiny apartment carved from the first floor of a clapboard Victorian-era home on Thirty-Sixth Street near Westfield Avenue.

The two-room apartment became our headquarters that first sweltering summer as we tried to figure out how to approach the men we were interested in talking to and convince them to trust us. The fenced-in backyard behind the house, equipped with a deck, plastic lawn chairs, and a picnic table beneath a large oak tree, served as the location for many of our initial conversations during the gradually cooling evening hours, our dialogue accompanied by the buzz of the fluorescent back-porch light and the occasional siren or thumping bass from a passing car. This intensive fieldwork, living daily life among the families of the men we interviewed while raising our own children there, shaped our initial ideas and forged the set of questions we eventually posed to fathers across Camden and Philadelphia.

Our goal was to build relationships with unmarried fathers and engage them in a series of conversations, thereby gaining an in-depth knowledge of their experiences and worldviews. We began with two years of ethnographic fieldwork—hundreds of hours of observation and casual conversation—in Camden, followed by five years of repeated, in-depth interviewing across Camden and a number of Philadelphia neighborhoods. As we were writing this book, we visited each of these neighborhoods multiple times to collect supplementary information. We drew fathers from across Camden, from Greater Kensington (including Kensington, West Kensington, and Fishtown), Port Richmond, Fairhill, Harrogate, North Central, Strawberry Mansion, Nicetown, and Hunting Park—all north of Center City Philadelphia; from the Pennsport, Whitman, Grays Ferry, and Point Breeze sections of South Philadelphia; and from Elmwood Park, Mantua, Mill Creek, and Kingsessing in West Philadelphia (see table 1 and map 1 in the appendix).

East Camden, where our study began, has the mix of housing typical of the Philadelphia metropolitan area. Row homes are the most common dwelling type, usually plain brick affairs. Twins come next—each side often in a different state of repair, with occupants seemingly eager to distinguish their side from its mirror image with different trim colors, distinctive siding, and layers of gingerbread. Here and there, only one-half of the twin now stands, creating an eerie asymmetrical look. Then there are the singles, most built in a simple Victorian-farmhouse style, but some in stone with pillars bracing roofs that reach over deep porches.

When we arrive in early summer, everything is in bloom—sprawling hydrangeas, climbing roses, lush crepe myrtle. In the deep backyards there are several aging aboveground pools, though few seem to be in use—one is totally covered with dead branches. To compensate, parents place plastic kiddie pools in their yards. But perhaps the most noticeable thing about the relatively quiet side streets for the newcomer is the trash—it lines curbs and sidewalks everywhere. We'll soon observe how the city's sanitary engineers seem to show their contempt for the neighborhood by ensuring that only a portion of the garbage they collect actually finds its way into the back of their trucks.

Homeowners ward off the neighborhood squalor by encasing every square inch of their property with chain-link fencing, sometimes adding the green plastic fill that creates a greater sense of privacy. Secure in these compounds, the more affluent residents—civil servants and immigrants running small businesses—tune out the neighborhood that surrounds them and focus instead on their little pieces of heaven. Cars usually park inside the fenced perimeters, not on the street. Few homes have garages, but many have freestanding metal carports with arched roofs, often listing to one side or another. Inside these dubious structures, we spot church vans for a dozen congregations, the trucks of food vendors, cement trucks, junk cars, and the like. One morning we see evidence of an informal restaurant alongside such a structure, with dozens of small tables in the backyard. In the driveway two black men wrestle a small cement mixer into the back of a truck ready for a day's labor. Later, they'll presumably drink beer and cook ribs for their patrons on huge half barrels serving as grills.

By the time we arrive in Rosedale, this once-desirable residential section of the industrial town has mostly lost the struggle against poverty and crime. The oldest, largest, and most notorious of the city's nine housing projects, Westfield Acres, located on Westfield Avenue at Thirty-Second Street, looms over the neighborhood's main thoroughfare, though the housing authority is about to demolish its high-rise towers. Over the years the area has earned a certain reputation; the *Philadelphia Inquirer* won't deliver to the local convenience stores because the drivers are afraid to enter the neighborhood, we can't get a pizza delivered, and even the Maytag repairman won't come, as we learn when our washing machine breaks down.

Like many inner-city neighborhoods, Rosedale is in a war between the homeowners struggling for a slice of respectability and the tawdry row homes and public-housing tracts that provide shelter for some of the most disadvantaged families in the metropolitan area. The homeowners arm themselves against blight in any number of ways: disguising rotting clapboards with aluminum siding, replacing 1920s single-pane windows with new vinyl models, converting the front yard into a concrete pedestal for the family car, and so on. Porches typically come last on the list of pressing home improvements. Some are encased in wrought-iron cages—often quite decorative—for added security, but others are left undefended and sagging. On main avenues homeowners' battle against undesirable, and possibly dangerous, passersby intensifies—those first floor windows not fortified by wrought iron are sometimes simply boarded up, with drywall applied right over the opening on the inside.

East Camden, the section of the city where Rosedale lies, was almost exclusively white until the mid-1960s. By the time its first black residents began to appear in the early 1970s, at the tail end of the great migration of African Americans northward, the city and neighborhood were still places of promise and hope. Separated from the rest of the city by the Cooper River, East Camden was laid out in the late 1800s by developers to attract immigrants and rural dwellers with modest means. Yet some of the twins and singles were almost opulent, made not of red brick but of stone—the native mica-infused granite that made these structures literally sparkle in the sun. Evidence of that time exists even now, for if one steps off of Westfield Avenue onto Rosedale or Merrill or any of the numbered streets, some of these distinctive structures still stand. In this residential area bordering an agricultural zone, one was more likely to hear a rooster's crow than a factory's whistle a hundred years ago. Even now, the neighborhood families sometimes raise chickens, so it is not unusual to hear the crow of a rooster.

If one walked the length of Westfield Avenue in 1950, its golden age, there were literally hundreds of shops.[20] On the 2600 block alone, where the avenue began, one could while away a Saturday afternoon browsing the Father & Son Shoe Store, Walen's Men's Wear, the Clover Children's Clothing Shop, Sun Shoe Repair, the Pastorfield Wallpaper Company, Jane Dale's Women's Furnishings, ABC Cleaners, the Sugar Bowl Confectioners, Devoe and Reynolds Artist's Materials, Westview Hardware, the New York Fashion Shop, Lester's 5&10 Cent Store and more. Most exciting for the neighborhood youth of the day was the lavish Argo Movie Theatre.

Fueling this heady prosperity was the mighty industry in North and South Camden. Originally a bucolic backwater in the shadow of its more powerful neighbor across the river, Camden became an industrial powerhouse in its own right by the late nineteenth century. By the end of the 1960s city leaders still believed Camden was on the upsurge. RCA Victor was the largest producer of phonographs and phonograph records for the first two-thirds of the twentieth century. New York Shipyards was the nation's largest shipbuilder during World War II, and the Campbell Corporation was the world leader in the production of canned vegetables and condensed soup. These three industrial giants, all founded in Camden roughly a century earlier, provided enough jobs for 75 percent of the manufacturing workforce. And while none of these firms had ever hired many African Americans, for more than a century black men had found their employment in their shadow, with jobs as teamsters, stevedores, and coopers that were contingent on the city's industrial economy.[21]

But just below the surface, signs of trouble were everywhere. A prime culprit was the residential trend toward suburbanization that had so many American cities in its grip. Camden's population had peaked at 125,000 in 1950 but was down nearly 20 percent by 1970. Young couples eager to establish themselves—spurred by Federal Housing Administration policies that made it hard, if not impossible, to secure a mortgage in the city but easy to finance a home in towns with pastoral-sounding names like Mount Laurel, Cherry Hill, or Audubon—offered a ready ear to suburban real estate boosters who proclaimed, "Why live in Camden or Philadelphia when you could live here?"[22]

Second, though city politicians were in denial, 1960s Camden was already beginning to hemorrhage manufacturing jobs, down 45 percent in that decade alone. Some of the city's shocking job loss was due to the abrupt closure of the New York Shipyards because of declining demand, but other, smaller manufacturers who felt pressure to modernize or expand were leaving as well.[23] Meanwhile, suburban industrial employment grew by 95 percent, luring even more of the city's younger industrial workers away from the Camden neighborhoods of their youth.

Third, businesses had already begun a slow exodus east to Cherry Hill, Morristown, Woodbury, and Voorhees, following their customer base. In the 1950s the city boasted large, prosperous department stores—nearly every major chain in the region was represented—elegant theaters, the grand 1925 Walt Whitman hotel, and hundreds of small family-owned shops along the city's major commercial spines: Broadway, Kaighns, Haddon, and East Camden's Federal and Westfield. Then, in 1961 the first shopping mall on the East Coast opened its doors, the Cherry Hill Mall, to a frenzy of acclaim, just a short five-mile drive from Camden's eastern border. "Shop in Eden all Year Long," advertisements read, referring to the mall's air conditioning. Over the next ten years, vacancies along Camden's commercial arteries grew rapidly.[24]

The year 1971, though, was when Camden exploded in racial violence, and this dealt its deathblow. The *Camden Courier-Post* had reported increasing racial tension in Camden during the prior decade, as Philadelphia (1964), Watts (1965), Newark (1967), Detroit (1967), Chicago (1968), Washington, DC (1968) and Baltimore (1969) had erupted, yet other than a series of civil disturbances in 1969, no major riot had occurred in Camden. Then, in the course of a routine traffic stop, a local Puerto Rican man was nearly beaten to death by two white police officers.[25]

By then Camden had a sizable Puerto Rican population, first initiated by Campbell's Soup's decision to cure their acute labor shortages during World War II by recruiting workers from Puerto Rico. Mayor Joseph M. Nardi, a Camden-born Italian American relatively new to his post, refused to suspend the officers involved. Throughout the day the crowd of Puerto Rican protesters gathered in front of city hall grew to as much as 1,200. Finally, around 8 p.m. Nardi agreed to meet with the group's leaders. While they were laying out their demands for more Puerto Rican men on the police force and better schools, housing, and employment, a bar fight overflowed onto the street and sparked a wave of looting, burning, and rioting that lasted three days. The city's entire 328-man police force responded, reinforced by 75 state police troopers and 70 officers from surrounding areas. By the morning of the fourth day, the *Camden Courier-Post* reported, "The city's major streets were bombed-out ruins, littered with broken glass, burned trash, objects hurled by demonstrators and spent tear gas containers. Water from firefighting and from fire hydrants turned on by residents made a soggy mess of the debris." Nearly every plate-glass window along Broadway from Federal Street to Kaighns Avenue was smashed.[26] In the years immediately following, almost all major retailers left the city and so did almost every large employer.[27]

Four decades later fewer than twenty-five thousand households remained in the city. Half of its residents were African American and more than four in ten were Hispanic—most of them Puerto Rican—with only a smattering of elderly whites and newcomer Asians. Median household income remained abysmally low—under twenty-nine thousand dollars—and more than a third of Camden's families lived below the official poverty line: 44 percent of families with children were poor. Unemployment between 2008 and 2010 averaged 22 percent. Roughly 15 percent of the city's households claimed government disability payments (SSI), and about 12 percent received cash payments from the welfare system, while nearly three in ten collected Food Stamps—all very high rates as compared with the nation as a whole. Four in ten adults lacked a high school diploma or GED, and the high school dropout rate stood at 70 percent.[28]

From the days of the Moynihan controversy onward, academic researchers and journalists who have focused on the lives of so-called fatherless families have looked almost exclusively at African Americans, lending the impression that "fatherlessness" is a black problem. By the mid-1990s, however, black rates of unwed childbearing had leveled off, while among whites (and Hispanics) the growth was substantial. By the end of that decade 40 percent of all nonmarital births in the United States were to non-Hispanic whites, while only a third were to blacks.[29] By the time we began our study, the so-called fatherless family, which Moynihan had labeled a black issue, had spread beyond America's disadvantaged minorities.

Thus, though we started in Camden, we expanded our focus to lower-income neighborhoods in Philadelphia, a city with minority neighborhoods with similar social ills as Camden's but also with predominantly white neighborhoods that, while not nearly as poor as some of its black sections, still had pockets of poverty.[30] Philadelphia was also an industrial giant, and it too peaked in the 1950s. As noted earlier, it also had an influential race riot in 1964 that coincided with dramatic changes in the economic and racial complexion of the city.

Today Philadelphia is a largely black and white city, with only a small representation of Hispanics and Asians. The median household income stands at just under thirty-six thousand dollars, and poverty rates are much lower than Camden's—20 percent (29 percent of families with children). A much smaller proportion claim government assistance in Philadelphia.[31] Unemployment, at 13 percent, is still above the national average. Nearly eight out of ten adults (79 percent) have at least a GED, but only 56 percent of the city's public high school students graduate within four years.[32]

Taken together, the metro area as a whole bears similarity to many rustbelt cities in the Northeast, Midwest, and Mid-Atlantic regions. In 2011 its unemployment rate stood at just under 9 percent, similar to rates in the Baltimore, Cleveland, New York, Milwaukee, Saint Louis, Cincinnati, and Chicago metropolitan areas. Out of the forty-nine largest metro areas, it ranks twenty-second by this measure.[33] Still, Camden and Philadelphia are among the nation's poorest cities—in 2007 Philadelphia was the ninth poorest of all large cities, while Camden was narrowly edged out by Bloomington, Indiana, as the poorest city in the nation, a designation Camden has earned in most years.[34] At this writing it has just earned the title again, edging out last year's winner, Reading, Pennsylvania. It is also America's second most dangerous city, but a recent spate of murders has put it very close on the heels of the first-place winner, Flint, Michigan.[35] Given the stark economic conditions of Philadelphia and Camden and the income restrictions we imposed on our sample—which we limited to men earning less than sixteen thousand dollars in the prior year in the formal economy (roughly the poverty line for a family of four in 2000)—our results must be interpreted with some caution; not all unwed fathers live in places with so many economic challenges, nor are all unwed fathers as disadvantaged as the men in our story. But because a disproportionate number of unmarried fathers are disadvantaged across a variety of domains, many men who have a child without benefit of a marital tie do so under similar conditions.

Nationwide, poor whites rarely live in neighborhoods of concentrated poverty, and Hispanics are also less likely than African Americans to do so. This substantial difference in neighborhood conditions sometimes leads to misleading comparisons, for while disadvantaged minorities usually come of age in communities with daunting challenges and precious few resources, poor whites are much more likely to enjoy the good schools, safe streets, plentiful jobs, and enriching social activities that are so beneficial to young people as they navigate the transition to adulthood. Philadelphia offered us an unusual advantage: the chance to study disadvantaged whites whose neighborhood contexts were somewhat more similar to those of economically challenged blacks. In selecting our neighborhoods, we took full advantage of this feature of the city.

## THE FATHERS

Over the seven years we spent on street corners and front stoops, in front rooms and kitchens, at fast food restaurants, rec centers, and bars in each of these neighborhoods, we persuaded 110 low-income unwed fathers to share their stories with us, sometimes over the course of several months, or even years. We recruited roughly equal numbers of African Americans and whites, the two groups who constitute the large majority of the population in the Philadelphia metropolitan area.[36] Fathers ranged in age from seventeen to sixty-four, yet we made sure that roughly half of the fathers were over thirty when we spoke with them so we could tell the story of inner-city unwed fatherhood across the life course. Their experiences were varied, but all were fathers with at least one child under the age of nineteen they did not have legal custody of, and all hailed from city tracts that were working class or poor.[37]

Because the men we were interested in talking with were often not stably attached to households, and some were involved in illicit activities they were eager to hide from outsiders, we did not attempt a random sample; instead, we tried for as much heterogeneity as we could.[38] Within each poor and working-class neighborhood we had identified using census data, we began by trying to solicit referrals from grassroots community organizations and social service agencies. But we soon learned that few of the fathers we sought were involved in these groups, and those who were—usually drug addicts in rehab or homeless men sleeping in shelters—were far from representative. We then visited local business strips, train and trolley stops, day labor agencies, and other employers in these neighborhoods in the late afternoons, when work shifts ended and many residents were out and about. We also simply walked the streets, striking up casual conversations with men we encountered and posting fliers on telephone poles and in corner stores, check-cashing outlets, liquor stores, and bars. We also invited early participants to refer us to other fathers whom we might have missed on our own.

With these unconventional recruitment strategies, it was surprisingly easy to convince fathers to talk with us. Getting them to speak candidly about their views and experiences required more work. No researchers enter fully into the lives of their subjects, and we do not claim to have done so. In the end what won the confidence of most men was our willingness to become neighbors and our eagerness to gain some firsthand experience with the contexts in which they lived. Our own backgrounds still marked us as outsiders but also allowed us to authentically claim the role of novices seeking the fathers' expertise in understanding the rhythm and risks of daily life.[39]

Our conversations with each father, usually stretching across several meetings, were wide-ranging and in-depth. We asked fathers to begin by describing their own childhoods and families of origin, and what it was like for them growing up. We tracked their paths through adolescence and early adulthood; their experiences with peers, school, and work; and the beginning and end of each romantic relationship. They described the circumstances surrounding the births of each of their children and the often shifting patterns of involvement in their children's lives. We asked how they had come to make the choices they had, what they wished had gone differently, and what they planned for the future.

The question that originally prompted our study—is it true that these fathers simply don't care about the children they conceive?—led to a deeper and more complex focus of inquiry: what does fatherhood mean in the lives of low-income, inner-city men? This query spurred us to chronicle the processes of courtship, conception, and the breakup of the romantic bond. We then looked at how fathers viewed both the traditional aspects of the fatherhood role—being a breadwinner and role model—and its softer side. Finally, we elicited the barriers men faced as they tried to father their children in the way that they desired, and how they responded to these challenges. Our goal was to offer honest, on-the-ground answers to the questions so many Americans ask about these men and their lives.

In this book we do not seek to portray the whole way of life in these communities. The voices of the women these men share children with only rarely enter in, for example, and this is intentional; their stories have already been told.[40] Nor do we discuss men who have earned college degrees, have managed to land and keep higher-paid manufacturing or white-collar jobs, or are raising their children within marriage, though men with these characteristics also reside in these communities. This is not a book about race; though we note racial differences when they occur, they are more in degree than in kind. In this narrative, where black and white men live in more similar contexts than in most places, racial differences are far outweighed by shared social class. This is not a work of history; we do not, and cannot, present the narratives of low-income fathers at earlier points in time such as the 1950s and 1960s—what some conceive of as the golden age of family life.[41] We do not offer an analysis of the individual characteristics or contexts associated with fathering a child outside of a marital bond—that question would have required a very different study design than ours. Nor do we engage with the rich literature on father involvement, though readers can find references to this literature in the notes to the book. Finally, this is not a book about the effects of fathers' behaviors on their children's well-being, though we do discuss the implications for children in the final chapter.

This is the story of disadvantaged fathers living in a struggling rust-belt metropolis at the turn of the twenty-first century. By examining each father's story as it unfolds, we offer a strong corrective to the conventional wisdom regarding fatherhood in America's inner cities. There is seldom anything fixed about the lives of the men in this book—not their romantic attachments, their jobs, or their ties to their kids. Only by revealing how they grapple with shifting contexts over time can we fully understand how so many will ultimately fail to play a significant and ongoing role in their children's lives.

The men in these pages seldom deliberately choose whom to have a child with; instead "one thing just leads to another" and a baby is born. Yet men often greet the news that they're going to become a dad with enthusiasm and a burst of optimism that despite past failures they can turn things around. Conception usually happens so quickly that the "real relationship" doesn't begin until the fuse of impending parenthood has been lit. For these couples, children aren't the expression of commitment; they are the source. In these early days, men often work hard to "get it together" for the sake of the baby—they try to stop doing the "stupid shit" (a term for the risky behavior that has led to past troubles) and to become the man their baby's mother thinks family life requires. But in the end, the bond—which is all about the baby—is usually too weak to bring about the transformation required.

Not surprisingly, these relationships usually end, but instead of walking away from their kids, these men are often determined to play a vital role in their children's lives. This turns out to be far harder than they had envisioned. Nonetheless, they try to reclaim fatherhood by radically redefining the father role. These disadvantaged dads recoil at the notion that they are just a paycheck—they insist that their role is to "be there": to show love and spend quality time. In their view, what's most important is to become their children's best friends. But this definition of fatherhood leaves all the hard jobs—the breadwinning, the discipline, and the moral guidance—to the moms.

As children age, an inner-city father's scorecard can easily show far more failures than successes, particularly because of the "stupid shit" he often finds so hard to shake. In this situation, it can require incredible tenacity and inner strength to stay involved. But few of these men give fatherhood only one try. Each new relationship offers another opportunity for "one thing" to "just lead to another" yet again. And a new baby with a new partner offers the tantalizing possibility of a fresh start. In the end, most men believe they've succeeded at fatherhood because they are managing to parent at least one of their children well at any given time. Yet this pattern of selective fathering leaves many children without much in the way of a dad.

By examining the unfolding stories of these men's lives beginning at courtship, and moving through conception, birth, and beyond, we come to see that the "hit and run" image of unwed fatherhood Moyers created by showcasing Timothy McSeed is a caricature and not an accurate rendering—a caricature that obscures more than it reveals. Some readers will argue that our portrayal is no more sympathetic, or less disturbing, than Moyers's. Others will find seeds of hope in these stories, albeit mixed with a strong dose of disheartening reality. But getting the story right is critical if we hope to craft policies to improve the lives of inner-city men and women and, of course, their children.

# One Thing Leads to Another

While witches and goblins lug candy-laden pillowcases and orange, plastic pumpkin-shaped buckets up and down the streets of Philadelphia, black thirty-one-year-old Amin Jenkins is experiencing the best moment of his life. It's October 31 and he's in the delivery room of the University of Pennsylvania hospital welcoming his baby Antoine into the world—a boy who he says "looks exactly like me." Though he admits the child was far from planned, Amin is proud that he "never said I wasn't responsible, that I had nothing to do with it"—"it" being Antoinette Hargrove's pregnancy. Far from it. "From the time that she was pregnant I was always involved, talking to her and spending time with her and rubbing her stomach."[1]

By the time the baby arrived, Amin and Antoinette were clearly a "couple." By then, Amin was certain that he "really, really loved" Antoinette and was cautiously optimistic about their future together. Eighteen months later, however, "the communication just stopped." Amin explains, "as time progressed we started having certain irreconcilable differences and that caused our fire and that spark to diminish." Soon both were "seeing other people" on the side, which led to a "retaliation-type situation." Finally, around Antoine's third birthday, Antoinette, fed up with the tit for tat, moved out, leaving no forwarding address. Antoinette's sister and mother weren't willing to reveal where she was living. A year later Amin is still crazy about Antoine but doesn't know his address; he can only see his son when the boy visits Antoinette's mother.

What brings inner city couples like Amin and Antoinette together in the first place? How well do they usually know each other before becoming pregnant? Is it usually true love or little more than a one-night stand? Faced with an unplanned conception, how is the decision made to go ahead and have the baby? Do the pressures of pregnancy fracture an otherwise strong relationship, or is it pregnancy that trans-forms a fairly casual liaison into something more—at least for a time? And what aspects of men's larger life stories—their childhood, adoles-cence, and early adulthood experiences and the neighborhoods they come of age in—both drive their desire and hamstring their attempts to forge a lasting relationship with the mother of their child? As we will see, the way in which men like Amin become fathers can tell us much about the many struggles they will face after their children are born.

Following a quiet career at James Alcorn Elementary, Amin's seventh- and eighth-grade years at Audenreid Junior High were pockmarked by suspensions for fighting, stealing, cutting class, and any other form of trouble available. By fifteen he'd been expelled from South Philly High and assigned to the Absalom Jones disciplinary school, and a year later the criminal justice system remanded him to a year in juvenile detention for burglary.[2] Immediately after his eighteenth birthday, Amin was convicted of robbery and served his first real time. Out at twenty, he managed to stay free just long enough to father his first child (Antoine is his second) with a woman he barely knew—a child he denied—and acquire a GED before embarking on another and more lengthy prison stint, this time on multiple charges including burglary and aggravated assault. He wouldn't see the outside again until twenty-seven.

Amin's behavior seemed inexplicable to his poor but respectable three-generation South Philadelphia family, ruled by a strict grandmother with high expectations—the one who helped raise the kids and "steer us right" while his mother worked long hours keeping house for well-off Jewish families in West Philadelphia. This prodigal son's older siblings embraced and even exceeded their grandmother's goals, staying out of serious trouble, finishing school, getting married, and going on to lead middle-class lives. The sister he's closest to because they share the same father pretty much stayed on the straight and narrow too; now she holds a coveted state job.

But Amin is the youngest and the only boy. For him the neighborhood— the racially charged Grays Ferry on the westernmost border of South Philadelphia—took a special toll.[3] In the mid-1960s his mother, Betty Jenkins, had been one of the first blacks to move into the hardscrabble working-class Irish community. With her mother and two oldest daughters in tow, Betty took up residence in Tasker Homes, a federal low-income housing development built for white war workers in the 1930s that, three decades later, had just begun accepting black applicants. Amin came of age there in the late eighties and by that time both the housing project and the surrounding neighborhood had taken a nosedive. Amin describes Grays Ferry as a "very, very rough community. Very racist, prejudiced. When you grow up in an environment such as that, it does have a tendency to affect and to *infect* your attitude and your disposition."

In this community everyone from peers to the police seemed intent on scapegoating black boys like Amin: for the declining economic fortunes of its industrial workers; for the deteriorating streetscapes; for the mounting racial tension; for the plunging property values and epidemic white flight. An enormous animosity toward whites who, in his view, were always ready to "start something" with the neighborhood's black residents and a bottomless anger toward authority figures were the contaminants that turned to poison in Amin's teenage years. Engaging in a little self-analysis, he says that it was these dispositions piled on top of the aching sense of abandonment he felt when his father simply drifted away that explained his compelling desire to find trouble whenever the opportunity arose. Not until age twenty-six, in Houtzdale

Prison, located in a remote area of western Pennsylvania, did Amin find the space for reflection that led to redemption. "The last eleven months of my prison term was when I began to realize that I was wasting time," he explains. "I had to do better things with my life."

After his release Amin moved back in with his mother, who was still living in the now nearly all-black Tasker Homes. To prove the sincerity of his jailhouse conversion, Amin immediately hit the streets looking for work and eventually landed his first real job stocking shelves at Rite Aid. Determined to do even more to ensure he could "take a different course in life," he enrolled in evening classes at the Community College of Philadelphia to earn certification as a dietary assistant, a career choice inspired by his twenty-three-cent-a-day job in the prison kitchen. This coursework eventually qualified him for a position in the dietary department at the University of Pennsylvania hospital, just across the Schuylkill River from Grays Ferry.

Flush for the first time with real wages, Amin then made another positive move. He and his mother decided to pool their resources and trade life in public housing for home ownership. Over a year's time, the two managed to put away five thousand dollars. Thanks to a special program offered by a community-development corporation, this was sufficient down payment for a mortgage on a renovated row house in the Strawberry Mansion section of North Philadelphia. Soon, Amin and his mother were fitting the key into the lock of their own home and marveling at the freshly painted walls, gleaming wood floors, and the kitchen equipped with brand new appliances.

Amin's new world was the 2900 block of Diamond Street, just east of Fairmount Park and a few streets away from the historically significant "Mansion Row" running the length of the 3200 block. There the traces of the neighborhood's nineteenth-century heyday as a wealthy Jewish streetcar suburb are most evident, albeit in dilapidated form. On Amin's own block, the decrepit "mansions" with their turrets and pillars give way to solid, spacious three-story brownstones, some with dusty red or white metal awnings. It is a relatively good block, unbroken by the gaps of vacant lots that lend a bombed-out look to most others in the neighborhood. In Strawberry Mansion, lots cleared of some of the most flagrantly neglected and structurally unsound structures in the city nearly exceed those with residences. This is not to say that the 2900 block doesn't have "vacancies"—as passersby, we can't help but notice as light reflects off the broken window glass that leaves several abandoned structures exposed to the elements.

Although Strawberry Mansion was well away from the peers that had led Amin astray in the past, "out of the frying pan and into the fire" is how many outside observers would see his first concrete step toward upward mobility. While there is no Grays Ferry–style racial tension here—the neighborhood is 98 percent black—there is little else to commend it: sky-high poverty, unemployment and crime, failing schools, abysmally low property values, and, other than the massive church and synagogue structures that anchor nearly every other block, almost no amenities.[4] Nonetheless, Amin viewed the move as an astonishing achievement and incontrovertible evidence that the prodigal son had returned home.

About this time, buoyed with newfound optimism about his future, Amin began to take notice of Antoinette, a coworker who was signaling her attraction to him. Flattered by the attention, he reciprocated. "She was attracted to me when I first saw her, and I made my approach," he recalls. We ask Amin to tell us how he and Antoinette met and what led to having a child together. His reply is noticeably succinct. "We began to socialize and communicate and then from there we began to affiliate and at some point in time we became intimate and my son was born."

In just a few words or a single sentence, inner-city fathers like Amin can often summarize what passes for courtship of the women who become their children's mothers. Perhaps this is because everything usually happens so fast: in Amin's case it was only fifteen months' time before "attraction" had led to "affiliation," then to an intimacy that resulted in conception. Nine months later Antoine entered the world. Amin's relationship with Antoinette is the most significant adult bond he has ever had outside of his tie to his mother, yet he, like most others we spoke to, uses vague, even bureaucratic language to describe his relationship in the period before pregnancy. In these accounts "affiliation"—a term indicating that a couple is "together"—often takes the place of other expected words like love or commitment.

Typically though, the two are definitely "together" by the time a child is conceived; Amin assures us that this was the case for him and Antoinette when Antoine was conceived. In fact, he can more or less pinpoint exactly when the two moved from "socializing" to togetherness. As men like Amin define it, this state is halfway between what middle-class youth refer to as a "hookup"—sex with no commitment—and a "real relationship." In the hookup phase, many men claim they use condoms quite consistently, and women in these communities confirm these assertions.[5] But once the couple moves to "the next level" of togetherness, condoms, defined more as disease prevention than birth control, are left in the nightstand drawer. Indeed, if both partners have "tested clean" from STDs, men who continue to use condoms might as well be calling their female partner a "cheater" or a "whore."

Kathryn Edin and Maria Kefalas's in-depth conversations with single mothers in many of these same neighborhoods suggest that women may overinterpret this signal and define what men deem mere togetherness as something more. It is perhaps because of this that their vigilance with regard to the pill, patch, or the shot so often falters once this level of couple cohesion has been achieved. Most—though by no means all—pregnancies brought to term among the men we spoke with across the Philadelphia metropolitan area were conceived in the context of bonds that, in their view, at least meet the minimum criteria of "togetherness," the point at which he, and then she, typically stops using protection.[6]

How selective are the men about the women who will bear their children? Do they "choose" their children's mothers with care, or do they just end up together by chance? Let's turn to the stories of Tim O'Brien and John Carr. These men have never met, yet their lives have amazing parallels. Both are as Irish as the shamrocks proudly displayed on the marquees and in the windows of their neighborhood's pubs—the Starboard Side Tavern, Dempsey Irish Pub, Shannon's, Bob's Happy Hour—and in the front windows of homes. Both Tim and John grew up in Greater Kensington, northeast of Center City Philadelphia, where tattoos and bumper stickers, like the bars and front windows, often feature symbols of ethnic pride. This area was an eighteenth-century industrial suburb that now encompasses the very economically and ethnically distinct Philadelphia neighborhoods of Kensington, Fishtown, and West Kensington. Tim and John were both raised by single mothers and have had little contact with their fathers since childhood. Both dropped out of Kensington High in the tenth grade due to utter lack of interest in school. Both have been touched by the area's feverish drug trade—John as a dealer and Tim as a user. Finally, both became fathers at a young age and in the context of exceedingly fragile, short-term relationships with girls they "stole" from their friends.

Kensington proper, where John resides, is enmeshed in a slow and bitter battle between its older inhabitants—the Irish and the Poles—and the newcomer Puerto Ricans, Asians, and African Americans, though whites are still the largest ethnic group and make up almost 80 percent of the population.[7] The nonwhites, whom John and many fellow Irish Americans view as "intruders," began permeating the northwest boundary between Kensington—the poorest majority-white neighborhood in the city—and the largely minority neighborhood of West Kensington in the 1980s, gradually eroding the de facto Berlin Wall of Kensington Avenue. This frightens young men like John, for across that divide lies West Kensington, once also a relatively stable, working-class, and staunchly white area and now 70 percent Latino and 20 percent black. It is also the poorest and one of the most violent areas of the city; the correlation between the area's changing complexion and social and economic conditions is one many white Kensingtonians take as causation.

John grew up just east of that line on the 1900 block of East Hagert between Jasper and Emerald Streets. Brick two-story row houses are tucked in here and there along the denuded street, dwarfed by multistory shells of textile mills that still create a decaying corridor five blocks long—the formerly proud homes of Albion Carpets and the Bedford Fast Black Dye Company at the corner of Hagert and Jasper, Job Batty and Sons Carpet Yarn and William Emsley and Brothers' Washington Mills at Hagert's intersection with Emerald, William Beatty's Mills one block farther on at Coral Street, Annot's Steam Power— later Standard Rug—between Coral and Amber, the Weisbrod and Hess Brewery on the corner of Amber Street, and many more.[8] Several are abandoned, though some have been converted into smaller manufacturing concerns or affordable live and work spaces for struggling artists. Built in the late 1800s, these are Dickensian four-to-six-story red brick affairs—some embellished with arched window openings and other fancy brickwork and topped with tall chimneys. Some area mills are still crowned by rusted iron water receptacles proudly bearing a defunct company's name. Neighborhood lore has it that in the turn-of-the-century golden era, one could walk down any one of Kensington's industrial streets like East Hagert and find a job in fifteen minutes. But more than fifty years of deindustrialization have taken a severe toll.

Any old-timer in John's neighborhood will tell you that as the jobs have fled, so has much semblance of social order. Middle-school kids sell drugs openly in broad daylight on major thoroughfares; John's street bears the mark of the addictions the trade spawns. At the base of Hagert Street, on the corner of Kensington Avenue, is the Saint Francis Inn, a soup kitchen well known for serving meals to the area's neediest, including the worst of the addicts. And just across the street, Inner City Missions offers drug referral and substance abuse counseling. The mean price of the neighborhood's homes sits at just under thirty-five thousand dollars, and given the low value and the very poor condition of so many of the narrow brick dwellings, lifelong residents have been known to simply abandon their houses to squatters or leave them to children or other relatives as cheap starter homes.[9] There are still enough stalwart white working-class residents in the neighborhood to keep its primary parish, the impeccably maintained century-and-a-half old Saint Anne, pulsing with parishioners—six hundred to seven hundred on a typical Sunday.[10] This fortresslike Romanesque Goliath and its parish house, graveyard, and school commandeer a wide swath of the beleaguered Lehigh Avenue, another of the neighborhood's old industrial streets and its northern boundary.

Tim was raised in a very different area of Greater Kensington, just south of Norris Street on the 800 block of East Thompson, in the more respectable Fishtown section, once the center of the shad fishing industry. Fishtown now houses families a bit too proud to live in Kensington proper: police officers and firefighters, along with nurses and other health care employees and craftsmen of various kinds—electricians, stone masons, plumbers, sheet-metal workers, teamsters, and skilled construction workers. It also claims an increasing share of young college-educated professionals with a taste for "authentic" urban living. The housing stock is the same aggressively plain red brick monotony of two- and three-story row homes that bleed into Kensington. So, eager to claim a separate identity from their Kensington neighbors to the northwest, residents carefully demarcate the area with potted plants and flower boxes, the occasional crisp metal awning, glossy new aluminum screen doors, manicured side lawns, decorative garden benches, and other flourishes that complement a streetscape neat as a pin. These outdoor environs host impromptu gatherings of residents who while away summer nights on lawn chairs chatting idly with one another.

Back in Kensington proper, we have our first conversation with John late on a weekday morning on his day off. The five hundred fifty dollar a month apartment he shares with a roommate—a female stripper—is simply furnished; the front room, where we settle on a couch and a chair, is dominated by an oversized television but is devoid of other decor. Coming up hard, John says he came to despise both of his parents. John's mother worked as a cop until recently, when she was suspended without pay pending investigation of a charge of police brutality. While she waits for the official adjudication of the charge, John's mom, whom he characterizes as a "bum," has been collecting welfare—illegally, it turns out, as she's also working full-time as a security guard. His father is a diesel mechanic who lives in central "PA," but John hasn't seen him in more than ten years.

John joined more than seven in ten of his classmates when he dropped out of Kensington High, one of the worst performing schools in the city.[11] This white youth was lured away from the tedium of school and into the work world at sixteen by a minimum-wage job at McCrory's, the now-defunct dollar-store chain that was all that remained of the local five-and-dime giant by the late 1990s. After that John worked one "chicken shit" job after another until landing his current position tinting everything from car windows to plate glass, which he got through a friend of his uncle. The summer he turned eighteen he was still working the chicken-shit jobs but had another source of income as well. He and a friend had turned a casual street-corner drug business into a modest empire, setting up shop in a cheap rental apartment where they and their "partners" could deal undetected day and night. John claims he was making money hand over fist and "blowing it" by buying drinks and weed for anyone who would party with him. While the business lasted only a couple of months—things with the police quickly got too "hot" to continue—he remembers it as a glorious time.

In the midst of that Mid-Atlantic summer haze, John met his baby's mother, seventeen-year-old Rayann, through a friend he hung out and partied with in the neighborhood; she was his friend's "girl." When she started hinting that she wanted him and not his friend, John claims he steered clear out of loyalty. "I didn't want to have nothing to do with it," he insists. The neighborhood rumor mill claimed otherwise, though. Soon, John's friend "heard some shit and started talking shit saying he would kick my ass." Furious at his friend's assumption of betrayal, John resolved, "Then I *will* be with your girl!" John concludes his story in this way: "Eventually, I just got stuck with her for a little while."

Six years later John's language reveals that even in the early days of courtship, he didn't feel that he had found the ideal match. Instead, in headlong pursuit of revenge, he "got stuck" with Rayann through pregnancy; just twelve months after they met, she gave birth to their daughter at the Cape May Regional Medical Center on the South Jersey Shore, where she had moved five months into her pregnancy—to get away from John. Little language of love or even attraction (except her initial attraction to him) enters into John's narrative, although there may well have been attraction involved. Though John says he badly wanted to "be in love" during this period in his life, things with Rayann just didn't click. Nor does his use of the phrase "a little while" indicate much commitment.

The conception that made John a father—occurring just three months into the relationship—was actually Rayann's second with John, following immediately after an early miscarriage. John suspects that in reality, Rayann's mother forced her to get an abortion. "Yeah, and then we're making *another* baby," John says. How did these conceptions come about so quickly? "You know, like she was always cheating on me. So whenever I would catch her cheating on me the first thing she would do is she would turn to sex because she was a nympho. It made me forget about the other guy," John recalls. In the afterglow of these postfight reunions, "She would start talking that she knows she wants to have a baby."

Despite these "discussions" John would hardly characterize the pregnancy that culminated in the birth of his daughter Naomi as planned. Indeed, John claimed surprise and even disbelief and insisted they make a trip to Planned Parenthood to confirm Rayann's news. When he told his mother, she called him "an asshole and stupid." Rayann's mother, the alleged impetus of the earlier forced abortion, hated John so badly that to preserve family peace, Rayann decided to name another man—the on-and-off boyfriend she had been secretly seeing on the side and that her mother liked better—as the father. John is proud to say that he finally put this false claim to rest with a paternity test he paid for himself when his daughter turned two.

In spite of these strong negative parental reactions, John claims that neither he nor Rayann even considered ending this pregnancy, perhaps because a surprise pregnancy after only a few weeks or months "together" is not unusual in the neighborhoods young men like John inhabit.[12] Here, families are often formed through a pregnancy brought to term in a relationship that is neither entirely casual nor serious. John's story hints at a common truth, that children can often ensue from relationships that have a haphazard, almost random quality. The women who bear these men's children seem to be indistinguishable from others that they "get with" but don't happen to become pregnant.

Tim, down in Fishtown, also "ended up with" his child's mother. At seventeen this high school dropout's main occupation was getting high. When Tim was introduced to Mazie he had just broken up with Andrea, his girlfriend of two years, because she had chosen an abortion over bearing his child. Andrea was also seventeen and was already caring for a son she had had at fifteen from another man; she didn't feel she could cope with a second child. This argument held no water with Tim, who discovered—after the fact of conception—that he was desperate to be a father.

One weekend shortly after the breakup, Tim met the woman who ended up fulfilling that dream. He was "hanging at a friend of mine's house, and Mazie and a couple of her friends were there." Mazie had just broken up with Tim's best friend: "My friend was trying to get back with her, and *I* ended up getting with her," he explains, as if poaching other men's girlfriends is fair game. "I really wasn't having sex with her too much," Tim confides. "She was only fourteen." But nonetheless, "we were only together for about two months, and she was getting pregnant!"

How did Tim respond to the news that he had gotten a fourteen-year-old he barely knew pregnant? "I didn't mind at all!" he declares. When pressed to explain his reaction, Tim notes that he "thought I really cared" for Mazie at that time. But, as he is careful to explain, this doesn't mean he ever considered Mazie a "real girlfriend"—he reserves that designation for Andrea, his first love. Nor is he willing to characterize his bond with Mazie as a "real relationship." In fact, he specifically asserts that it was not.

Like John, Tim only "ended up getting with" his baby's mother—he didn't choose her. The courtship was exceedingly brief—only two months in duration—but the two were more or less "together" when conception occurred, and there was just enough cohesion to prompt a positive response to the pregnancy. Plus, in Tim's case, Mazie's pregnancy was a way to satisfy the strong desire for a child evoked by Andrea's conception. Mostly, though, Tim is perplexed by the question we pose. Why *would* he mind, the tone of his answers imply.

## BEING TOGETHER

So what does "being together" imply? Generally, it means that the two are spending regular time with one another and view the relationship as something more than a mere sexual encounter.[13] Being together is more than a "hookup," borrowing from the terms more privileged high school and college students use; hookups have no distinct beginning or end, while the termination of these liaisons requires a "breakup."[14] There is an expectation of fidelity, at least in theory; outside relationships are still usually designated as "cheating," though this norm grows a lot stronger once a baby is on the way or has entered the world. Tim clearly knows he's done wrong when he's caught having sex on the couch with Andrea one night when he thinks Mazie and his child, Sophia, are asleep in bed. But, as the ambiguous language men use to describe these ties suggests, at the point of conception, Tim and his peers seldom view their unions as serious or "real relationships."[15]

For simplicity we refer to this stage in men's romantic relationships as "being together." But blacks and whites use somewhat different terms. In poor black neighborhoods across the Philadelphia metropolitan area, like Amin Jenkins's Strawberry Mansion, youths and adults alike frequently use the description "associate" to denote persons they spend time with but who are not "friends."[16] In the same way, the terms "affiliate" and "associate" depict a bond that is more than just a one-night stand but not exactly a boyfriend or girlfriend relationship either. In economically struggling white neighborhoods like John's Kensington or even Tim's more respectable Fishtown, the language tends to be simpler—Tim "gets with" his baby's mother, while John and Rayann are simply "together." These terms are as distinctive in what they include as what they do not: much evidence of a search for a life partner.

We asked each of our 110 fathers to tell us "the whole story" of how he got together with the mother of each child, what the relationship was like before pregnancy, and how things developed over time. As was the case with Amin, the prepregnancy narrative is often startlingly succinct: the couple meets, begins to "affiliate," and then "comes up pregnant." Few men even mention, much less discuss, any special qualities of their partners or any common tastes or values that drew the two together. Usually, the girl lives on his block, hangs out on the stoop near his corner, works at the same job, is a friend of his sister's or the girlfriend of a friend, and is willing to "socialize" with him.[17] Obviously, there is a spectrum here; Amin was with Antoinette much longer at the time of conception than Tim was with Mazie. It is also true that some conceptions are to very stable couples who may already share children, while others are the result of one-night stands. In the typical scenario, however, couples are usually together, but for only "a minute"—just a few months is the norm—before their first child together is conceived.[18]

In sum, a common feature of our fathers' narratives about the nature of the relationship before pregnancy is the brevity and modest cohesion of the tie.[19] Only rarely do such couples "fall in love," get engaged, or get married *before* conceiving a first child together, though they may do so later on. Indeed, they rarely even refer to each other as boyfriend and girlfriend. As we have already indicated, and show in chapter 2, planned pregnancies are rare, yet once the pair deems themselves "together," any serious attempt at contraception usually fades.[20] Then the inevitable occurs: the woman "comes up pregnant."[21] Precious few men are consciously courting a woman they believe will be a long-term partner around the time that pregnancy issues a one-way ticket to fatherhood. Indeed, there is little evidence that many were even attempting to discriminate much among possible partners based on who they felt would be the most suitable mother to their child.[22]

## COMING UP PREGNANT

Given their haphazard origins, these relationships might well have been short-lived had it not been for an unplanned conception. As the stories of Byron Jones, Will Donnelly, and Jack Day will illustrate, pregnancy, and not a shared history, similar tastes, or common goals, is what typically galvanizes partnerships in the low-income neighborhoods of Philadelphia and Camden, though this is not always the case. An unplanned pregnancy and the decision to carry it to term transforms relationships of mere "togetherness" into something more.

Byron Jones was born in rural South Carolina, but his parents moved to Philadelphia when he turned three. He was raised in "The Bottom," the local nickname for Mantua, the working-class West Philadelphia neighborhood that black southern migrants began flocking to in the 1920s. His mother was only fifteen when she gave birth to Byron's sister, and his father was just a shade older. His parents married soon after and had five more children together, Byron right in the middle. While his father labored for a Jewish factory owner in the neighborhood (given racist unions and mill owners, holding a factory job was a rare accomplishment for a black man in Philadelphia at this time), his mother worked as a domestic for a wealthy Jewish family living nearby, whose matriarch took a shine to young Byron. Each summer she paid his way to the leafy Golden Slipper Summer Camp, where he marveled at its gleaming lake, heated swimming pool, and pristine playing fields. Byron grins as he recalls that part of his childhood. "Golden Slipper Camp—I'll never forget it—all the way up in the Poconos. The majority of the blacks that was there, their families worked for the Jews 'cause it was a Jewish camp."

While at camp during the summer between fifth and sixth grade, Byron learned that his father had died of a terminal illness, and the news had a seismic impact.[23] "I didn't know he was really that sick! They sent me up to summer camp, and the next thing I know he's dead. I was just starting to get to know him," Byron says of the man who worked long hours to ensure his family's survival. "I started getting in more trouble when he passed. I felt like he abandoned me."

A widow with six dependents, Byron's thirty-two-year-old mother returned home to her family in South Carolina. "I had a good childhood," Byron insists, expressing especially fond memories of the three middle-school years he spent down South among extended family: the sound of the ax as his grandmother chopped wood in the backyard and the sizzling of greens fried on a woodstove, Sundays spent sweating for hours in an "old, hot country church" with no air-conditioning, church "suppers" that lasted all day long, and trips of several hours to his uncle's place even deeper into the up-country of the South Carolina piedmont. The adults in his life there were uniformly strict. "Every child had responsibilities, and the parents made sure we fulfilled them. You had to get your job done, or you would get your tail cut," Byron says before adding wryly, "There wasn't no child abuse back then!"

Trouble didn't find Byron while he attended school down South. His teachers ruled their classrooms with an iron hand, and he thrived within this structure. "There wasn't any such thing as getting suspended or getting a note home. They beat your butt. They didn't spare the rod," Byron says in an approving tone. But once the family moved back to Philadelphia, Byron was assigned to Sulzberger Middle School for ninth grade, where chaos reigned. He began cutting class with increasing frequency, a practice that accelerated when he entered the tenth grade at West Philadelphia High. "I didn't get into a lot of trouble until I came back up here for ninth grade when I played hooky. Then in tenth grade I started hanging out with a worse crowd. I started drinking."

It is tempting to speculate about what might have been different had Byron's mother decided to stay in the South, surrounded by this exacting but supportive extended family. Did the sudden separation from kin rekindle Byron's feelings of paternal abandonment? Was it the fact that his mother now had to work several jobs to support the family and seemed to have no time or patience for her children? Perhaps it was simply the added temptations of city life. Reliving that return, Byron quips, "The city didn't have that much brotherly love, as they call it— you know what I mean?"

After showing up drunk at school on several occasions, Byron was expelled from West Philly High. The School District of Philadelphia then transferred him to Bartram High, which was taking on increasing numbers of black students in Kingsessing, an area of the city experiencing rapid racial turnover. Like in Grays Ferry, racial tensions in Kingsessing were palpable. It should be said, though, that Byron didn't get into any really serious trouble during these years—he drank a little too much and at the wrong times, he once stole the tires off a car to put wheels on the junker of a friend, he went joyriding when an absentminded motorist left his keys in the door of his car, and he got into a knockdown, drag-out fight with four other youth in a convenience store—all of them intoxicated. But after the convenience store altercation (which earned him a night in jail), the antics of Byron's peers escalated further. Byron was convinced he needed to get out of Philadelphia. With his mother's blessing, he dropped out of Bartram in twelfth grade and joined the marines.

Discharged after four years of service, Byron took a job as a bookbinder, but the business soon closed. While searching for another job, he subsisted on revenue from an informal speakeasy he opened in the basement of the house he rented in Kingsessing, where he had gone to high school. It is there that he met Shari. "I had my little house. I used to sell a little wine, a little weed. She and one of her girlfriends, they'd come over. She was a lot younger than me. She said she was eighteen, but she wasn't. When she came over to the house with her friend, me and my cousin was there, and I was like, 'Dag. I like her, man!'"

Despite Byron's initial attraction, he was "messing with" a number of other women and didn't add Shari to his roster for a long time. Meanwhile, he found a job as a truck jockey for a suburban U-Haul franchise, servicing, delivering, and picking up trucks, and, after that business closed, as a caretaker at a downtown apartment building. After that job fell through—he was drinking too much to perform his duties reliably—he met his expenses through part-time cab work, putting in only enough hours to pay the bills and support the alcohol habit nurtured by four years in the military. He was selling weed on the side, often to fares who assumed a black cab driver would know where to find it.

Byron can instantly recall the date that he and Shari first had sex—April 14—and the clear memory hints that he imbues the event with some significance. A couple of months later Shari was pregnant, and while he was twenty-five, she was only sixteen. In Byron's section of the city, remaining fatherless for that long merits an explanation. Men like Byron with less than a high school education have more than an even chance of becoming a father before that age.[24] "I waited until I was twenty-five years old before I had my first child, but I always wanted to be a father," Byron says, careful to emphasize that delaying fatherhood longer than most of his friends was not due to lack of desire—he just hadn't had the opportunity yet.

Upon hearing the news that the woman they are "with" is expecting, men such as Byron are suddenly transformed. This part-time cab driver and sometime weed dealer almost immediately secured a city job in the sanitation department and quickly worked his way up to what he viewed as an exalted post on the back of a garbage truck. "I was doing the right thing," he brags. "After I found out I had that baby coming, shoot! I was giving up my money to *her!* You know what I mean?" In addition to working more, many feel a sudden urge to clean up their personal lives. Byron, for example, stopped "messing around with certain people," meaning other girls. Suddenly, his relationship with Shari was "all I wanted. Shoot! I was talking about getting married!" We ask how the pair got along during pregnancy. "We had a good time, man," he recalls, grinning. "While she was pregnant, I couldn't go *nowhere*. Shoot! She wanted me to do this, wanted me to do that. I was like a puppy anyway. I waited on her. I'd do certain things that she wanted me to do, getting pickles and ice cream. I didn't mind at all. I was *glad,* man!" Note that Byron's description of the relationship before and after conception stands in sharp contrast. Shari, once just another girl Byron found himself with, suddenly became "all I want"—a potential marriage partner, and Byron was her willing servant.

### A "REAL" RELATIONSHIP

Getting a job and settling down are part of a deeper metamorphosis triggered by news of a pregnancy. Suddenly, what was mere "together-ness" is becoming transformed into something more: the "real relation-ship" that building a family requires, as the stories of Will Donnelly and Jack Day show. Will and Jack were raised in nearly all-white enclaves at opposite ends of the city—Will in Northern Liberties just west of Fishtown and Jack in Elmwood Park, located just below Byron's Kingsessing neighborhood in Southwest Philly. Both come from lower middle-class white families—Will's stepfather owns a used-car lot, while Jack's father works as a cop. In childhood, both saw their neigh-borhoods change almost overnight from white to black, though Will's family stayed while Jack's fled. Both dropped out of school to help sup-port their pregnant girlfriends, Will at sixteen and Jack at twenty-one. Finally, both experienced relational transformation after conceiving children within haphazard unions and encouraged their girlfriends to go ahead and have the babies. Rather than cutting and running at the news of a pregnancy, or denying paternity, the news galvanized both of these tenuous unions into something that looked more like a "real relationship."

Will now lives in the Fairhill section of North Philadelphia, has four children by the same woman, and works as a part-time mechanic and a boxing instructor. Fairhill is a beleaguered section of the city just two neighborhoods north of his childhood home. Its only real claim to fame is that the Fairhill cemetery contains the remains of several famous Philadelphians, including Quaker abolitionist and proponent of women's rights Lucretia Mott, and Robert Purvis, the unofficial "president" of the Underground Railroad. Fairhill is overwhelmingly poor—more than 50 percent—and largely Hispanic and black; only 2 percent of the neighborhoods' residents are white. Yet Will, like the handful of other whites living there, says he was drawn by the cheap home prices—the median value for owner-occupied units is fifteen thousand dollars less than in the cheapest majority-white neighborhood in the city—which allowed Will to purchase the apartment where he lives despite marginal employment.[25]

Will recounts his relationship with Lori this way: "I had just come out of a juvenile institution. I think I just turned seventeen… and I started going with her friend. And then one day she came around and we started talking, then I went with her and left her friend, and me and her got together and started having kids together and then we got closer and closer. Then we started living together." Will's story, like Byron's, reveals a typical sequence of events: attraction and a moderate level of couple cohesion produce a pregnancy that is taken to term. For Will and most others, it is at this point that the real relationship commences. Getting "closer and closer" and then "living together" are things Will and his peers often accomplish only after they conceive children and not before.

Jack went through eighth grade at Mary Mother of Peace Catholic School in the heart of Southwest Philly, a Polish and Irish residential quarter organized around a cluster of Catholic parishes that developed during the first half of the twentieth century. In 1985 two Elmwood Park families broke the unspoken neighborhood code by selling their homes to the "wrong" buyers, one to a black family and the other to an interracial couple. Local whites rioted and Wilson Goode, the city's first black mayor, declared a state of emergency in an effort to quell the violence, but to little avail. Ultimately, though, the white-hot protest of residents like Jack's parents could not prevent the neighborhood's transformation: between 1990 and 2000 the white population was cut in half, with corresponding increases in nonwhites. Jack's father, the Philadelphia police officer, and his mother, who worked for the school district, fled north along with other white civil servants from the southwest side, moving to the working-class enclave of Manayunk, with its tiny row homes perched precariously on steep streets reaching up to the bluffs above the Schuylkill River.

Jack rebelled at the move and was kicked out of the prestigious Roman Catholic High in his freshman year for cutting class, exhibiting a belligerent attitude toward authority figures, and bullying other students. His parents felt they had no choice but to enroll him in what they viewed as a second-best educational option, the local public school, Roxborough High. Given the relative ease of the classes, he breezed through with almost all As. Penn State was his next stop, the "party school" where he spent three years studying journalism and "polishing my drinking up to a fine art." Like Will, Jack's baby's mother was just a "girl" he met by chance on a weekend visit home. "My grades weren't great, but I was getting through. I was going back home every other weekend.... Met some girls, and in turn met my baby's mother. Shortly afterwards, she became pregnant, so I quit school, got a job to support her."

Jack elaborates, "I was coming home one day, and I was pulling up to my driveway, and my next-door neighbor, Michael, was out front with this guy and a girl, and he says, 'What are you doing tonight?' And I go, 'Nothing.' 'Why don't you hang out with us...?' After a couple of drinks I told her that I thought she was gorgeous." Marie was working at an eyeglass manufacturing plant when she happened upon Jack in the driveway. She was also a new bride of four months but was contemplating leaving her husband. "She was unhappy at the house where she was. She kind of married this guy—her words: 'I never really liked him in the first place, but I wanted to get out of the house and have a baby and start a whole new life....' Then we met, and the next day we moved in together," Jack recalls, of the move to a tiny apartment financed by

Marie's wages. According to Jack, Marie's family is, "I hate to say this—kind of a lower-class white trash." Jack comes from an "educated" family and is proud of the increase in status he provided her at the time. "I pulled her out of that situation."

Eager to spend as much time as possible with Marie, Jack began leaving State College each Friday for the three-hour drive east. After three months of this arrangement, Marie turned up pregnant. We ask whether they'd discussed having children beforehand. "No, that was a subject we never talked about," Jack replies. "But I knew she wanted to get pregnant because she didn't want to use any protection." For Jack, Marie's failure to employ birth control is the equivalent of a bullhorn broadcasting her maternal desire and no direct conversation is necessary to establish that fact. When asked to describe how he felt about this, Jack simply says, "I was OK." The two decided to terminate this pregnancy due to their ages—both were twenty at the time—but another pregnancy almost immediately followed. This time, both were adamantly opposed to an abortion. Jack then dropped out of college.

"We were made for each other," Jack crows, recalling this time, evidencing more than the usual level of romantic feeling. Yet he admits, "I don't think we'd agreed that we were going to stay together forever." Marie had never bothered to get a divorce from her husband, yet once they decided to carry the pregnancy to term, Jack and Marie were firmly a couple who "though never married in the eyes of the law" nonetheless thought of themselves as a family.

## ATTRACTION, AFFILIATION, CONCEPTION, BIRTH, AND BEYOND

For the middle class, pregnancy is usually the outgrowth of a relationship, not its impetus. It is a reflection of a couple's decision to commit to each other, not the cause for commitment. On Philadelphia's affluent Main Line or in well-heeled New Jersey suburbs like Cherry Hill and Haddonfield, shotgun marriage is largely a thing of the past.[26]

Unplanned pregnancies that occur before marriage are typically avoided or terminated. And while poor men like Byron often become fathers in their early twenties, their middle-class counterparts typically put off parenthood until their late twenties and beyond, and then almost always within the context of a relationship that is years in duration, one in which the signals of commitment—that is, marriage—are unequivocal. But in the neighborhoods we studied, with their lack of opportunities and many challenges, nothing seems to work the way it should. It is not so surprising, then, that this order of events is often turned upside down. Here, once a young "couple" becomes pregnant and decides to take the pregnancy to term (a decision generally ceded to the woman), the bond between the two typically coalesces into more of a "relationship," though often in dramatic fits and starts.[27]

While pregnancy often serves as a galvanizing force that transforms "togetherness" into more of a "real relationship," the birth of a baby can solidify a disadvantaged young man's dedication to his partner even more, at least in the short term. Take the story of David Williams, a black thirty-year-old father of five, as an illustration. David grew up in Hunting Park, just one mile north of Will's Fairhill home, across the street from the park the neighborhood is named for. Because his parents were still teenagers when he was born and were soon overwhelmed with the responsibilities of raising him and his three younger sisters, all close in age, David was brought up in his paternal grandmother's home on Lycoming. This tidy row home built of native sparkly granite "shist" on the first level and with pristine aluminum siding on the second was further embellished by a two-story bay window on the side. The property was secured by a chain-link fence and the pincushion front lawn was filled with freshly trimmed shrubs and well-tended flowers. "My grandmother had a *nice* house," he recalls. The neighborhood, now half-black and half-Hispanic, centers on the park, which is its jewel.

Hunting Park was still a desirable residential neighborhood when David was a child—a far cry from the industrial neighborhoods of Fairhill and West Kensington just to the south, known colloquially as the "Badlands" because of the drug activity there. But by the mid-1990s, when David hit his teens, the Badlands had clearly crept north and the jewel of a park had become little more than a haven for drug dealers. Its western boundary, Old York Road, with its imposing three-story Victorian twins and occasional grand stone singles, began to draw prostitutes, pimps, and street hustlers like a magnet.

The father of five children by three different women, David describes his current girlfriend, Winnie, as the "best" of his children's mothers and refers to her as his common-law wife. Yet their relationship and entry into joint parenthood also had a haphazard quality. "When I was first with Winnie I had a girlfriend on the side too, Kathy," David explains. "She's somebody that I met at a Narcotics Anonymous meeting. We got close and we were helping each other with our addictions. One thing led to another, and we got intimate. Me and Winnie would get into an argument; she'd tell me to leave; I'd go stay with Kathy." "So how did you end it with Kathy?" we ask. "Winnie got pregnant, and I had to do what was right, stand by Winnie."

David may have been "together" with Winnie at the time his son Julian was conceived, but the relationship was hardly ideal—why else did he find himself so often with Kathy? It took a pregnancy to resolve the dilemma of which woman David should choose. Suddenly, because of an unplanned conception, his course was clear; he "did the right thing" and chose Winnie. The two then began to form a family around the promise of a shared child. As evidence of this decision, David left Hunting Park for South Philly, where Winnie had secured a unit in the Wilson Park Homes, a newly renovated mix of two-story family townhouses and high-rise buildings for the elderly just a stone's throw south of Tasker Homes (from which Amin and his mother had escaped), where the two now live. He views the Wilson Park location as a big step downward in the local prestige hierarchy from his grandmother's semidetached Hunting Park residence.

Nonetheless, "each month of the pregnancy, you know, we got closer and closer. I wanted to be with her more. And then like two or three o'clock in the morning, she had me running to a Pathmark grocery store buying different foods. So that brought us a lot closer too. And then, watching him born brought us even closer. On her last push he came spinning out like a bullet!" David recounts, beaming at the memory. "Nothing was more beautiful than Julian. The way he came out of his mother, that was amazing. And I held him, I didn't want to let him go."

The child has become David's obsession, despite the fact that he sees his daughters, now in their teens, only once a month or so and has no contact with his sons, who are ten and twelve. And Julian's birth has further stoked David's desire to stay with Winnie, whom he now professes to love. Despite the lack of a marital tie, the two have begun to "go for" husband and wife. The way he sees it, his new job description is "being there for her. Um, ah, um, helping her, when things is rough you got to be in her corner, sharing, compassion, closeness, communication. That's what I'm trying to say: communication."

There are many things David says he loves about Winnie. Her culinary skills get first mention: "What's the saying, 'the way to a man's heart is through his stomach'? She's a good cook. That's the truth." And besides, he adds, "She's a good housecleaner—she keeps the house clean. We work our problems out together. Most of the time she's pretty cool." But what quality does he treasure even more? "She takes care of the kids—she's very firm—she's there for them. That's what I love about her the most."[28]

David is making what he views as a bold attempt to form a family that can withstand the test of time. Yet his background, his current circumstances, and the fragile relational context into which his child is born all dramatically reduce the probability that he will succeed. When we last speak with David he is still together with Winnie—Julian has just turned one—but by the time Julian celebrates his fifth birthday, a father like David has less than a one in three chance of still being together with the mother of his child.[29]

The experiences of Amin, John, Tim, Byron, Will, and Jack all bear these statistics out. Things between Antoinette and Amin grew impossibly strained when Antoine turned three. Not only had the "retaliation-type situation"—both of them cheating to get back at the other—become unbearable, Amin had also been laid off from his job. Due to his felony convictions, he had had a hard time finding another. Now, a year later, the two still haven't spoken; though he sees his son at Antoinette's mother's home, Amin doesn't even know his son's address.

John's girlfriend left him during the pregnancy, infected by her mother's downright hatred of John. And Tim's relationship blew up when Mazie found him on the couch having sex with Andrea—only one in a string of poorly disguised infidelities. Byron hung on for thirteen years and enjoyed a fairly good relationship with Shari, but then lost his city job due to drinking, and she put him out of the house. He blames her actions on the fact that he was suddenly unable to contribute financially, not on the drinking that cost him the job. He also blames her for "cheating"—though her so-called infidelities occurred after she had broken up with him and kicked him out.

Will went on to have three more children with Lori, who then became an addict and left Will to move in with her drug-dealer boyfriend, trading the children back and forth every other day. Finally, the mother of Jack's two children, ages nine and eleven, moved out after twelve years together—she could no longer deal with his outbursts of anger. He is hoping to reconcile. In the meantime, he lost his job when a judge ordered him into a residential rehabilitation program: just after the breakup Jack was charged three times in a single week for driving under the influence.

Through the life stories of these men, whose backgrounds and circumstances are fairly typical of the range of fathers we spoke with, some of the seeds of relationship destruction—the first deadly strike against those who wish to stay involved with their children and father them well—are revealed. Tenuous relationships and a lack of sufficient desire to avoid pregnancy produce unplanned conceptions and births. Drawn by the possibility of a profound connection to another human being, a child of one's own, future fathers and mothers—young people who may barely know each other—often work fairly hard to forge a significant relationship around the impending birth. The new baby often spurs these efforts further, at least for a time. But the conditions under which these conceptions occur make the odds of success very low. Next, we explore in greater detail how these so-called unplanned pregnancies actually come about, how fathers react to them, and why.

# TWO

# Thank You, Jesus

"Guess what?" Charlene called to her young nephew Andre as he burst through the front door and bounded up the stairs to his room. Fifteen-year-old Andre and his older brother, as well as his two younger half sisters, mother, and stepfather, were all living with his Aunt Charlene, the seven-member extended family jam-packed into one of the fourteen-foot-wide, shotgun-style row homes that populate much of Camden. In 1970 the Green family had followed the path of so many other African American families in the migration up the coast from their home in Rocky Mount, North Carolina. Ever since, Andre's mother and her sisters have often offered one another shelter during hard times. In fact, Andre cannot remember a time when he hasn't shared quarters with some combination of grandparents, aunts, uncles, and cousins. "What?" he replied cautiously, noting the disapproving tone in Charlene's voice. "You know your old girlfriend?" Andre pictured Sonya in his mind and recalled their on-again-off-again relationship with mixed emotions, impatient now with the way his aunt was drawing out the drama. "Yeah, what about her?" As if unable to hold back the news a second longer, Charlene blurted out just two words: "She pregnant!"

This was indeed a surprise, a shock really, not only to Andre but soon to everyone who heard the news. Andre was the exception to the other kids in the neighborhood—a serious, church-going boy who made the grades in school, stayed off the streets, and carried himself "like a young man," he tells us later while recreating the scene. "I was always a gentleman type. I was never a gangster type with my pant hanging down and all that." As the information about Sonya registered, Andre gathered as much shock, disappointment, and anger into his voice as he could muster and shouted, "Oh, man!" before stomping off to his room and slamming the door for added effect. But, as he tells us with a sly chuckle, it was all a performance for his aunt's benefit. "I was just doing that as a front around her. When I went to my room I was like, '*Yes!* Thank you, *Jesus!*' Boy, I was jumping around, couldn't tell me *nothing!* I was *happy!*" He grins, recalling the moment. "When my aunt and them came around me I be sitting there like, 'Ah, man, what I'm a do?' But meanwhile, on the inside I was *happy.*"

What prompted such enthusiasm in a boy just starting high school? Andre says simply, "Because that was me. I always wanted my own child. People didn't understand me. They like, 'How you gonna take care of this baby? This baby is going to be born in poverty' and all this stuff. That's what they was saying." But Andre shrugged off these negative assessments. "To them it was a mistake, you know. My daughter wasn't no mistake to me!" He adds, pointing proudly to the sleeping child, Jalissa, "My daughter, she is the bomb!"

Andre makes clear he is no "hit and run" father for whom children are mere trophies of sexual prowess. "I want to be a *real* father to my kids. I want to not only make a baby but I want to take *care* of my baby. I want to *be* there." He is dedicated to ensuring that Jalissa will grow up "with stuff that I didn't have," especially "love from her father. I didn't have that. She's got a father that's *there* for her, that she *knows,* that she *loves,* that she calls 'da da.' Oh, she knows her da da!"

Andre is determined not to be like his own father and uncles who are, in his words, "dogs." "They will create their kids—and they got kids all over the place—but they never really took care of them or spent time with them." Andre points to four boys around his own age that he's run into by chance—half brothers he didn't know existed. He spied the first boy while walking through the neighborhood on the way to visit his cousin. Noting the striking resemblance to himself, Andre asked who his father was. The name the boy offered was the same as Andre's own father's. Not long afterward, Andre and his mother were at the grocery store, "and this boy was helping us bag. I said, 'Mom, that boy look just like one of my dad's kids.' I ask him what his dad's name is. What he say? *My* dad! I asked him how old he is and he said he was around the same age as me and my younger brother!" Several months later a fight in the schoolyard that pitted Andre and his younger brother against two other boys landed all four in the principal's office. The school called in Andre's paternal grandmother—the only adult on the emergency contact list who answered the phone—as part of the disciplinary process, which led to the following scene: "She came to the door and the other boys was like, 'Grandma!' And we was like, 'Grandma?' And she was like, 'Ya'll are brothers.' We was like, 'Brothers?'" After these experiences, Andre started to wonder, "Dag, how many kids do my dad got?" Contemptuous of his father's behavior, Andre vowed to do right by his kids when he became a father. "I started saying, 'If I ever have a child I refuse to let my child go without a father. I want to be there for my child, for her to know that she or he has a father that she can come to, and I'll be there when she needs me.' It's just like I was inspired by my dad treating me wrong to take care of my kid."

Fast forward two years. Jalissa is seventeen months old, and Andre is more involved with her than ever. In fact, Andre's mother now has custody. Andre had visited Jalissa one afternoon when she was still an infant and had immediately seen that things were not right. "I happened to go over there one day, and she was lying on the couch. But I could have sworn that it was a doll baby 'cause she was real skinny and her head was big. Her head was big 'cause her body wasn't at its right weight with her head. And I was like, 'Oh no.' I was like, 'Where's my baby?' They was like, 'Right there!' I was like, 'Where?' They was like,

'Right there on the couch.' I said, 'Give me my baby!' I took her to the hospital and everything." The hospital's social worker reported Jalissa's condition to the Department of Children and Families, who levied a charge of child neglect and removed the child from Sonya's care. At Andre's prompting, his mother went to court to seek custody.

In a tragic and ironic turn of events, just after Andre intervened to rescue Jalissa from Sonya's neglect, his older brother Charlie was killed for coming between a child and his father. "Charlie had a girlfriend," Andre tells us, "and he was taking care of her and her son. The son wasn't his and the father found out that my brother was being a father to the little boy. He shot Charlie in the back." Andre's mother has struggled for years with a drug addiction (one reason why Andre, his mother, and his brother and sisters are doubled up with his aunt Charlene), and while she had managed to get clean before the shooting, Charlie's murder has driven her back to her old habit. While his mother struggles for sobriety, Andre has dropped out of school to care for Jalissa. By all accounts, he is performing the role well. "Every time I take her to church, people say, 'Oh Andre, you're doing a beautiful job. That baby is gorgeous. You're taking care of her; you're doing her hair nice and stuff.' I say, 'Thank you.' They're like, 'Andre I'm very proud of you' and stuff like that. It feels good."

When we moved into East Camden and began to study the lives of inner-city fathers, we were eager to learn how they reacted to the news of a pregnancy. Did they "hit" and then "run" like the stereotype exemplified by Timothy McSeed, or did they grit their teeth and determine to face up to their impending responsibilities? Both of our guesses proved wrong; most greeted the news with happiness, and some, like Andre, even with downright delight. But the "happy" reaction, and the complex realities that prompt it, is molded by men's often-troubled childhoods and the challenging neighborhood environments in which they came of age. If one listens carefully enough, the happy reaction speaks volumes about these men's highest hopes and deepest desires, and how these will animate men's subsequent efforts.

Andre was one of the first young men we spoke with after arriving in Camden. We were stunned by his story. We had to ask ourselves whether this guy was for real. Although Andre had not set out to become a father—his liaison with Sonya was a brief and mostly unhappy one—when he hears the news of her pregnancy he is overjoyed. His mother and aunt are not so thrilled. After all, Andre is still in high school, has no job, lives in a neighborhood full of violence and crime, and has long since broken up with the girl who is about to become the mother of his child. Most Americans would probably agree with Andre's elders that raising a baby under these circumstances is a profound mistake. Yet young men like Andre have their own reasons for welcoming these children into the world.

In our conversations with each father, we explored the story behind how he became a dad, some for the first time like Andre, and some for the second, third, or even the sixth time. We asked each father about every pregnancy he claimed responsibility for. We wanted to know if he had wanted to have a child right then, if and when he had used contraception, and if he had talked about having a baby with the woman he was with at the time. We asked him to think back to the moment when he first heard about the pregnancy and to describe what went through his mind. And we inquired about the reactions of both his and the mother's family, as well as any advice these kin gave.

## REACTIONS TO THE NEWS

Men's responses ran the gamut—from vehement and panicked denials of paternity to loud shouts of joy—when they first heard about the pregnancy.[1] Only a handful outright rejected the news. A pervasive sexual mistrust—the conviction that women couldn't be trusted to be faithful—featured large among men who responded this way.[2] Another handful said they were either shaken or scared or didn't quite know what to think when they heard about the pregnancy.[3] Craig, a black twenty-eight-year-old day laborer was just fifteen, like Andre, and had recently been kicked out of the tenth grade at Camden High when he learned that his girlfriend was pregnant. We ask if he had felt ready to become a father. "No, no, I am not going to sit here and lie to you. No, I was not ready at all." Craig then says, "When can you actually say that you are ready to have a child at a young age?" Lee, a black forty-two-year-old, part-time construction worker was already twenty-four when his girlfriend conceived. Thinking back, he says his first reaction was, "Run!" explaining, "I didn't have no job!" Several others say they were unsure how to respond because the woman in question kept changing her story about who the father was.

For one pregnancy in five, men say they responded by "accepting" the news, a generally positive reaction but one tempered with a sobering realization of their new responsibilities. When Marie told Jack, the thirty-three-year-old white father we met in chapter 1, that she was expecting he says he was "excited." Yet, he admits, "I was a little scared." When we asked what had him worried, Jack replied, "Responsibility. Staying home all the time instead of hanging out with my friends, the financial costs—diapers, diapers, diapers. Formula! Ow! But I was looking forward to having a little baby running around my house. That's what I focused on." Jack took the news in stride, dropped out of college, and got a job. Alex, age thirty-six, was raised in Camden by the oldest of his six siblings; when he was three his mother died and his father abandoned the family. This black father of three was eighteen when he learned his girlfriend was pregnant the first time. Alex's initial emotion—delight—was quickly overtaken by a second: an almost overpowering sense of duty to his unborn child. "The first thing that hit my mind was, I did not want to be like my dad. This is the summer between the eleventh and twelfth grade, and I said, 'look ain't no sense in me going back to school. I need a job.'"

Unadulterated happiness—even joy—was by far the most common reaction though; more than half of all pregnancies were welcomed in this way without reservation.[4] Byron Jones, age forty-six, whom we met in the previous chapter, is clear about his response to the news: "Shoot!

I was *happy*, man!" Thirty-nine-year-old Amin Jenkins, also from chapter 1, says that during a brief interlude in his late teens when he was not incarcerated, he fathered a son with a woman he was not even together with at the time. Nonetheless, he tells us, he reacted with considerable enthusiasm to the news that this mere acquaintance was pregnant with his child. "Even though I was not in love, I wanted a son." Many fathers were surprised that we would even ask them this question. "I was glad! It was no major obstacle!" says thirty-three-year-old Steven, a black father of three who works as a casual laborer for a city contractor, describing his reaction to the news that he was going to become a father at age twenty, as if the answer to our question was so apparent that it could be assumed.

In story after story, happy reactions abound. Thirty-six-year-old Omar, perhaps the most troubled, violent, and criminally involved man we spoke with—a black hustler who had even pimped out the mother of his three children—was also puzzled by our query. He exclaimed, "I was happy! All the other girls killed my babies. They had abortions. I said, 'She's my first—I'm gonna give her everything.'" Joe, a white forty-five-year-old father of four who drives a horse and carriage for tourists, says simply of his reaction to the news that his first child was on the way, "I wanted a son, and I had a son!"

Forty-six-year-old Roger (who manages a thrift store), twenty-six-year-old Little E. (who works at a butcher shop in the Italian market), and Ozzy, age thirty-five, who does odd jobs and collects SSI (or "disability") for mental-health problems—all white men—each claim a strong underlying desire to have a child that was galvanized by the news. "I always wanted one!" Roger tells us, to explain his ecstatic reaction. Calvin, who combines maintenance work with occasional jobs with a moving company, was twenty-five when his first child was conceived. He recalls a similar response: "I loved it. I love kids!" This white forty-five-year-old now has five children.

James says that he planned it all out. This white forty-year-old father of four has his own home business assembling computers. Although he was only nineteen at the time his first child was conceived, he claims, "I wanted to have a kid. I wanted to get my girlfriend pregnant and have a baby. Nobody made me that way—that is me, how I came up. I was a working kid. I thought I made a lot of money. I was ready for it." At the time, he suspected that his girlfriend was having sex with several other men on the side, yet he says, "When I found out she was pregnant everything changed. I was like, 'I don't care if she is cheating,' and at first I was so happy."

## WERE THE PREGNANCIES PLANNED?

Taken together, the happy and accepting reactions to a pregnancy comprise over three-quarters of all responses (see table 2 in the appendix). At least some of the men who were happy at the news thought that they were "ready to become a dad," as James had, or said they had "always wanted" kids. Yet recall that Andre Green had clearly not set out to have a baby with Sonya. Nonetheless, when faced with the opportunity to embrace a pregnancy, he seizes it with both hands.

A critical ingredient to our story's arc—high hopes, yet often failed ambitions in relation to fatherhood—is the fact that precious few pregnancies are either actively avoided or explicitly planned. We asked each father to tell us the whole story around each conception, whether he had talked about the possibility of children with his partner beforehand and whether either he or she was using any birth control at the time. We then sorted fathers' answers into four categories: "planned," "semiplanned," "accidental," and "just not thinking at the time" (see table 3 in the appendix).[5] Planned pregnancies—cases in which men said they wanted to have a baby at the time and had talked with their partner about it—account for only 15 percent of the total.[6]

Accidental pregnancies—where the couple actively avoids a pregnancy (with birth control) or believes they can't conceive due to infertility—are as rare as planned pregnancies. Note though that both condoms and the pill are highly effective at preventing pregnancy; thus "accidents" due to contraceptive failure are likely the user's failure and not the product's.[7] When William, a twenty-five-year-old African American father of four who works as a dietary aide at a nursing home, is asked about the conception of his oldest child, he responds, "My girlfriend told me she was taking birth control pills every day faithfully. Somehow she just got pregnant. I don't see how. I told her I didn't want none, not yet, and she said she ain't want none neither."

Bruce is a white forty-five-year-old father of twins who occasionally finds jobs through a temp agency. Even though he didn't particularly want children, he didn't "believe" in safe sex either, because "every time I had any kind of relationship, there is no babies born." Imagine Bruce's surprise when after only two months with Debbie, she announced, "I am seven weeks pregnant!" Forty-two years old at the time, Bruce responded with disbelief—"I am shooting blanks!" he exclaimed. "You can't be pregnant!" The argument was settled when they went for a DNA test. "That was when she found out," says Bruce, "that I was the father and she was the mother."

When accidental pregnancy occurs, discussions of abortion often follow. Although some of these pregnancies are terminated, disagreement among the couple often forestalls abortion.[8] Intriguingly, these men are more likely to oppose than advocate for ending the pregnancy in these circumstances. Taken together, the planned and accidental pregnancies account for only 30 percent of the total. Just over a third are somewhere in between; we call these "semiplanned." We asked Michael, a forty-one-year-old African American father of an adult son and a four-month-old daughter, whether the conception of his oldest child, at the age of eighteen, was planned. He responded, "Semiplanned. We didn't sit down and say we wanted to have a baby. It just happened." "Did you think she might get pregnant?" we asked. "Yeah, but I didn't care. It was good. I was still a young man. I wasn't wearing no protection, so it happened." Men like Michael feel fatherhood's pull to some degree but haven't seriously discussed this desire with the woman they are with at the time. Although these men say they were well aware that unprotected sex would lead eventually to a pregnancy, they didn't seem daunted by the fact (see table 4 in the appendix).

In sum, while a handful of pregnancies are either clearly intended or unintended, many are "semiplanned" or somewhere in between. Yet a rather large number—nearly four in ten—are not on this continuum at all. In these cases men say they were "just not thinking" about the consequences of their actions when conception occurred. Like those in the semiplanned situation, these men say they had no lack of familiarity with the birds and the bees but admit to using condoms only occasionally if at all. They also admit they knew or suspected that their girlfriends were not using birth control, though few say they had bothered to ask. Thomas, for example, is a white twenty-seven-year-old father who says he has worked at practically every type of fast-food franchise in Philadelphia. His first child was conceived when he'd been with Laurie, whom he met at a party, for only six months. Thomas claims he never even considered the fact that she might get pregnant, though he knew she wasn't consistently taking the pill: "She was missing it," he says. "We talked about it for just maybe a minute or a half an hour. We said, 'Let's have a baby.' It wasn't serious—just one of them things, you know?" When asked how he reacted to the news, Thomas recalls, "I was confused, like I wasn't sure I wanted a child. But I didn't want an abortion. No, I was against that. It's not right. If you get pregnant, you get pregnant—you know what I'm saying? And not out of careless sex, 'cause if you don't want to get pregnant you know what to do."[9]

Yet what is striking is that relatively few men who conceived while "just not thinking" denied paternity, and none who acknowledged responsibility said that they didn't want to have the child. Furthermore, nearly all expressed a determination to be actively involved in their child's life.[10] Bart, for example, a white twenty-seven-year-old who processes orders in a warehouse, has only a tenuous relationship with his two oldest children by a prior partner. He describes his response to his new girlfriend's pregnancy in this way: "I said to myself, 'I want to be there for the pregnancy. I want to be there through everything—when she goes to the doctor, when she has the baby, to wake up with the baby in the middle of the night.'"

As we've hinted at, though one might suppose that the degree to which the pregnancies were planned or actively avoided would heavily influence men's reactions to the news of a conception, the correlation is far from perfect. While those with planned and semiplanned pregnancies almost universally welcome the news, those who are "just not thinking" when conception occurs still respond positively—with either happiness or acceptance—more than six times out of ten. Even more amazing, about a third of those who had been explicitly opposed to having children and were taking measures to prevent conception were either happy or accepting when the pregnancy was announced. What are we to make of the surprisingly positive nature of men's responses?[11]

Perhaps the men who most eagerly embrace the news of a pregnancy are simply those who are in the best life circumstances. To see if this is so, we turn to the stories of Ozzy and Terrell, who, like Andre Green, were especially enthusiastic. Ozzy, who collects SSI and does odd jobs, is a thirty-five-year-old white father of one. He was twenty-seven when he met Dawn one night on South Street, a strip of loud bars, live music venues, and tattoo parlors, and thus the favorite congregating spot for many of Philadelphia's working-class youth. Ozzy was out with a group of his friends and Dawn was with her friends, and after the collective laughing, teasing, and flirting was over, the two ended up exchanging phone numbers. Four months later Dawn was pregnant.

There were bigger problems though, aside from the fact that they had known each other such a short time. The first was that Ozzy was an unemployed high school dropout who still lived at home and had developed a problem with a variety of substances, including alcohol, Xanax, Valium, cocaine, and marijuana. The second was that Dawn was only sixteen years old. "I lied to her about my age," Ozzy admits. "I told her that I was like twenty. Then after a couple of months I started to like her a lot so I told her the truth." Despite his problems, Ozzy was thrilled—without reservation—by the news of Dawn's pregnancy.

"I always wanted to have a kid," he told us. "But before I met Dawn I never really found the right person to have one with."

Terrell, a black nineteen-year-old supermarket stock clerk, was just seventeen when he heard the news about the conception of his oldest child. But this came as no surprise to him, as he had lobbied hard for his girlfriend to have a baby. He had just begun his sophomore year at West Philadelphia High School when he met Clarice, a friend of his cousin's. "I come home from school one day, and I saw her sitting on the porch. Ever since that day I've been liking her. I had it in my mind that I'd get her."

Terrell was surprisingly sure of himself, seeing as how seventeen-year-old Clarice was pregnant with another man's child at the time. Meanwhile, he was doing poorly in school and cutting classes regularly. After he violated a contract that required attending a certain number of days per month, the school finally kicked him out. It was when Terrell was "sitting at home with nothing to do" that he began to "get with" Clarice, who had just broken up with her newborn's father. The first thing he did was to try and convince her to get pregnant by him right away, despite the fact that he had just left high school and had no job or any prospects of one. "I wanted a son so bad. I saw all these guys with kids, especially with boys," Terrell explains. "I always wanted a son, especially when they start walking." Clarice was understandably reluctant, but Terrell was persistent. "She came around to it, came to her senses," he says with satisfaction. "We sat down and had a long talk about it. Two months later she was pregnant."

Ecstatic that he was about to become a father, Terrell immediately signed up for Job Corps after hearing the news. After spending several months in Pittsburgh acquiring some of the skills of the construction trade—drywall and plaster work—Terrell quit and returned to Philadelphia to witness the birth of his son. Several months later, just as he was adjusting to being the father of a newborn, Clarice had some additional news for him: she was pregnant again, this time with twins.

What the stories of Ozzy and Terrell reveal is that men's willingness to embrace, or occasionally even pursue, pregnancy does not always, or even usually, hinge on their life circumstances. In fact, it is often men in some of the worst and most desperate situations who are also the happiest when learning of a pregnancy. Why would this be so? How would the prospect of bringing a child into the world under these circumstances be an appealing one?

The answer lies in the way men answered one important question: "What would your life be like without your children?" One might expect that men would complain about lives derailed, schooling foregone, and job opportunities forsaken. Yet we heard very few tales about sacrificed opportunities or complaints about child support and the like. Overall, children are seen not as millstones but as life preservers, saviors, redeemers, and the strength of the sentiment behind these fathers' words makes them all the more remarkable.[12]

Kervan, a black twenty-one-year-old who had been working construction but has just finished bartending school, says that without his kid, "I'd probably be in jail." Quick, who is black, twenty-four, and a student at the Community College of Philadelphia, says, "I'd be dead, because of the simple fact that it wasn't until Brianna was born that I actually started to chill out." Apple, a black twenty-seven-year-old who washes dishes six days a week at Jim's Steaks, a hoagie shop on South Street, says, "I guess after I got caught up in the bad life, as far as jail, the kids helped me keep my head up, look forward. I got something to live for. Kids give you something to live for." Lee, who was just laid off from an optical lab and is currently working odd jobs to get by, is an African American forty-two-year-old father. He says, "Without the kids I'd probably be a dog. I hope not with AIDS." Thirty-seven-year-old Seven, the black on-and-off house painter, tells us, "I couldn't imagine being without them because when I am spending time with my kids it is like, now that is love. That is unconditional love. It is like a drug that you got to have."

For these men the imagined alternative to becoming a dad is not a college degree or a job as a CPA, it is incarceration, death, rehab, "the bad life," "a dog with AIDS." Kids, on the other hand, are something to live for, to fight for, "a drug that you got to have." Self is a twenty-one-year-old African American who is certified as a home health aide but can only get part-time work at a nightclub. He recalls, "What influenced me to have children was that I felt alone. It's a good feeling to always know that I have somebody to relate to. A child at that. Somebody that's going to look up to me, to learn from me and things like that."

White metal finisher and part-time construction worker Alex, age twenty-two, says that without his children, "I would be out getting high because I would not have anything. I would have my girlfriend but my baby is the most important thing in my life right now." Will Donnelly is white, twenty-four, and works part-time as a mechanic. He teaches boxing on the side at the Joe Frazier gym.[13] He says, "I think I'd probably be in jail. My little brother is in jail, and I figure without kids, whatever he was doing I'm sure I would have been doing it with him." A white building superintendent and jack-of-all-trades, Bill is thirty-eight, and white carriage-driver Joe is now forty-five; both offer particularly poignant responses. Bill says, "I'd still be out there. I'd still be fucking off, drugs and all. I think about my kids and there's just this *hope* I have now of getting a good relationship with them." Joe responds, "Man, I wouldn't even know how to answer that, they are such a big part of my life. I would probably be in jail down on Eighth and Race."

We ask Lacey Jones, a black forty-two-year-old who cooks at Jessie's Soul-on-a-Roll in North Philadelphia, "How did you see your future before you became a father?" "I didn't have no future," he replies. "I didn't care. I lived for the moment." We ask, "Did you think you would live to see forty-two?" "No. Nobody did," Lacey admits, and then adds, "Nobody expected me to be there to see seventeen." Lacey now lives with his fiancée and her daughter plus the nine-year-old child whom he gained custody of a year ago. He gets up at 5 a.m. to ensure he's on time for his 7 a.m. shift, works forty hours a week, never touches anything stronger than beer, and spends most of his leisure time with family—visiting with his eighteen-year-old daughter and her kids, offering advice to his seventeen-year-old son, or spending time with his fiancée and the two little girls who live in his household. "I spend as much time as I can with my family," he says with satisfaction.

His life wasn't always this way, though. The two oldest children—only nine months apart—were conceived on the heels of his release from prison at age twenty-three, after his murder conviction was over-turned on a technicality.[14] Both women lived on his mother's block, and "it was back and forth. I'd mess with her for a minute. I'd go mess with the other one for a minute. Once one got on my nerves, I went with the other." In both cases, Lacey says, he was "just not thinking" when conception occurred. By age twenty-four he was incarcerated again for robbery. He began seeing the mother of his nine-year-old while in prison, where, somehow, she got pregnant; Lacey wasn't released until the child was five. Lacey treasures all his kids, but especially the youngest, because she offers him the opportunity to watch one of his children grow up. When asked what his life would be like if he didn't have children, he says, "I can't imagine that one. I really can't. I can't imagine it. 'Cause my life without them, it would be empty. It would be empty. That's what kept me going in prison, knowing that I had to come out and be there for them."

How can men like Lacey even consider bringing a baby into the world when their lives are so chaotic, their relationships so fragile, and their means of support so unstable? Don't they understand that these are not good situations for a child to be born into? We asked each father what they thought was the best time and circumstances to become a dad. Ironically, almost every response pointed to standards that the men themselves had not met when they had their first child. Andre Green is a good case in point. He counsels that men should become fathers "when they are older and married. Just wait till they get older and married." Monte, a white twenty-one-year-old with three children already says one should be twenty-five and established before thinking about children. "You know, some people like to go to college, so that's four years. Finish them four years of college, and then look for a job, take a job, and get some money out of that job. Then if you have a kid you'll be able to take care of that kid." William, white and twenty-seven, is the father of an eleven-year-old. "We were fourteen, fifteen years old," William says, referring to the period when he and his child's mother conceived. "You don't have a kid that young. I believe if you're going to have a kid, wait until at least you're twenty-three, twenty-four years old. Because then you're done with high school; you can go to college; you can do what you want. And then you can get yourself situated and have the kid, you know what I'm saying?"

Most men at least pay lip service to the norm that the ideal age to begin having children is in one's late twenties or early thirties (though one put it as high as thirty-seven), because by that time one is done with school, established in the workforce, and settled down. Not until this stage, fathers claim, are men prepared for the responsibilities of fatherhood. A few even say that one should be married first, and should wait until several years after the wedding (past the "jittery years" of marriage, according to one who had some experience in that department).

Hill, a thirty-year-old black father with a four-year-old child, tells us, "I would say thirty because, at least for men, between thirteen and thirty years of age the world is like a playground—you don't really know what you want to do, you just want to see how much you can do, how much you can get away with." Thomas is a white father of a nine- and six-year-old and is currently in a halfway house finishing out a prison sentence. He is one of ten siblings, each of whom have the same mother but different fathers, and has been to jail five times in his twenty-eight years. At first Thomas refuses to give a precise age, saying only that it's when "you're ready to settle down." He continues, "You'll just get tired of partying, and even if you don't party you want to slow your life down a little bit. Instead of going out to dinner you just want to sit home and watch the news. You know, just settle. Actually, right now would be the ideal time for me to become a father.

I'm twenty-eight. Yeah, right now would probably be good, 'cause I'm done with the fast life."

## EMBRACING FATHERHOOD

The portrait of low-income fathers that emerges from these responses is striking—many clearly have a thirst for fatherhood, though they might not discover it until their partner delivers the news that she has conceived. Despite the fact that most are in very tough circumstances and believe strongly that situations like theirs aren't the kind to bring a child into, a large majority still respond positively to the pregnancy. How do they resolve the dissonance between their desire for fatherhood and strong cultural norms—norms that they themselves seem to espouse—about the proper conditions for having children?

On the one hand, these men often show surprising optimism about the future. Yet at the same time, their narratives reveal deep uncertainty about the probability that their circumstances are going to get better with time. When one's future is so uncertain, it can be hard to muster the self-restraint required to put off having a child. Sure, he may not be in the best situation right now, but given the nature of life at the bottom rung of the ladder, when will that be? And how long would the good times last anyway? Byron Jones, from the last chapter, articulated this point when we asked him his thoughts on the ideal time to become a father. He replied, "When you are financially able to take care of the children. And that's when, nowadays? I have no idea, because, when is it? I mean, shoot, for the average guy stable employment don't last long. You might work this week and be out the next week, you know?"

Another dynamic helps resolve the tension men might otherwise feel over having children in these circumstances. Recall that most pregnancies are either semiplanned or happened because the men were "just not thinking about" contraception at the time. Were they simply assuming that their partners were "taking care of it" in some way? For some, this is clearly the case. Kanye is a twenty-eight-year-old African American father of at least two children and is currently receiving General Assistance. He had his first child in high school when he was sixteen and the child's mother was fifteen. "A guy grows up thinking if he is intimate with a female, she is supposed to be on birth control."

Yet most men admit they had no reason to assume that their girlfriends were taking precautions, and they still failed to initiate a conversation with their partner about the possibility of pregnancy. Consider the case of Jones, a white twenty-year-old working two part-time jobs, and his former girlfriend Jessie. One evening before their now one-year-old daughter was conceived, Jones and Jessie had been walking together down the aisles at Wal-Mart, browsing through racks of baby clothes and accessories. Jessie had taken the opportunity to almost casually inform Jones that she had stopped taking her birth control pills nearly two months earlier. Although he was surprised, Jones took the news in stride and told us later that he didn't think it was "really any big thing. Like I wasn't saying, 'Uh-oh, better get back on the pill.' And we totally knew the consequences, I mean, there's no doubt about that. I don't need sex education; I know how it works." Jones summed up their outlook this way, "We were fully aware, but I guess you could say we weren't really worried about it."

From these and many other accounts, it seems that low-income couples often practice a kind of "don't ask, don't tell" approach to birth control. From parallel conversations with mothers in these neighborhoods, Kathryn Edin and Maria Kefalas learned that a woman often stops taking birth control because she wants kids and lacks sufficient incentive to wait.[15] A man may want a child badly too, at least eventually. But each wants a child for his or her own purposes—the desire often has little to do with their relationship with each other. And neither party usually seriously discusses their desires openly until a pregnancy occurs—he prefers instead to let her take control over whether or not birth control is used. He typically continues to relinquish control once the pregnancy is confirmed, as he almost always places responsibility for the next set of decisions on her.

Men rarely counsel their partners to have an abortion—this usually occurs only when a woman is very young or still in school. While most fathers we spoke with believe abortion is wrong, even those who are strongly morally opposed are typically careful to say that because she is the one bearing the child and giving birth, the woman has the ultimate say. While this sounds quite progressive, there is often another logic in play. Because she is the one who chooses to stop using birth control and then decides whether to bring the pregnancy to term, she also bears the ultimate responsibility for those choices; the buck stops with her. By stumbling into fatherhood without explicitly planning to do so, men's sense of responsibility for bringing a child into the world in even wildly imperfect circumstances is significantly diminished. He can always say, "Well, I didn't set out to become a father, it just happened. She wasn't taking birth control, and when she got pregnant it was really her decision to have the baby."

## WHAT HAPPINESS MEANS

Whether or not they harbored a conscious desire for children prior to pregnancy, conception presents a man with a profound choice. How is he going to respond? What are the possible futures flashing before his eyes? On the one hand, he typically sees a clear opportunity to do the right thing, to step up to the plate in a way that he has never been challenged to do before. For a man to welcome a pregnancy in what is often an astonishingly challenging situation is to embrace the chance for a certain kind of salvation. In fact, the less intentional he was about the pregnancy, and the worse the circumstances, the greater the magnitude of that possible rebirth. Sometimes, a palpable need for redemption is evoked by the mess men have made of their lives—Amin Jenkins is a perfect example. But for young men like Andre Green who haven't yet had a chance to make many mistakes, a child—so pure and innocent—is a symbol, almost a magic wand that has the power to vanquish the oppressive sense of "negativity" that quite literally surrounds those who come of age in the inner-urban core.

To illustrate what the "happy" response to pregnancy might mean, we return to Andre's story and—to an extent—to our own. What became clear from Andre's account, and what made it so remarkable to us, is that Andre clearly doesn't see himself as deviant for having fathered a child in almost impossible conditions. Instead, he sees himself as a hero of sorts; that is how he tells his own story. To understand why Andre sees his actions in such a positive light and why he has embraced fatherhood so eagerly, we had to look to other events that occurred in his Camden neighborhood around the time Andre and Sonya conceived their daughter, Jalissa, events that Andre and we witnessed together.

The year begins with a sensational double homicide and hostage standoff on Thirty-Sixth Street near Westfield Avenue, just blocks from Andre's aunt's home and, coincidentally, just two houses down from the first-floor apartment into which we are about to move. The Les, one of the handful of Vietnamese couples who have bought wood-framed, 1920s-era single-family homes in the neighborhood at bargain basement prices, are celebrating the New Year with relatives right after midnight on January 1. A burglar, later identified as the assailant in two execution-style murders, breaks in through the cellar window, lured by a rumor that Mr. Le has just gotten a large insurance settlement for a work-related injury. When his wife hears the noise and investigates, the would-be thief shoots her in the chest. As her husband tries to call for help through a window, the intruder shoots him in the head and then runs out of the house, taking the couple's four-year-old child as a hostage. He is killed by police after a standoff on a neighbor's porch.[16]

Then in March a man is spotted by firefighters standing calmly by with a doughnut and coffee in hand while a roaring blaze consumes a two-story row home near McGuire Courts, a low-rise red-brick public housing project just minutes from Andre's aunt's home. Four children are trapped upstairs by the flames. While the two older children escape through a second-story window, the younger ones, ages two and four, perish. The children's mother is unable to help with the rescue effort, as she is getting high in a nearby crack house. Police later learn that the onlooker is the former live-in boyfriend. He had entered the house while the children were asleep to seek revenge on their mother, who had just "put him out." He had doused the kitchen, living room, and the stairs to the second floor with accelerant and had then struck a match.[17]

In May an antiviolence group unveils a piece of public art at city hall—nameplates of over 180 recent homicide victims linked together by large metal chains symbolizing the chain of violence in the city. Those named include Samalica Ortiz, an eleven-year-old East Camden girl who was killed three years before by a stray bullet while waiting for her piece of cake at a birthday party.[18] In June a rare piece of good Camden news makes the *Inquirer:* Eboni Burnett, a shy but bright girl who attends Davis Elementary, down the street from Aunt Charlene's row home, has won a brand-new bike for 182 days of perfect attendance. In the news photo, she wears her relaxed hair in a scraped-back ponytail and stands next to her friend, a slight Vietnamese youth who has relatives across the street from our apartment.[19] Two years later the two girls will be united again, but this time in tragedy. In the space of a single week, Eboni's father will be killed in a drug-related shooting, and her friend's uncle will be shot down in his own front yard while trying to settle an altercation between his son and two other Vietnamese teens.[20]

August offers up the most heinous murder of the year. Shaline Seguinot, a thirteen-year-old middle-school honor student and cheer-leader, takes a bicycle ride and never comes home. She is found three days later in the high weeds behind her school. She has been stabbed ten times, her throat is slit, and her body offers evidence that she has been raped by at least two different men.[21] Families like Andre's take notice, as his own half sister is also only thirteen years old.

Into the fall the drug trade is humming, and Camden police are making an average of ten drug-related arrests a day. On the street the addicts are as visible as the dealers. In October sixty students from Camden schools gather at the new Camden Waterfront Entertainment Center—practically the only venue besides the New Jersey Aquarium that attracts outsiders not looking for narcotics to the city—to pledge to stay free of drugs for life, an annual event sponsored by the Drug Enforcement Administration's Network 3 school antidrug program.[22] The featured speaker is eighteen-year-old Tavon Johnson of Baltimore, who has made national news for seeking custody of his thirteen-year-old brother, headed to foster care because his father's incarceration and his mother's drug addiction have left no one to care for the boy. Young fathers like Andre take inspiration from the story. Andre plans to apply for custody of Jalissa when he turns eighteen.

Finally, as the year winds down, compositions written as part of the Stop the Violence Educational Forum essay contest at one Camden elementary school are judged. "Every day I look at the news I hear about something that happened in Camden, whether it's a shooting, a drug bust, a missing kid, a fight or a robbery, and it upsets me," writes LaCondia Catlett. "Every time I hear about someone getting killed, I picture that person being someone in my family or someone I really care about." Catlett ends her essay with the following message: "Put down the guns and pick up the babies."[23]

In Andre's environs the rhetorical contrast of guns versus babies—rejecting violence and death and embracing innocence and new life—gives an almost mythic aura to the act of becoming a father. Compared to all the negativity that Andre could be involved with, what could be more positive than diapering a baby, making up formula, and skillfully fashioning her hair into twists? Picking up the babies is exactly what Andre Green thinks he is doing, and the context of his Camden address is why he cannot conceive of his actions in a negative light. By embracing a less than perfectly planned conception, becoming a father, and attempting to meaningfully engage in a child's life, young men like Andre Green are embracing the chance to do something *productive* to counteract the problems they see all around them.

Now we can understand what the positive reaction to a pregnancy means and how it goes far beyond a simple emotional state, as well as why so many men who did not react positively express such deep shame later on. "I was happy" is shorthand for a recognition of a rare opportunity for a clean start in a new role, immense gratitude for that opportunity, and a symbol of one's determination to take up the gauntlet and attempt to "do right" by a child. The neighborhood context throws the decision of how to respond into sharp relief. Against these often-lurid backdrops, embracing new life offers young men a chance to participate in something viewed as utterly good.

Those who have lost their way in these environments may especially welcome the chance to turn their lives around. They may look at their past and regret "rippin' and runnin'" with the wrong crowd, dropping out of school, getting "caught up" in dealing or using "substances," or having sexual liaisons on the side. Some, like Amin Jenkins, can clearly see how they failed their other children. But with each new pregnancy there is a possible child who exists only as pure potential, and this is where men's optimism shines. Being a father to *this* baby is a saintly calling in an evil and chaotic world, and a relationship he hasn't screwed up yet. Who wouldn't be excited by such an opportunity?

How does this turn out in the long run? Unfortunately, not so well for most of these fathers. As we've hinted at before, the story we tell in the following chapters is much like a Greek tragedy in which the fatal flaws that bring about the hero's demise—both as a partner and father—are evident from the beginning. Flaw number one is that he typically conceives in the context of a bond that, while not purely casual, is not really serious either—which commences a shotgun relationship. As we show in chapter 3, such relationships have little "glue" beyond a shared child and are thus exceedingly fragile. Flaw number two is conceding the responsibility for conception to her. The fact that he also typically deeds the decision about whether to carry the pregnancy to term to her alone constitutes flaw number three. While relinquishing power in these domains may be an effective way of warding off criticism for bringing a baby into a harsh set of circumstances, and while this rationalization may suit his purposes at the time, these actions also set up a dynamic that will work against his efforts to claim rights to his child later on. As we demonstrate in the pages that follow, when couples break up, as they usually do, and he wants some say in the parenting, he will frequently complain that his ex-partner acts like she "owns the child." But how can he really protest that she's in the driver's seat when he is the one who put her there in the first place?

In this chapter we have explored these men's surprising reaction to the news of a pregnancy—happiness—and what such a response really means. Now we must ask what transpires between these men and women during pregnancy and after the baby is born. The happiness response offers the first clue of the powerful hopes for forging an "ideal family unit" that suddenly come into play, but over the long haul will men's actions conform to these desires? Do these men even aspire to marriage? If so, what are their criteria for a marriage partner, and are these criteria ones that their children's mothers are likely to meet? We take up these questions in the next chapter.

# THREE

# The Stupid Shit

Robert aka "Bear" Mallory earned his nickname in childhood. While on an errand for their father, he and his brother were jumped by three older boys. In self-defense Bear started "biting and biting" one of his opponents and held on with his teeth—"like a bear," according to the police officer called to the scene—until he tore off the other boy's nipple. Bear revels in the retelling of this story and admires those who exhibit their toughness with violent exploits.

Despite the origins of his nickname, Bear reports an amazingly conventional adolescence for a white boy from Kensington. Surrounded by troubled peers, Bear nonetheless went to school regularly and earned solid Bs while working diligently at a number of after-school jobs, taking pride in the "possessions"—the sound system and small TV—he was able to accumulate with his earnings. Aspiring to a military career, Bear joined the Army Reserves at sixteen and completed the first half of his training in Basic Combat between his junior and senior year. To qualify for phase two of the training he had merely to finish high school.

Just three weeks shy of graduation, however, Bear had a violent fight with his stepfather, a sadistic man whose abusive behavior began the evening the two first met, when Bear was eleven. During that encounter Bear had made the mistake of bringing an action figure—his prized toy—to the dinner table, and as punishment the man pushed Bear's face into a plate of mashed potatoes. After years of being on the losing end of vicious beatings, Bear won this fight—Army training had left him physically fit—but lost the battle. In retaliation his stepfather kicked him out of the house, handing him a one-way bus ticket to North Carolina, where Bear's father had kin, on the way out the door. But Bear didn't board that bus right away. For the next three days, Bear, now homeless, struggled to stay in school. He showered surreptitiously in the neighbor's backyard with a garden hose and made sure he woke in time for classes. "I propped myself up against this store door that opened up at 6 a.m. and for them to get in they had to wake me up. So it was like my own little alarm clock," he recalls. But this grueling routine proved too hard. Admitting defeat, Bear boarded a Greyhound headed south, where his biological dad—recently dead from cancer—had a half brother.

As the bus lumbered down Interstate 95, Bear convinced himself that there was a bright side. Perhaps he could bring comfort to the family, as his uncle, a sanitary engineer and father of three young children, was struggling with the same disease his father had died from. Bear would do more than rise to that challenge; soon after he arrived the uncle died, and then "one thing just led to another"—he began having sex with his newly widowed aunt by marriage. Within a year of his arrival, Amber gave birth to Alyssa, Bear's first and her fourth child.

Meanwhile, Bear was learning that jobs for high school dropouts were in short supply in rural North Carolina. A half dozen relatives back home offered him help finding work, and Bear decided the best way to fulfill his impending family responsibilities was to return to Philadelphia, where he secured a job at a print shop for eight dollars an hour. Eager to keep the family together, Amber decided to join him. The two even managed to buy a rattletrap row home at a rock-bottom price, courtesy of his uncle's life insurance policy, just eight blocks southwest of his mother's house. But the overwhelmingly poor and predominantly Puerto Rican neighborhood they settled in was a world apart from Bear's childhood home in largely white Kensington. Their new address was in North Philadelphia's Harrogate section, not far from the infamous drug-infested "Badlands," and the choice of location proved to be a fateful one. As Bear tells us later, "*that* was our downfall."

Just a month or so after they had settled into their new home, Bear was laid off from his job. Then there was "nothing else to do but sell drugs," or at least that's what he told himself at the time. Truth be told, he had leads to some low-end jobs. Getting involved with the drug scene, which quite literally surrounded the small house just off G Street and Allegheny, was a youthful adventure and a rebellious rejection of the expectations suddenly foisted on this nineteen-year-old who had—more or less by accident—become "head of the house" of a family of six overnight. "There was just so much, well, kids mainly," says Bear, identifying the main source of stress that spurred his descent into deviant activity.

Soon Bear had transformed this dwelling from the happy home of a newly formed family to a "weed house," at least while Amber worked her four p.m. to midnight shift as a waitress at a diner a mile away. The home's location was perfect. Whites who wanted to satisfy their addictions in drug-rich North Philadelphia had to venture only two blocks west of Kensington Avenue, which marked the boundary of the typical white's comfort zone. And customers could do business with fellow whites, which added to the feeling of safety. Bear didn't perceive much danger in the enterprise—after all, they didn't sell "hard stuff," only marijuana they purchased for under-market value from a twelve-year-old Puerto Rican kid who "wasn't too bright." So while Amber was waitressing full-time to supplement the monthly two thousand dollars in Social Security death benefits she received for herself and the children she had had with Bear's uncle—Bear, who was supposed to be looking after the kids, carried his infant daughter strapped to his chest, letting the older kids run wild while he and a handful of childhood friends who lived nearby developed the business. Bear figured that he might as well blow the proceeds—on alcohol, drugs, and old cars, so he and his friends could stage their own "little crash-up derbies"—because he knew Amber wouldn't approve of where the money came from.

Then the Phillies made it to the World Series and Bear decided to celebrate, gathering his buddies to watch the final game. They downed a shot of Canadian Windsor for every base hit and RBI. The Phillies were winning, and Bear's friends—who were "so screwed up it's unreal"—and the whole neighborhood went wild. "People are shooting guns 'cause the Phillies are winning, shootin' in the air. We decide to take our clothes off and run around the block naked." This is what pushed the street's "old ladies" over the edge. A week later at a meeting of the neighborhood watch, they made sure Amber, who had been serving cheesesteaks and fries during that final game, got wind of what happened. Suddenly, the truth about everything—the parties, the weed, and Bear's own growing drug use—was revealed. Amber ejected Bear from the house.

But several months later, while Bear was serving an alternative sentence on a drug possession charge at Eagleville State Hospital, a rehabilitation center just outside of Philadelphia, Amber had a change of heart and came for a visit. Once the two were alone, one thing led to another yet again. Bear had heard rumors that men are more potent when they are "cleaning their systems out," so was not totally surprised when, upon his release, Amber had news. Despite the fact that he was, by his own admission, already overwhelmed by paternal responsibilities, learning the child would be a boy still made Bear giddy with anticipation—and determined to set things right with Amber. Upon release he talked his way back into the house and traded his fairly lucrative life as a low-level drug dealer for a part-time job at his uncle's salvage yard. This job paid only $50 a day, but he hoped he'd have better luck in the legitimate labor market eventually. He also stayed clean and tried to steer clear of his old friends—several had become addicts, and some were living on the streets. One close friend was even dead by this time, a victim of a lethal overdose.

Luck didn't strike until two years later when Bear, demoralized by his failed quest to secure a better job, got a tip from Amber's aunt's boyfriend and landed a position as an off-the-books roofer. The job paid relatively well—$125.00 a day—but was dangerous; it was also miserable in midsummer, when the blistering sun heated the asphalt shingles like a frying pan. But Bear's primary lament was that he could only scale Philadelphia's rooftops to do the work when it was not winter and not raining or when his boss, a recovering addict, didn't suddenly feel the urge to take off a day to attend a Narcotics Anonymous meeting. He ended up earning only about $15,000 a year from that job. Those higher-up and "on the books" in the construction trade are often unionized and better paid. Plus, they can claim unemployment benefits when the weather gets cold. These perks were off-limits for Bear; he had no formal training, no valuable skills, and no union card; he didn't even work on the books. He rued the fact that "my income ain't that great" but managed to supplement his earnings by scoring side jobs on weekends. A friend owned a power washer, and the two developed a small referral chain among homeowners whose domiciles were encased in aging aluminum. Bear has begun taking his son, nicknamed Cub, along on these weekend power-washing junkets, delighting in any opportunity to impart fatherly wisdom, such as "teaching my son to pee standing up in the bushes." Meanwhile, Bear dreams of becoming a firefighter, a job where he can pull down real money, and fantasizes about becoming the father whose progeny respect him because he's done something truly worthwhile, like rescuing a child from a burning building.

Bear is still clean and spends nearly all his leisure time with his family. And there is now a real spark in his relationship with Amber; they have just gotten engaged. But mainly it is Cub, now two, and, to a lesser extent, Alyssa, age five, who provide the motivation to stay on Amber's good side and surrender to the demands of a relationship. As we will see, this fact is not lost on Amber.

### "DOING STUPID SHIT"

The easiest way for fathers to be involved with their children is to stay in a relationship with their mom, a simple logic that has not escaped Bear. Thus he strives to form an "ideal family unit" in the wake of the birth of a child, and he is not alone. Despite the near ubiquity of unplanned conception, most fathers like Bear do make some effort to forge lasting relationships with their baby's mother. Survey research shows that at the time of the birth, more than eight in ten men who have a child outside of marriage are romantically involved with the mother, and about the same proportion say there is at least an even chance they'll eventually marry her. Half have found a way to live together by the time the baby arrives, and even more have tried living together by the child's first birthday.[1] Many men in Bear's situation are well intentioned. They want their relationships with the mothers of their children to work. But while good intentions may be a necessary foundation for stable family life, they are rarely sufficient. Of the men we spoke with, only a few were unambiguously "with" their child's mother at the time—although hopes for reconciliation are common.[2]

What goes wrong between the euphoria of a baby's arrival and that child's fifth birthday, when surveys reveal that only one in three men will still be in a relationship with their child's mother? This chapter, an autopsy of relationship failure, doesn't focus on the proximal causes that feature again and again in the narratives that appear throughout this volume—substance abuse, serious conflict, infidelity, incarceration, and so on (see table 5 in the appendix).[3] The corrosive effects of these factors have been well documented.[4] Instead, we attend here to the more subtle relationship dynamics that underlie the often-tawdry finales that blow their relationships apart.

Let's return to the story of Bear, who like many economically disadvantaged men, began his career as a father young; he was only nineteen when Alyssa was born. In his teens, he kept his partying in check, stayed in school, and steered clear of the law even though his family tree offered any number of felons ready to serve as alternative role models. "Half are on death row, all derelicts, OK? Drug dealers, pimps, I mean, you name it," he explains. In fact, among the fathers we spoke with, Bear's adolescent years were unusually orthodox. But just a few months into fatherhood, and after losing the print-shop job, he began to behave like most of the other Kensington youth he'd grown up with—he "started doing stupid shit." He whitewashed his act while Amber was around, but the farce was exposed by the neighborhood's "old ladies," who may have turned a blind eye to the drug dealing but stood firm against a gang of white drunks running naked in the street.

In these contexts both mothers like Amber and fathers like Bear often claim that their children have transformed their lives. But there is no denying that the men typically "rip and run" a lot before the baby comes and are far less likely than the mothers of their children to stay on the straight and narrow after the birth. Women usually see children as their chief source of meaning and identity and often hope—even if it is clearly against the odds—that their baby's father will emerge from the crucible of pregnancy and birth as deeply transformed as they are, willing now to put the interests of his family ahead of his own.[5] Men like Bear, though, often fail to fully embrace the new life or to cast off the old.[6]

What happens next is illustrative. Just after Bear and Amber's engagement, six years after their first child Alyssa was conceived, Bear injures his back and can't work. Lacking health insurance, he decides to ease his pain by scoring a small quantity of the Percocets that are so readily available on the streets of North Philadelphia. Amber is also uninsured and suffering from an abscessed tooth, so she gives Bear money to purchase painkillers for her as well. Finances are tight, so the cash she entrusts to Bear is especially precious. Things do not go as planned. While waiting for his contact to arrive, Bear spots another dealer and decides that he has enough extra cash to purchase a small quantity of cocaine—due to the pain, he tells himself. A police officer observes him making the buy, beats him up, and locks him in a paddy wagon for several hours before releasing him—minus the cocaine and the rest of the money. When Bear finally drags himself back to the house, Amber takes a dim view of his story, convinced he has wasted her hard-earned cash and that he has spent the intervening hours getting high. And there is other evidence that Bear may be veering off the righteous path; just the other day he and his brother had tried to score cocaine for resale to pay off his brother's child-support debt. A rival drug dealer confronted the pair and shattered a two-by-four over Bear's head, only to be met by Bear's irate brother, who beat the assailant in the head with a cinder block, rendering him unconscious. "He messed that guy up good," Bear chuckles, with brotherly pride. But Amber fails to see the humor in either situation. Not surprisingly, Bear ends up living back with his mother.

We have chronicled how eagerly men anticipate children despite the fact they seldom plan them. We have also shown how much they believe they have to lose if they break up with the mother of their child—the chance to create the "ideal family unit" and the opportunity to enjoy "the whole fatherhood experience," despite the fact that they were seldom in a "real relationship" when their first child together was conceived. Cub, especially, is clearly the apple of Bear's eye. How do we then account for Bear's failure to fully shape up the way that a family man should? Why can't these men try harder?

In many ways, we argue, the speed at which couples break up only reflects the essential truth of these relationships—that beneath the facade of familylike ties, these men seldom have a strong attachment to their children's mothers. We run into Amber after a lengthy final conversation with Bear, and she confides that something vital has always been missing in the relationship: "I see the way he looks at his son. I wish he would look at me that way some time," she says poignantly. Amber has always sensed what the trouble is: though he's clearly attached to his children, she's less sure that he's devoted to her.

## FRAGILE BONDS

Despite men's apparent resolve to reform, weak attachment to one's child's mother is a key part of their failure to do so. What can account for the shortfall in this basic ingredient of couplehood? First, consider that young people across the class spectrum break up every day over any number of things, from whether the toothpaste tube is squeezed in the middle or rolled up from the bottom to dissimilarities in moral outlook. Conversely, even seemingly trivial things like similar tastes in music or food or bits of common biography may form the glue that helps keep relationships together. One piece to the puzzle of low attachment is the incredible brevity of most of these unions prior to conception; young disadvantaged couples who have children together may emerge from the euphoria of the delivery room only to find they have astoundingly little in common—a seemingly obvious, yet crucial fact.

Potential points of friction, both large and small, are often submerged in the months leading up to delivery as the couple scrambles to get ready for the baby.[7] Bear and Amber, for example, were too busy arranging an interstate move for the very pregnant Amber and her three young children to think much about the large difference in their ages—not to mention maturity levels. But in the late stages of pregnancy or in the aftermath of the birth, variations in background and outlook often come raging to the fore. What might have been little more than "togetherness" at the point of conception—at least from his point of view—has been prolonged and intensified, first by the news of the impending birth, then by midnight demands for pickles and ice cream (recall Byron Jones from chapter 2), followed by a flurry of activity to get ready for the baby, and then, finally, by the event itself. But as the day-to-day routine of being a "family" sets in, many fathers—and no doubt mothers—are often surprised by the fact that they've joined their lives with a veritable stranger's.

Self, the African American twenty-one-year-old from North Philadelphia we met in chapter 2, earned his GED and certification as a home health aide while in Gary, Indiana, where he was assigned to Job Corps after an expulsion from University City High. He's never managed to find a full-time job in that trade (or any other) so he scrapes by working three nights a week as a nightclub waiter. Self is highly articulate and defines himself by his art (performance of the spoken word), his love of learning (treatises like *Black Men: Obsolete, Single, Dangerous?*), and his spiritual orientation (a blend of prayer and relaxation exercises).[8] His story illustrates how the birth of a child often forces a young couple to consider important issues that they have avoided before.

Self met his first baby's mother on her front stoop when he was eleven and she was thirteen. Seven years later, after Self returned from Job Corps in Pittsburg, the two reconnected and almost immediately conceived. But once mother and child came home from the hospital, the couple began to wrangle over "money issues," and Self also suddenly became aware of how different her background and outlook were from his own.

Self considers himself a self-made artist and intellectual. His mother had struggled to put herself through college after he and his siblings were born, and his goal is to do likewise. Meanwhile, in his ample spare time, he sits in on public lectures at Temple University and performs spoken word at local clubs. His mother's bachelor's degree and her occupation—an administrative assistant at Drexel University—lend his family a certain level of status. In contrast, Self's baby's mother is an aimless high school dropout from a family with no such pretensions. After the baby was born, Self tried to provide the intellectual "uplift" he thought she would benefit from. She felt belittled by his efforts and a rift opened that rapidly widened.

"How did the birth of your first child affect your relationship?" we ask. "It's crazy, man, because the birth of the child gave us more issues to approach. So that opened up the door to agree or disagree." What kind of issues? "Money. Also, I think at that point, I started looking at her more as somebody I wanted to uplift. So after the child was born, since I took on that point of view, I would do things like get books for her and teach her the things that I was learning. And at the time, she may not have been as open to that, and I may have taken that personally. So I think after the child was born, it created a certain bitterness in our relationship."

Recall Ozzy and Dawn from chapter 2, who got pregnant only four months after exchanging phone numbers one night on South Street.

When their daughter Roxanne entered the world after a protracted labor and painful cesarean section, Ozzy, who was forced to wait anxiously outside the delivery room during the surgery, was on top of the world. But over time the differences between Ozzy and his child's mother emerged. He continued to flit between any number of low-level, part-time jobs—changing oil at Pep Boys, setting up and taking down shows at the convention center, washing dishes at an Italian restaurant—which, combined, seldom brought in more than two hundred dollars each week. He lived with his mother rent free, so had little motivation to work more. Dawn, though, was far more ambitious. She had enrolled in community college and was pursuing a nursing degree and, in addition to her studies, she had taken on the night shift at Kmart so the couple could get a place of their own. "She was mad 'cause I wasn't working enough," he recalls. "She said I was lazy, that I didn't want to work."

How did Ozzy respond to these taunts? "I started treating Dawn like crap, treating my family like crap, getting into fights with everybody—fistfights, like arguments with my mother and everybody. Pushing Dawn around—like I would hit her and stuff—I didn't mean it. The next day I would feel really, really bad. You don't go and hit somebody if you love her, if you are going to marry her." It was during one of these violent episodes that Dawn, after five years together, finally broke things off.

Having too little in common isn't the only source of friction that emerges soon after the baby is born. As new parents like these embark on the serious business of building a bond, certain expectations come into play—his and hers—and stark gender differences emerge in how each thinks a father ought to respond.[9] Mothers are now thoroughly engrossed in the tasks of caring for a newborn and begin to set their sights on the "marriage bar"—standards regarding what it will take to make them ready for marriage.[10] As Christina Gibson-Davis and her colleagues have shown, both parties agree that the relationship must be of suitable quality and that the couple's finances have to be "right" before the wedding. These standards are fairly high, and new parents are aware it might require several years to meet them.[11] Now that they share a child, the mother is often chomping at the bit to start making progress toward these objectives. After all, she reasons, isn't this why they are together?

What effect does this have on the new father? Think back to the stories of Ozzy and Self, whose haphazard partnerships led to relationships with women they shared little in common with. Note that after the baby is born, Dawn promptly enrolls in school and takes a job to save money for an apartment of their own. Meanwhile, Ozzy's desultory attitude toward work doesn't change at all—he seems happy if he's just getting by, content to remain living with his mother. No wonder Dawn begins taunting him, charging that he's lazy because he can't get a full-time job. Similarly, when Self's first child is born, he is also less than motivated to find full-time work. "I think I was more into performing at the time," he admits. "You know, as an artist. I may have had a part-time job somewhere in there, but I don't remember working really that much." Meanwhile, his baby's mother is forced to take on full-time employment at a clothing store. Is it any surprise that there are suddenly "money issues"?

Kathryn Edin and Maria Kefalas have told the mother's side of the story in this way: for her a baby is instant maturity—if she doesn't get her life together and figure out a way to support the child, she could lose custody to the state. Plus, she, he, and the community at large assign her—not them—ultimate parental responsibility. She usually welcomes this opportunity to prove herself, because it is a chance to move away from the chaos of a life spinning out of control toward one that is ordered by the routine demands of a child. Once she becomes a mother though, she begins to evaluate her partner in a new light—where does he stand in relation to the marriage bar? A sharp sudden rise in expectations—in terms of both the relationship's quality and financial viability—is the result.[12] Suddenly, she's set standards for his behavior that she may never have given voice to before, and he seldom sees this change coming.

Debuting in 1955, the television sitcom *The Honeymooners* kept American households in thrall for more than two decades. Alice Kramden is the grown-up in the relationship and keeps the family together, while her working-class husband Ralph bumbles hopelessly along, pursuing one get-rich scheme after another. In the 1960s American children were offered their own helping of the same theme; Wilma Flintstone and Betty Rubble had to constantly bring their foolish, accident-prone husbands up to speed in the important matters of life. For decades, even centuries, popular culture has served up the notion that wives must fix up their men. To the extent that this actually happens, most American husbands seem to be rising to their wives' demands without too much resistance—after all, married men earn more, drink and carouse less, and commit less crime than their unmarried counterparts do.[13]

But men at the bottom have a sharply different reaction. Women's new mandates are not met with the grudging acceptance of a Ralph Kramden—or that of the typical American husband, who has become increasingly involved in the day-to-day activities of family life in recent decades.[14] Instead, our men become bewildered, aggrieved, and enraged—one mark of a deep fragility that has its roots in men's often-troubled families of origin and will manifest itself again and again as this book tells the rest of its story. The sudden change in a woman's expectations may, in fact, be read as a betrayal, conclusive evidence that she is lacking in commitment, willing to throw him over as soon as he fails to meet her mounting demands. Men often counter with the charge that their new baby's mother is an overbearing know-it-all.

Dayton is thirty, black, and has three children aged four, five, and seven. Donald is also African American, and is a thirty-seven-year-old substitute teacher's aide. What the printed page cannot fully capture is the sharp emotion both Dayton and Donald express as they share this part of their stories. Dayton, a day laborer, says that he broke it off with his youngest child's mother "because she is the type of female that don't want to listen. She think she know everything. But I am not that type of guy that tolerates things like that." Donald and the mother of his fourteen-year-old child tried living together for a short time when his child was young, but "it ain't' work," he states bluntly. "It lasted about three or four weeks. I couldn't take it." What went wrong? "I couldn't deal with her 'I'm the boss' attitude. She is a very controlling person, always trying to run my life and everybody else's life."

Thus, as soon as a woman has the baby, she can easily be perceived as just one more authority figure—the kind they've been rebelling against all their lives—who insists that he shape up and toe the line. And on the financial end she may be viewed as a mere mercenary, just out for his money. Boy Boy, a black twenty-year-old father of a four-year-old child, sums up the sentiments of many when he tells us, "it's all about the Benjamins now. If you don't got no hundred dollar bills, you don't got no woman." He responds grudgingly, in part, because this all comes as a surprise—it is remarkable how men consistently fail to anticipate that their children's mother's expectations will rise after a birth, even if this baby is not their first. Some, like Dayton and Donald, break things off quickly for this reason, while others labor for several years under the weight of her expectations, as Bear did, only to falter later on.

The one-sided revolution of rising expectations, which places women in the judgment seat and men in the supplicant's role, makes it easy for him to blame the relationship's demise on her "I'm the boss attitude"— and even to extend the character assassination to the entire female half of the population. For example, Jeff Williams is a forty-six-year-old African American father of a two-year-old boy and an eighteen-year-old daughter. He works as a cook at Essene Market and Cafe on South Street and says that participating in the birth of both of his children was a "blessing." "I was stunned! I was just at a loss for words. It was so beautiful just to see my daughter coming out of her mother's womb. With both of my children, *I* was the first one to hold them." Clearly relishing the memory, Jeff continues, "I really felt good. With my youngest, my son, I asked the nurse to take pictures of him, the whole nine yards. And I have all of this in a little folder. I'm talking about before and after he came home—down to the bracelet, with his name, the name card on his crib—I kept all of that, because it was such a wonderful feeling."

Yet Jeff is only tentatively attached to the mother of that boy, though they live together in a tiny apartment in North Philadelphia. His hesitancy is due in part to a philosophy he's derived from the hard knocks he received from the mother of his first child, who he feels treated him as little more than a paycheck—pressuring him to turn his earnings over to her. Reflecting on this situation, Jeff says, "I don't have no trust, no faith in women, behind the fact that to me, a woman is like a snake. They'll try to manipulate you; they use whatever they have to use to take advantage of you. My daughter's mother taught me that love is like running water. It turns off and on. I really believe that behind the fact of so many breakups is that they can love you when you're doing—providing financially—but when you don't do, they don't love." Now Jeff sees this same characteristic in his eighteen-year-old daughter. Despite the fact that he has always paid child support whenever he has had work, "My daughter had told me on numerous occasions that her mother's boyfriend does more for her than I do, and I felt hurt. Irregardless, if this person is doing something for you or not, he can't fill my shoes. I'm still your father. If I give you a million dollars or I give you a penny, I'm still your father."

Men on the economic edge, even in multiyear partnerships with several children together, often obsess about the younger guy with the nicer car who has a better job and might turn their girlfriend's head. Bill, a white thirty-one-year-old father of six, emphasizes the nearly universal belief that love is not enough; when the money is gone, love disappears. He is haunted by the fear that a younger man with a better job will woo his children's mother, Michelle. "I hear a lot of people say that love is good, but I am telling you, money will rule over a relationship real quick. If the money is gone, the love is gone, and a lot of women will do that to you. Don't get me wrong; there might be maybe two relationships out of a hundred that will survive without money. Even if a man works part-time and he is doing what he has to do—he could be the greatest man in the world—and a woman will overlook that for somebody driving in a new car, a young guy. That guy might have a little bit of money now, but sooner or later down the line he could wind up like I am at any time, no guarantees at all. Yo, that concerns me a lot. I love my girlfriend a lot. I call her my wife because we have been together for twelve years off and on, and we have six kids."[15]

## THE NEW PACKAGE DEAL

There is more to both of the stories we've just told. Jeff was using drugs when his first child was born, a habit that presumably consumed a lot of his cash, and Bill is an alcoholic who falls off the wagon of sobriety at regular intervals—the couple conflicts his drinking provokes can be dangerously fierce: "Since we moved to this house four years ago, there has been cops at my house maybe thirty, forty times because we were fighting," he confides. So we are still left with the question of why so many of our men can't just find a decent job, settle down, and bring their money home? Bear's narrative is another case in point—after all, how much is Amber really asking of him? Fleshing out this part of the story requires us to consider what kind of bond these men really think they are building and how they react to the familylike relationships they suddenly find themselves in when their children are born. On the surface it may appear that the new father is fully on board—Bear's attempts to build a relationship with Amber, to steer clear of drugs and "stay legit" despite the paltry wages from salvage and roofing work, are actually quite typical of men's efforts in the wake of a birth. But dig just beneath the surface and you will uncover a deeper truth: Bear's primary attachment has always been to his children, and never to their mother.

This is not how things used to be. American men were partners—usually husbands—first and parents second. Fatherhood was a "package deal."[16] And it was the tie with the mother that bound men to their obligations to children, obligations they might otherwise have ignored. Scholars studying the lives of men living apart from their children in the fifties, sixties, seventies, and early eighties argued that the "package deal" version of family life worked reasonably well as long as the mother and the father remained together. But when couples broke up, men seemed unwilling, or even unable, to engage with their children. "It is as if men only know how to be fathers indirectly, through the actions of their wives.... If the marriage breaks up, the indirect ties between the fathers and children are also broken," wrote family scholars Frank Furstenberg and Andrew Cherlin to explain the paltry rates of father involvement among divorced men in the 1970s and early 1980s.[17] Similarly, Elliot Liebow, the ethnographer of poor black street-corner men of the 1960s, wrote, "It is almost as if the men have no direct relationship with their children independent of their relationship with the mother."[18]

For men across the bleak terrain of Camden and the economically distressed neighborhoods of Philadelphia, the package deal has been turned upside down. Here it is often the child who is at the center and who binds men to their obligations to their children's mother. Usually, shared children, and not couple affection or commitment, are the glue, at least in the men's minds. For men like Self, there is little direct relationship with their child's mother independent of their relationship with their child (Bear's union with Amber, which began as a mere relationship of convenience, only recently generated a real spark). In some fundamental sense, it is not a "package" at all—but family life à la carte. Yet the purest expression of the desire to parent their children well and get what one man called "the whole fatherhood experience" is their willingness to try to make a go of it with their baby's mother—to try and form the "ideal family unit" that they view as supreme. They believe it is vital to participate in "all of it"—to witness the first words spoken, the first steps taken, and other crucial milestones. But will a shared child be sufficient to transform these more-or-less coincidental unions into lasting bonds?

The stories we turn to now—of Lavelle and Bruce—show how the couple-level "expectations" that the "real relationship" suddenly imposes on him can begin to chafe quickly, turning from a bad cough to a terminal disease almost overnight. The first symptom of the malady is often quite subtle—in the weeks and months following the birth of the child, men are often profoundly vexed by one of the fundamental expectations that usually accompany the transition to family life: the comonitoring of routine activities. Overnight he's accountable to another person 24–7, when he would rather merely revel in the bond he is forming with his new baby girl or boy. Suddenly, he feels smothered by the weight of this basic expectation. He just can't stand "all that togetherness."

Lavelle and Big Toya share a pixieish four-year-old with a shy but mischievous grin. This thirty-four-year-old black man hails from East Camden, but he grew up in rural Bucks County, Pennsylvania, the middle child of a baker's dozen born to a stable African American, working-class, two-parent family. When we meet Lavelle, he has been working for four years in the shipping department of a local electronics warehouse and has recently gotten a raise to just over nine dollars an hour. His goal is to move further up the ladder, and he works hard to look the part of an aspiring manager, cultivating a clean-cut, conservative look.

Little Toya's mother, Big Toya, is someone Lavelle knew from the neighborhood—five years ahead of him in school—who walked into a bar where he was drinking one day, handed him a slip of paper with her phone number on it, kissed him on the cheek, and left. The two were barely together when Lavelle was informed he was about to become a father. Once the baby was born, Lavelle fell head over heels in love— with the infant, Little Toya. Lavelle and Big Toya then experimented with being a couple by moving in together, but the way he tells it, Big Toya was so possessive and jealous that he could barely leave the house to get to his job as a door-to-door salesman. Suffocated by the situation, Lavelle abruptly fled, moving from Bucks County to Camden, where he had just found the warehouse job he now holds.

Lavelle had no intention of letting the breakup, or the geographic distance, get in the way of his relationship with Little Toya. But soon Big Toya—an unsmiling woman whose toughness and rough origins are broadcast in her manner and style—made it clear that she was going to restrict Lavelle's access to his daughter unless he included her in the relationship. She "wanted to play it off as a package deal," Lavelle complains, mocking her manner and tone, "'you can't take her here without me. You can't take her there without me.'"

Once resigned to Big Toya's insistence on the mother-daughter "package deal," Lavelle began to make considerable efforts to invest once again in a relationship he had run away from a short time earlier. He proposed marriage but she turned him down flat, saying that she didn't want to lose her freedom, her food stamps, or her subsidized apartment. Recently, he has persuaded her to let him call her his fiancée. What has he gotten out of the deal? She is now willing to spend weekends with him in Camden with Little Toya in tow. "She's fun to be with," a smiling Lavelle says about his daughter before his countenance clouds and he adds, "She's better than her mother." Lavelle readily admits to us that he would never have chosen to stay with Big Toya if she hadn't happened to be the mother of his child, and then hadn't insisted on making Lavelle's parental relationship contingent on his connection with her. "Big Toya feels that she gave birth to her, so it's her way or the highway," he explains.

Bruce, the white father of two-year-old twins who works day labor and sells blood for extra cash, ends up in a similar situation. Seven weeks after Bruce and Debbie started seeing each other, she declared that she was pregnant. This required a significant mental adjustment for Bruce who, at forty-three, was resigned to childlessness ("I thought I was shooting blanks!"). Then came the second bit of unexpected news: Debbie was carrying twins. Bruce didn't have much time to recover from this one-two punch before the babies were born. Bruce gloried in fatherhood, but in the weeks that followed he realized that living with the mother of his newborns entailed more constraints than he was prepared to submit to. Despite his age, he had never been in a long-term relationship, and he found that Debbie's growing claims on his time and attention were driving him wild. "If I would go someplace, she would want to go with me. And that is the main reason that broke us up. I would go in the bathroom, and she wanted to know what I am doing. Why should I have to answer to her? I just couldn't put up with it." Not having Lavelle's fortitude, Bruce managed to stick it out for only a little while; he packed up and left right after the twins' second birthday.

Thus far, this chapter has asked why new fathers' romantic bonds are so fragile and why so many can't seem to stop engaging in the "stupid shit" that breaks their relationships apart. In 1969 Travis Hirschi famously turned the tables on the study of delinquency: rather than asking why individuals *deviate* from conventional norms, he posited that criminologists should focus on why most people *don't*.[19] According to this view, life is a vast cafeteria of appetizing temptation. Thus, people need a strong reason—a stake in conformity—to abide by society's rules.

The key to desistance from deviant activity, Hirschi argued, lies in the strength of one's social bonds: the depth of one's attachments, involvements, beliefs, and commitments to mainstream endeavors.[20] Robert J. Sampson and John H. Laub have taken this idea one step further, arguing that key moments in young adulthood, such as the transition to marriage, stable work, or even parenthood, can alter one's trajectory—they can become a "turning point" where one can "knife off" the past and start fresh. But the transforming power of these key life events is contingent on the strength of one's social bonds.[21]

But even in the "real relationship's" earliest days, there are multiple signs that the bonds of disadvantaged fathers with the mothers of their children are not strong. First, at the same time these fathers are attempting to form a relationship with the mother of their child, their *attachment* to their partner is often remarkably low. As we have seen, this is in part because they don't know each other that well and may have little in common, but there are also other dynamics at work.[22] Second, her rising expectations are often met not with begrudging acceptance, but with bewilderment and anger. Here, men seem to be actively resisting the notion that they ought to *invest* more of their time and energy in the activities generally associated with becoming a family man—getting full-time work, settling down, and the like. Third, and perhaps most important, these men reject traditional beliefs about the enterprise they are supposed to be engaged in. They've turned conventional *beliefs* about family life—the package deal—upside down and have embraced a radical alternative, where the child is at the center and the mother is peripheral at best.

And as we show in the pages that follow, their *commitment* to their child's mother—the decision-oriented part of the bond—is also often low. We demonstrate that while on the one hand, most men at least go through the motions of forming real family ties, many are actually trying *not* to make a real choice. While they hold on to one relationship, they simultaneously hold out for something better—the soul mate they believe marriage requires. We show that aspirations for marriage, which seem to have endured even among the segment of the American population least likely to engage in it, as well as men's high standards for the institution may, in fact, be a driving force behind their unwillingness to fully commit themselves to the women they find themselves having children with.

## WHAT MARRIAGE REQUIRES

Many Americans assume that the institution of marriage has no relevance in the inner-city neighborhoods our men hail from. This is not so.[23] We asked for men's opinions on several aspects of marriage, including what he thought the ideal marriage relationship was like, how the ideal husband and wife performed their respective roles, the circumstances in which one should get married, and if they could identify any marriage relationships they admired. The answers are illuminating, not only for what they say about men's attitudes toward marriage itself, but also what they reveal about the true state of their relationships with their children's mothers.

Thomas, an unemployed white twenty-eight-year-old father of two children, ages six and nine, says he is holding out hope for marriage and longing to find that special "somebody who wants to be with me for the rest of their entire life." White fathers like Thomas have generally not lacked exposure to marriage; a substantial minority of those we talked to had short-lived marital unions themselves, and many have witnessed the marriages (and the divorces) of kin and friends. But they have seldom seen a marriage they admire. Thus, most conclude that marriage ought to be approached with great care.

Black fathers, by contrast, have almost never had any firsthand experience with marriage, which is also less common among their parents or close kin. Yet this does not mean that it is something they don't someday aspire to. Michael, a black twenty-seven-year-old stock clerk and the father of a seven-year-old child, says, "I dream about marriage. I dream about like me going to work, me going to work and coming home, and like my daughter and my wife and eating and talking and watching TV, playing. That would be like my day. Just being together." Michael's vision of the day-to-day realities of marriage is striking in its simplicity. Yet the conclusion that he and other black fathers like him draw from their lack of experience with marriage is remarkably similar to that of their white counterparts: achieving the status of marriage is an exceedingly lofty goal and should be contemplated only when one is absolutely sure that he's ready and only when he's certain he's found the right woman.

Men assess their readiness for marriage the way a patient checks his temperature. Being ready is not a matter of will; he must instead observe the symptoms of his own desires and behavior. "Am I really ready to settle down?" is the first question he asks of himself. "Settling down"—limiting sexual activity to just one woman—is a challenge many fathers feel men are congenitally unable to accomplish in their twenties; as one father said, "you gotta get all of the whoring and the hoochie mamas out of your system first." Boy Boy, a twenty-year-old black father of one, became a father at sixteen—with a thirty-two-year-old relative who seduced him at a family reunion. He says it's good to have children fairly young, since young men like him are "dropping like flies." He grew up "on the rough side of things" in the heart of West Kensington, and Boy Boy's childhood memories are punctuated with shootouts between the local dealers and the police. He was raised by parents who were so embroiled in the drug trade that they didn't pay their six kids much mind. He's got a girlfriend his age now and says he is in love; thoughts of marriage have even entered his mind. But he claims he can't get married to Danea just yet because he's got too many "needs" for one woman to satisfy. "The girl can treat me nice and everything. I may love her, but I ain't gonna get married if I know I am going to still be cheating on her. I like different things, man. Some things she don't do right. Some things the other girl might do."[24]

The difficulty of finding sexual satisfaction with just one woman is a common complaint among our younger black fathers, and some of their white counterparts too. But there is often more to these declarations than meets the eye.[25] As a deeper exploration of Boy Boy's story will show, giving license to one's "needs" in this domain may salve deeper anxieties about one's ability to meet a larger set of mainstream expectations. After nearly two years with Danea, the two have taken the relationship to the next level—they have even moved in together. But Boy Boy, who has always tried to stay on the right side of the law, has recently been laid off from his $7.50-an-hour job at a box factory and hasn't been able to find another job, despite considerable effort. To shore up the family finances, he has begun selling drugs for his father, a long-time neighborhood dealer. Danea has been pressuring him to leave the streets and search harder for legitimate employment. He cites his ninth-grade education as the reason he's been unable to secure any formal sector work. Meanwhile, how does he deal with her growing reproach? "When we argue and stuff, I go outside and get more phone numbers from girls so that it can ease my mind."[26]

Young men like Boy Boy are often eager to claim their status as men, yet have little to show for themselves, a state of affairs that can continue for years. "Talking to girls"—which can mean anything from flirting to sex—is a chance to claim some regard for his looks, his wit, his "game," from a woman who knows only what he has told her about himself, who isn't aware of his financial situation, his less than stellar past, or the child he has done little to support lately.[27] Likewise, keeping multiple women on a string—as Boy Boy was prone to do before moving in with Danea—dramatically increases the chance that at any given time he will be able to find at least one woman who will be in the mood to put up with him ("ease his mind") and make him feel like a man. Thus, marriage entails not only disciplining one's sexual desire but forfeiting a significant source of esteem as well. Sometimes a marginal young man may simply need someone to believe that he is better than he really is, particularly when the level of his finances or his ability to resist the "stupid shit" begins to fall short of the escalating demands of his child's mother, who may come to view him as a disappointment.

But readiness for marriage is more than being able to settle down with one woman. To be marriageable a man must have reached the point where he knows how his economic prospects are going to turn out—he's got to be settled. He doesn't simply want to go for the best woman he can manage to attract; it is a matter of fit between a potential partner's characteristics and his own—he doesn't want to overshoot and end up being a disappointment. Paul's opinion on the matter is an interesting case in point. His prospects looked relatively good in his twenties—he worked the entire decade as an under-the-table delivery truck driver in "the food industry," bringing in ninety dollars a day. In addition, the route facilitated a lucrative illegal sideline; currently, he is finishing up a sentence for drug distribution in a prison halfway house.

This black father of a four-year-old child is firm in his belief that "you should only get married when you are like thirty-five," because by then "you know what you are going to do and what you want to accomplish in life." At twenty-one talk is cheap, he says. "You said that you would accomplish this thing and that thing, but now you are thirty-five. You know whether you are on that track, and you see a light at the end of the tunnel in the future: 'OK, this is where I am going to go.'" Paul believes marrying in his twenties might have been promising too much, that a man who weds while in this hopeful phase might prove a disappointment a decade later. At the age of thirty-four Paul is now finally "open to" marriage and believes that if he can manage to secure employment, he'll have more to offer than most; his grandmother recently died and left him her home in the Mill Creek section of West Philadelphia where he was raised, and the once heavily blighted neighborhood (and site of the worst mass murder in the city's history) is now gentrifying.

Holloway Middleton, a thirty-nine-year-old black father of a six-year-old daughter from the Nicetown section of North Philadelphia, expresses similar concerns. He had a good job cleaning office buildings before he was laid off. Since then he has only found work through temporary agencies. He is adamant that "the only way that marriage works is when two people make the same amount. Like if you got a job making $20,000, and she's got a job making $20,000, then everyone's happy. If she's got $20,000, and you making $1,200, you know what I mean? It's like she takes care of you, and that's not going to work."

One study of a cohort of low-skilled men who were first identified while in high school and then followed over time reveals that for men at the bottom of the skills distribution, it is often not until their late twenties or early thirties that they enter into "careers"—a stable pattern of employment. This is particularly true for African Americans.[28] In our study African American men are the most likely to say that marriage ought to be put off until the thirties, the forties, or even beyond.

What most men are seeking in a marital partner is someone who is on "the same level." Listen to how Lee, a forty-two-year-old black father with three children, enumerates the "minimum criteria" for a marriage partner. "You each have to have a job, your own home, your own finances. I don't have a car, so you don't have to have a car, but, you know, we're meeting on the same level." Lee's ideas about the importance of equal status extend to the smallest detail. "I want a ring too—a diamond. I don't want no wedding band. If you're getting a diamond, I want one too. That way, if we break up, then both of us have a rock."

While it is vital to have settled down, and to have become settled, before marriage, men emphasize that it's critical not to settle—to marry without being absolutely certain that they have found the right partner. First, there are certain status considerations that must be addressed. As outlined earlier, men don't want to overshoot, but they don't want to undershoot either. In the neighborhoods we studied, it is marriage and not childbearing that signals one's status in the community. To the degree that pregnancy can be deemed "accidental," the characteristics of the woman he has children with say nothing about a man. But one can't exactly get married by accident, and it is this aspect of choice that makes the wife's attributes weigh heavily on a husband's social standing.

Ultimately though, men's demands in the status domain turn out to be rather modest because their own situations are also modest. Usually, they end up simply wanting to find a woman who is "decent"—doesn't do drugs, drink too much or run around, has a job and an asset or two. The job is particularly vital, since most men insist they shouldn't be expected to support a family on their own; in fact, men often avoid attachments to women who hold the expectation that the man will be the sole provider.[29]

More important, they say, a man shouldn't settle for someone who has not absolutely proven that she is trustworthy.[30] It is at this moment in fathers' narratives that the generalized mistrust of women they have developed over the years comes through loud and clear. Byron Jones is the black forty-six-year-old Mantua native who washes store windows and cars for a living. We ask this father of a young adult son and twelve-year-old child what kind of woman he would consider marrying. "A woman that I can trust. They all lied to me. I want a woman I can trust, an honest woman. And I don't think they make them anymore." Lee, the man who says he'll insist on his-and-her diamond rings, is just as adamant in his description of his "ideal woman." For him she is "somebody who's in my corner whether I'm right or wrong. Good or bad. Like I could lose my job, and she's still there for me. If I'm sick, to be in my corner and help me get better. Don't leave me. If I'm dying or whatnot, be there for me." We ask Bob, a twenty-two-year-old white father of a fourteen-month-old baby, about who would make an ideal wife for him. He says, "Someone who is caring and trustworthy. Someone that's not going to dick you over, you know. Someone that's going to be there through thick and thin, no matter what happens. 'Cause that's the vow, through sickness and health and richer and poorer."

Why do men like Byron, Lee, and Bob feel that this level of commitment and trustworthiness is so vital in a potential partner? Because marriage makes a man enormously vulnerable. Marriage involves asking a woman to accept him as he is, with whatever he has to offer. Hill is a thirty-year-old father of a four-year-old and works part-time at an art-supply store. When we bring up the topic of marriage, Hill says, "A lot of men are terrified of it." When we ask what's so scary about marriage, Hill replies, "The fear comes in that you get stuck with a wife, she feeds you a game that she loves you and then next thing you know, you're in court because she doesn't like you anymore. She's found something better." "She's cheated on you?" we ask. "Either she's cheated on you," Hill says, "or you're not good enough. You know, you haven't reached the potential that she felt you could've reached." Hill believes that it is simply impossible for most men to live up to a woman's expectations. "You can't do it," he states emphatically, "and a lot of men spend their whole life trying to measure up to what they consider the level that their woman would appreciate them more."

While trustworthiness is an indispensable foundation for a marriage, it is far from sufficient in men's minds. Ultimately, a bride ought to be one's "soul mate" or "best friend." As Bob puts it, "That's your mate, you know. That's supposed to be your other half." Quick, a twenty-four-year-old black father of a three-year-old child who may or may not be his, and another baby with a different woman on the way, says, "I would like to get married and stuff, but the way it is going I don't think I ever will." His pessimism stems from the fact that he is looking for someone "willing to be my best friend. Not only be my girl, but you have to be my best friend." Kensington-resident William, a white thirty-three-year-old "picker" at a warehouse that stocks dollar stores, is the father of an eleven-year-old and expecting another child with a new partner in July. He explains that for two people to marry, "they got to care about one another. The more you're friends, the more you can open up to one another and talk to one another and be there for one another. When you got something on your mind you got to be able to talk to your mate, because if you don't, it's just going to drive you nuts, and you're going to explode, you know what I mean?" William feels lucky that he's finally found a woman who satisfies this require-ment—his pregnant girlfriend—and he is about to propose; he envisions a June wedding just ahead of the arrival of the baby.

Ernest is currently in rehab at the Salvation Army. This black thirty-two-year-old father of a twelve-year-old son offers the most compel-ling diagnosis for why marriage in his neighborhood has become rare. "I mean people really don't know nothing about love. Oh, they know about the four-letter word. They know that's what they supposed to say, you know, 'I love you.' But I am talking about that insane love. The love to where you will do anything for this person. You will stand out in the rain until she stand at the window, until the lights go out. That's how much you love this person. Just unconditional love to where there is nothing, nothing that you wouldn't do for this person."

Like William, Ernest too feels that he's finally discovered that undy-ing devotion, and from a surprising source—his twelve-year-old son's mother. She's stuck by him through thick and thin, even ending a mar-riage that had occurred while he was in prison once he was released and wanted her back. While one might question Lynn's judgment, it is her willingness to stand by him for more than a decade, despite all that he's put her through, that has convinced Ernest that she is trustworthy enough for marriage. "I love her. I love my son's mother, man," Ernest says.

While the process of "getting together" is usually described in vague, bureaucratic terms—any mentions of love are often conspicuously absent—discussions of marriage are often rife with the kind of love language Ernest employs.[31] This is what exposes the "real relationship" with the child's mother, a union contracted primarily for the sake of a shared baby, as being not all that real after all. The "soul mate" relationship that Ernest believes is the key to true fulfillment casts his baby's mother in a very unflattering light. Holding out hope for eventual marriage seems to keep many of our men "in the market" for a wife even while trying to make a go of it with their children's mothers. Thus, the younger guy in the flashy car isn't the only threat to the relationship—there is also the soul mate who can make your marriage dreams come true.

## BROKEN BONDS

How successful are these low-income, inner-city fathers at forging an "ideal family unit" while operating under the logic of the new package deal? After all, only about a third will still be together by the time their child turns five, and only a handful—fewer than one in five—will marry the mother. This chapter has examined what happens to the other two-thirds. Ultimately, fathers' rejection of the old package deal—where the mother-father relationship is central and binds men to their progeny—seems to be the core cause of breakup. If men hold to this view, it is reasonable to speculate that they may be more willing to risk having children with virtual strangers who they then have trouble getting along with, less motivated to step up to the plate when her expectations rise, and more able to justify holding on to their current relationship while holding out for a better one later on.

Like the shotgun marriages of old that were initiated to legitimate a premarital pregnancy, these relationships fail in droves. Part of the problem is that, in some sense, nearly all these men see themselves, through circumstances they haven't done much (if anything) to try to control, as "just getting stuck with" the mothers of their children—these are the words John Carr, from Fishtown, used to describe the onset of his relationship with his child's mother, Rayann, in chapter 2.

Here, we must ask whether these for-the-sake-of-the-baby liaisons are really the modern equivalents of shotgun relationships. The answer is not really. In the shotgun marriages of old, marriage was supposedly prompted by the enraged girlfriend's father forcing the man who impregnated his daughter to the altar. In truth, it was the strong social norms shared by all parties involved. Today, there is virtually no support, much less pressure, from either his or her side for these young couples to stay together and form a family unit around their child. Often, it is much the opposite; the mother's kin often warn that the baby's father is "no good" and may even advise their daughter to "get away from him," while the father's kin may dismiss the girl as "trifling" and not worthy of their boy. They may even urge him to get a paternity test, warning "you know what they say, 'momma baby, daddy maybe.'" If these young couples are going to make it, it is going to be entirely because of their own resolve. Indeed, the only one holding the shotgun is the baby itself—and the father's own desire to have the "whole fatherhood experience" by living with his child. But this norm is not a mandate, as the shotgun metaphor would imply, so perhaps the best imagery is not a shotgun but a slingshot.

Beyond the new package deal, what else can account for these distressingly low levels of relational commitment, especially given how much these men believe they have to lose? A notably common theme in their narratives—particularly the black men we spoke with—is a profound, abiding mistrust of women. This seems to be driven, at least in part, by a deep division of expectations and goals that emerge after mom brings baby home. Suddenly, he's potential marriage material, and the relationship becomes a "project" as she tries to create enough momentum to spur him to begin to do what it takes—both in the relational and financial domains—to clear the marriage bar. Men seldom share this sense of urgency. "What's the hurry?" he asks. "Can't I simply enjoy the baby right now?" Over time, he comes to read these efforts as rejection and evidence that she's merely an opportunist incapable of unconditional love. These men's mantra is, "If men don't do, women don't love." There is "no source of commitment in a relationship," they claim. And surveys do show that unmarried fathers' economic troubles are, in fact, associated with break-ups.[32] The "men don't do, women don't love" narrative is especially strong when men talk about what is keeping them from marrying. Ultimately, they say, it is the lack of trustworthy women that is killing marriage.[33]

As for the specter of the younger guy in the flashy car, here fathers' fears might not be entirely unfounded. The Fragile Families and Child Wellbeing Study, a survey of parents with nonmarital births, shows that when unmarried women do break up with the fathers of their children, those who find new partners often manage to trade up and find men with fewer personal problems and better jobs, the sought-after characteristics that the flashy-car fear symbolically speaks to. Unfortunately, there is little evidence that these new relationships will prove more stable than the old.[34]

But even in the earliest days of the relationship, men often manifest their underlying discomfort with the familylike bonds that they suddenly try to embrace. They just can't seem to tolerate all the "togetherness" and are irritated by the idea that they are accountable to their partner for their time. The underlying motivation behind women's desire to monitor and men's desire to evade it, is, when one gets right down to it, a central norm borrowed from marriage: fidelity. Relationships between unmarried couples only rarely take on the full set of normative expectations that marital relationships do—for example, they seldom embrace the ethos of "til death do us part" or even pool their finances. But both partners recognize that two people who have decided to forge a real relationship to raise a child in an "ideal family unit" shouldn't really stray; the norm of sexual fidelity is stronger here than in the "together" phase.[35]

But there is a good deal of subtle ambiguity still. On the one hand, new fathers certainly know what is expected of them and recognize that the revelation of "cheating" is an almost certain trigger for breakup. On the other hand, and unlike their female partners, they only strongly associate fidelity with marriage, not the onset of parenthood or even living together. As we will show, the belief that a man should forgo marriage until he is ready to "settle down"—that is, be satisfied with just one partner—is nearly ubiquitous. Thus, the simple fact that the couple *isn't* married yet offers the tacit leeway that often gets men in a bind. And when the relationship is "all about the baby" and the mother is viewed as a mere complement to the father-child bond, temptation has a much stronger pull.

Finally, there are men's views about marriage, and the kind of relationship a lasting marriage is going to require. Men seldom get lucky enough to stumble into a soul mate through the haphazard partnering process that so often produces children. And their observations of their own behaviors and desires tell them that they're not even close to being able to settle down, or to find themselves settled, during their early twenties. For these men, even more than for the women that Edin and Kefalas interviewed in many of these same neighborhoods, childbearing and marriage have become radically separated. Thus, it is almost difficult to imagine that one's soul mate—the kind of woman a man might envision meeting and marrying in his thirties or forties—will end up being the mother of one's child.[36]

Taken together, each of these factors plays a role in creating a self-fulfilling prophecy: if a man suddenly finds himself thrown together with a woman he barely knows and may not even like, if her rising expectations in the wake of the birth leave him feeling it's impossible to please her, and if he believes she views him as expendable if a better catch comes along, she will be seen as a poor source of commitment. Such a man will likely fail to invest—shape up, overlook differences, and be content at home—to the degree required. And when it's only the baby who is holding the shotgun—or the slingshot—while kin often war against the couple's survival, a man's own desire to live with his child is very nearly the sole source of relationship stability.

In sum, when men assign a high value to their relationships with their children but are hesitant to invest too much in the relationship with their children's mother—the new package deal—a perilous situation results. Many disadvantaged men prove eager to capitalize on unplanned births as a pathway to fatherhood—though they will readily admit it is family on the cheap and not the "right way" to go about things. They do so because they fear that a discount version of fatherhood is all they may ever be able to afford. Being the baby's daddy gives them certain leverage with the child's mother—suddenly they have something (a biological tie) that the next guy doesn't. This is a reason for her to give him more of a chance than she otherwise would. Meanwhile, her leverage—control over the child—is sufficient to motivate him to try to turn mere togetherness into something more. But there is seldom anyone in the larger community who is really "for" this young couple and works to ensure their survival. In the end, the expected payoff of the partner relationship is too uncertain, the normative pressure is too low, and visions of the soul mate he has not yet encountered too compelling, and he fails to give himself fully. While men try to convince themselves that the partner relationship will work—observe the desperate efforts of Lavelle and Self and especially John in this regard—they know deep down it probably won't.

Following the dictates of the new package deal, at the same time couples are making the effort to get the relationship together for the sake of the baby, men embrace the belief that in the end, their relationship with their child is pure and unassailable and should have nothing to do with their relationship to the mother of that child. As we'll show in chapter 6, the dramatic falloff in father involvement in the aftermath of breakup should warn that this belief is a profound form of self-deception.

# FOUR

# Ward Cleaver

It is just after 8:00 on a clear and bright July morning, but despite the early hour and promising weather, Will Donnelly is getting angrier with each passing minute. "Why does Lori *always* pull this shit?" he mutters to himself as he grips the phone receiver. He listens one more time as his ex-girlfriend's recorded voice informs him that she is not available at the moment and to please leave a message. He knows that his kids, five-year-old Will Jr. and the toddlers, Destiny and Tom, are awake already, though the baby might still be asleep. The kids live with Lori, but they have recently started staying with him every other night, the three older ones splayed out across the overstuffed sofa sectional that dwarfs the living room, while Jonathan, the baby, sleeps with him in the apartment's one tiny bedroom. Given this arrangement, he is all too familiar with their early rising habits.

Since Lori moved in with her new boyfriend, Will has been calling the house each morning they are with her, just to make sure the kids are OK. Some might feel he is overprotective, but Will believes that he has good reason to be: Lori is a heroin addict, and Will suspects that her boyfriend is her supplier. After a minute or so he considers trying Lori's cell phone one more time but decides instead to take the ten-minute walk and check on them in person. He exhales with annoyance and strides to the front door. Will knows Lori and the new boyfriend won't like him coming over there again. Just last week Ruben protested his presence with the laughable assertion that his dumpy little place was a "house of business," and Will couldn't just come over and pound on the door whenever Lori failed to answer the phone. "Yeah," Will thinks, "I have a pretty good idea what your 'business' is."

He smiles grimly as he pulls his door closed and descends the front stoop, recalling with some satisfaction his response to the guy: "If my kids are in here, I don't give a fuck what you are doing; I'll come and knock on your door any time I want." As Will turns the corner of Allegheny and heads up Fifth Street, he thinks back to the weekend with the mix of fondness and exasperation that often accompanies parenting small children. The kids had been up early, of course, watching those stupid cartoons over and over again until he came out of the bedroom and turned the TV off. Then came the whole production of getting them fed, cleaned up, and dressed. Finally he herded them over to the bus stop and they set off to Kelly Drive for a walk along the Schuylkill River bike path. Sometimes, but especially on these outings with the kids, Will regrets selling his car to raise bail for his younger brother. A lot of good that did anyway, with him now up on State Road serving two to five on a robbery charge. "Another heroin addict," Will sighs. After that, he took them over to Penn's Landing, along the Delaware, where a local radio station was having some kind of promotional event complete with music and games. Will Jr. loves the water, so Will had agreed to shell out ten bucks a head for a ferry ride across the river to Camden and back. But the kids had spent the trip running around and screaming, pretending that they didn't hear him when he yelled at them to get their asses back over here and settle down. "Well," Will thinks, "at least I got them out of the neighborhood for awhile."

This sentiment is underlined as he comes up to the corner of Fifth and Westmoreland, across from the Chinese takeout with the deep yellow awning. At this time of the morning it is deceptively peaceful, only the tiny vials scattered around the pavement serving as a reminder of what usually goes on here. Will is suddenly angry again, this time at the takeout's owners for letting the dealers use the grimy linoleum and Formica-lined lobby as an alternative place of business when it rained. "If that was my store," he says to himself, "their ass would be out of my lobby and out on somebody's steps getting wet." Will grew up just a couple of streets over and so is well aware that this is one of the worst drug corners in the city. However, Will's knowledge about the local narcotics business goes quite a bit deeper than merely that of a lifelong resident, even of such a notoriously drug-ridden area as Fairhill.

Six years ago, right after he found out that Lori was pregnant with Will Jr. and just two weeks into the tenth grade, Will had said a not-so-fond farewell to high school to hit the streets and find work. His cousin was manager of a Burger King in Center City, so that was a logical place to start. But Will didn't have much tolerance for the "soft skill" demands of the job. "You take what you get" was his attitude toward the customers, especially for a measly $5.75 an hour. After three weeks he had dropped his hairnet and apron on the counter and walked out, telling his cousin, "I ain't got that kind of patience. 'This drink has too much ice in it!' It's not like they are going to the fucking Olive Garden!"

Transferring to an industry without such exacting standards of customer service, Will had ended up selling crack in an abandoned house for almost a year. The money had been amazingly good. He had started as a lookout earning fifty dollars each shift, and when he began selling he could sometimes see as much as eight hundred dollars a day. But the strain of watching people go to jail all the time and wondering when he would be next finally got to him. Of course, he had ended up in jail for nearly two years anyway. But that was a little later on, when he was nineteen, and it wasn't for drugs but for a gun-possession charge over a stupid incident that had to do with a neighbor of his mother.

All of that seems like ancient history now as Will continues up Fifth toward Glenwood, almost in the homestretch. Proprietors from the various used furniture and appliance stores along the street are just beginning to line the curb with selected items from their inventory: plastic shelving units, dented washers and dryers, bar stools, armchairs with tattered upholstery, baby strollers, and floor lamps. There is a crib lying among the items now clustered on the sidewalk, and Will reflects that the hardest part of being in jail was that he missed out on two years of the kids' lives: Will Jr. was only two when he was convicted and Destiny was actually born while he was inside. But he was the one who made the decision not to let Lori bring them on visits, telling her, "I'll be damned—when I'm locked up, I'm not letting my kids see me in prison." When he was released and moved into an apartment with Lori—the first time they had actually lived together—the other two kids came along in quick succession.

Will's mouth twists in a rueful smile as he considers the irony of his current situation. Now he's got plenty of time to spend with his growing family, but the fast current of drug money has been replaced by the slow, often-unreliable trickle of a part-time mechanic's wages. When it doesn't rain he works for his uncle, who runs a car lot over on Berks and Hancock, a job that may bring in three or four hundred dollars a week. Plus there's the hundred dollars a week or so he makes teaching kids to box over at the Joe Frazier gym on Broad and Glenwood. Lately though, he hasn't put in so much time there because the violence on the corners around the gym has gotten so bad.

Between these two jobs he barely makes enough for himself, let alone to provide for four kids, especially when it seems like they need new clothes every few weeks. "It's like a goddamn Chia plant," Will had exclaimed to a friend recently. "They grow in front of your face!" Just the other day Will had taken the kids over to the Gallery in Center City to buy summer clothes—swimming suits, sandals, and shorts. Despite looking for sales and other bargains, he had ended up dropping more than three hundred dollars at Sunshine Blues for his own kids plus his niece, who he is raising while his brother is in jail.

With these thoughts of finances darkening his mood further, Will arrives at his destination. Mounting the front steps to the crumbling porch, he can already hear the hyperactive soundtrack of a cartoon radiating through the aluminum storm door. He pounds on the corroded metal with a rapid series of blows, like a cop with a warrant. While waiting for what is sure to be an infuriatingly slow response, he turns and surveys the pathetic scene—wrought iron bars on the front windows, dented aluminum awning overhead, accumulated trash on the sidewalk. And nothing green at all. Even a weed that managed to struggle through all the concrete would die of loneliness on this block. Leaning against a battered post holding up the awning, Will thinks, possibly for the thousandth time, that he should have gone ahead with his plan to get custody of the kids. But when he had informed Lori, she had started the usual routine—crying, begging, and making bullshit promises—to the point where he simply gave up. "Screw it," he had sighed with resignation—she always knew how to get to him. "We'll just keep things the way they are."

Finally, Lori's boyfriend opens the door. Seeing that it is Will and not a potential customer, he lets the storm door slam and calls over his shoulder loud enough to be heard over the manic TV, "Lori! Will's outside—he wants to talk to you!" "No!" Will quickly and forcefully contradicts him. "I *don't* want to talk to her. I just want to know where my kids are." But before the boyfriend can turn and yell again, Will Jr., still in his underwear, slips by him and charges into Will's legs at full speed, delighted to see his daddy.

An ex–drug dealer with a prison record, no high school diploma, and a history of unstable, part-time employment—a father of four who chose to dump his children's mother rather than help her seek treatment in the face of a heroin addiction—may not seem like much of a father. But upon closer inspection, there are admirable and even exceptional aspects to Will's efforts as a parent. His concern about his kids' well-being is clearly evident, both in word and in deed. A month ago he got his own place and now cares for the kids under his own roof every other night, expending his scarce resources to ensure they have the shelter, clothing, food, and other things they need. And this fall, when Will Jr.

started having behavioral problems in school—frightening outbursts of aggression—Will began sitting in the classroom when he could to help keep the boy in line.

So how should we rate Will's success as a father? There is no doubt that he is a fairly good provider, assuming fully half of the responsibility for his children's needs at present. He offers discipline, and he works hard to protect his kids: by getting them out of the neighborhood and by monitoring possible risks in their mother's new home. Like all parents Will sees fatherhood as both a tough challenge and a great reward. "Sometimes it's rough and sometimes it's fun," he notes.

Dealing with his razor-thin financial margin, the treacherous streets, or even the difficulties of coparenting with a heroin addict, are not the roughest parts though, he says; it's the challenge of being a good role model. Will knows that children are very close observers of their parents' behavior. "If you are just a normal person," Will says, "with no kids or nothing, you don't have to try to put an example out for anybody." His desire to show, not just tell, his children the path they should follow has slowed Will down a lot. "You have to make the kids the number one priority in your life. You *always* put them first. And that's what is hard sometimes," Will says.

Before he had children, Will lived by the following credo: "You just do what you got to do for yourself." Putting children first is especially hard in a corner of the world where so many men have abandoned any semblance of effort. Will's own biological father, for example, disappeared when he was still a baby. "Do a lot of dads around here run away from their responsibilities?" we ask. "Hell yeah! They get scared; they don't want the responsibility so they leave." Yet in the midst of an otherwise difficult life situation, the constant pull of his children—their seemingly unending needs and demands—makes life immeasurably richer. "As a father you will always have somebody stable in your life, someone who you can care for. You know your kids are always going to be there. It's just—you wake up in the morning and you see a part of you laying there and it makes you feel real good."

"I don't think I take *good* care of my kids. But I do take care of them to the best of my ability," Will tells us. When we ask him to explain, Will insists that a two-parent family with father as breadwinner is best: "I should be able to provide a *family* for them. Like, with their mother. Instead of leaving her, I should have just tried to work it out, put her in a program and stayed with her. Instead, I got rid of her. And I should have a full-time job and shit, but I don't." Pressing a bit further, we ask Will to describe the kind of father he would like to be. "Ward Cleaver," Will says without hesitation. "Because he is like the ideal dad. He was always smiling, always happy, never had a worry in the world; his kids were always happy and always cheerful. They had everything in the world. Now *that's* an ideal dad."

Suburban Mayfield, the fictional home of the Cleaver family in the 1950s sitcom *Leave It to Beaver,* bears little obvious resemblance to North Philadelphia's ravaged Fairhill neighborhood in the early years of the twenty-first century. Men like Will, however, often draw on idyllic old-fashioned cultural images of the family—he isn't the only one of the men we interviewed to mention the iconic television show—as they work to define their role as fathers. Some can also point to exemplary men they know personally, such as their father or stepfather, an uncle or a brother, a boss or even a former school principal, as people they strive to emulate. But often as not, men's close ties provide more negative than positive models. In general it is far easier for men like Will to summon up specific examples of bad fathers than good ones. As we'll see in the next chapter, the sharpest critique is leveled at those men who fail to "be there"—who abandon their kids, like Will's father did, or fail to spend "quality time." No amount of money, they say, can compensate for that loss.

When we asked each of the men to describe what they thought good fathers ought to do for their children, their responses were remarkably consistent, with core features surfacing again and again. Good fathers, they say, provide for their children financially, offer discipline and protection, dispense wisdom and advice, serve as moral guides, show love, facilitate open and honest communication, and spend quality time. The obligation to provide—that traditional definition of what a good father ought to do—was usually mentioned first, but they also spoke of the features that Ward Cleaver surely would have espoused as well. In this chapter we consider how men fare in traditional aspects of the role, such as providing financial security as well as the other "father knows best" tasks that fathers throughout the last half century have traditionally shouldered. In chapter 5, we'll take up love, communication, and quality time—traits that reflect a definition of fatherhood that has emerged in recent decades and that, as we'll see, have extraordinary salience for men like Will Donnelly.

In the 1950s a father's primary job was to "bring home the bacon." Correspondingly, nearly every father we spoke with believed good fathers must "provide," though as we'll see, what this means has been sharply, even radically, redefined. Lacey Jones, the cook at Jessie's Soul-on-a-Roll, a stone's throw from Temple University and just south of Will's Fairhill apartment, has three children, ages eighteen, seventeen, and nine, and offers a straightforward assertion of what good fatherhood entails: "A good father is someone that's able to provide for their family." Jabir Rose, a black forty-eight–year-old who sells beer by the glass out of his South Philadelphia Point Breeze row home—at double the rate he pays at the state beer distributor—is the father of two, ages six and twenty-four. He quips, "I had sworn that I would never breed them if I couldn't feed them. Yeah, we say giving a child time is more important than money. But when that child is with you, and they ask you for something and you are not able to give it, how do you feel then? So sure, the dollar is paramount."

But what does "providing" for a child actually mean? Certainly, the full-on *Leave it to Beaver* version—where the man makes all the money and the woman stays at home—is out the window. These men are typically quick to insist that financial provision is both parents' responsibility and, in fact, often avoid women who expect to depend on a man financially. Most offer strong lip service to a fifty-fifty ideal. But, in reality, what a father feels he is obligated to provide strongly depends on his "circumstances." With respect to financial provision, Will Donnelly, who does manage to cover half of the costs of his kids' care, is at one end of a very long continuum.

Lacey Jones, whose closely cropped hair, clean-shaven face, and serious bearing all seem to speak "family man," freely admits he hasn't paid a penny in official child support to the mothers of either of his two older children—even now, when he has left prison and landed a job. Still, he insists, he provides. Occasionally, he'll give his seventeen-year-old son "little dollars or fives" or, more rarely, spring for a pair of sneakers or jeans the boy may need. As for his eighteen-year-old daughter, who is struggling to attend college while raising two kids of her own, "Every now and then I do buy her something. And I come get her children off her hands and give her a break." Until recently, the same went for his youngest—though he stopped by her mother's house nearly every day, even if just for a few minutes, he helped financially only when the child "needed" something: that is, something out of the ordinary like money for school clothes or a field trip.

The "as needed" approach to financial provision, which seldom puts cash in the hands of the child's mother but is directly responsive to particular needs of the child, is the method of support nearly all men prefer, unless they have an exemplary relationship with their ex-partner.[1] Jabir Rose explains that giving cash to his children's mothers only encourages them to misappropriate the money: "Let me tell you something: the average dollar that those females get does not go to that child," he asserts. "Where it's going is on their dresses. It's going on their jewelry, their drinks, their habits, and every damn thing else. The average dollar is not going on the child like it was supposed to."

Given the very tight budgets of their children's mothers, it is hard to put much stock in these claims. But that is beside the point. The frequency with which men fixate on the luxurious trips to fancy restaurants or splurges for jewelry or cosmetics at the mall—frivolities that they imagine are consuming their hard-earned money—speaks to the strong current of mistrust that pervades these relationships from start to finish.[2] This is especially true for men who are caught up in the net of court-ordered child support like Jabir. Lacey, who is not subject to any child-support order he is aware of, is free to adopt the "as needed" approach. But "as needed" doesn't mean he is always responsive to his children's needs; cash passes out of his hand only when he has the money to spare. "Everybody can't get something in one day, in the same day. We ain't got it like that," Lacey explains.

A year ago Lacey assumed custody of his youngest daughter, Amani, now nine, after her mother, whom Lacey repeatedly derides as a "loony tune" and a "mental midget," proved unable to care for the child. Though he certainly didn't plan to raise Amani himself, he is now glad he took her on: "When I came home from prison, my older kids were all like sixteen years old. But now, I basically got a chance to see one of them grow up." When Amani moved in, she joined a household of three—Lacey, his fiancée, and her eight-year-old daughter, Tasha. Lacey's steady full-time job and his frugal habits—he indulges in only a couple of beers a night—allow him to cover his share of the household bills, meet his daughter's expenses, plus buy things here and there for Tasha. With two live-in "daughters" to provide for, "I'm always seeing something for little girls, and I'm always getting it," Lacey says. Does Lacey think he's a good father? "*Now* I do," he says. "I'm trying to do the right things like a law-abiding citizen. Providing for them." Taken together his contributions over the past eighteen years total only a tiny percentage of the amount required to raise his three children. Yet this is clearly not the denominator he uses to calculate the value of his contributions.

Jabir Rose had been in and out of jail for more than two decades on charges of drug possession but has now left dealing and using behind and is trying to become "a productive member of society." But his extensive criminal history stands in the way of a legitimate job. So he hustles work as a speakeasy barkeep and jack-of-all-trades. As part of his quest to be an upstanding citizen, he makes sure to pay the amount the child-support system requires of him—twenty-nine dollars a week—even though he has no legal income. And because he is in compliance with his child-support order, he has been able to approach the family court to secure visitation rights for the six-year-old daughter, whose birth finally generated his determination to stay out of "the joint." The ability to use formal channels to obtain visitation is virtually the only reason that men prefer to pay through "the system"—the Bureau of Child Support Enforcement, which acts as a collection agency on behalf of the mother—instead of the informal "as needed" method.

This "old head" of nearly fifty, who is both a wordsmith and a joker, appears blithely unaware that despite his pledge not to "breed" unless he can "feed," a mere twenty-nine dollars a week won't come close to covering the cost of food. But he estimates he makes only about five hundred dollars each month at his various entrepreneurial ventures—selling beer by the glass, repairing porch railings and awnings, and even taking in ironing and making meals for his neighbors in South Philadelphia's Point Breeze. Clearly, Jabir would be hard-pressed financially if his live-in girlfriend didn't pay 70 percent of the household bills.

Jabir discusses at length what he believes makes for a good provider. "I try to be *all man* in that I support *myself,*" he says. The weight he, and many others, assign this seemingly obvious duty—providing for himself—takes us aback. But, he says, merely meeting his own needs is no easy task, given his limited earning potential. He takes pride in his ability to cover his 30 percent share of the household bills, his own clothing and shoes, plus the twenty-nine dollars a week in child support with his proceeds from odd jobs. In Jabir's case this arrangement works, in part, because Jabir controls another huge asset: the subsidized apartment he "inherited" after his mother died—a unit the family has held for three decades. This resource is so valuable—only a fraction of poor households are lucky enough to have such a perk—that he feels it earns him the right to claim the role of "the man of the house," a somewhat ironic assertion, as the presence of the fiancée and child are the key to his ongoing eligibility for the unit. As for the twenty-nine dollars a week he sends to the child-support office for his daughter, that makes him a good provider to her too—after all, he's doing the best he can.

Given certain circumstances fathers can take pride in even exceedingly modest and infrequent contributions. Ahmad, a black South Camden resident who is six foot two with closely cropped hair, is a case in point. He is only nineteen but has a two-year-old child by a woman he has "been with" since he was twelve. After months without work, he has finally found temporary employment with a local masonry company and is eagerly awaiting his first paycheck. Ahmad sums up the bare-bones definition of what most men mean when they say that a good father "takes care of his responsibilities as far as taking care of the child financially." "Don't leave *everything* up to the mother," he explains. "It's like a team. Both of y'all have to be there."

Ahmad stays most nights with his baby's mother, Leticia, in a two-story row just down from the United House of Prayer for All People, one of the few thriving endeavors that remain along largely abandoned Broadway Avenue in South Camden—the most vital commercial artery in all of South Jersey a half century ago. Leticia and the child, Gabrielle, live with Leticia's mother, her aunt, and her two brothers. Ahmad has been more or less living off of her family, and Leticia's steady job, since he graduated from high school, but he helps out with diapers and formula when he can. Ahmad firmly believes that as long as a father is making an effort, and is at least *part* of the team, he ought to be golden, no matter what portion of the bottom line his contribution constitutes. Note that he does not count the cost of his keep against the value of his sporadic donations.

Taken together these stories illustrate a very broad, and somewhat unexpected, working definition of what providing entails. First, there is the subtle yet critical point—most evident with Jabir but at least implicit in many fathers' stories—that a provider's first responsibility is to provide for himself. For those with a criminal history or other impediments to employment—a physical disability, a run of bad luck, a lack of a stable place to live, a mental-health problem, or an addiction to alcohol or drugs—this may be more easily said than done, especially when men rarely qualify for any meaningful form of government assistance.[3] In fact, men like Jabir sometimes say that simply meeting their own needs can constitute a nearly overwhelming burden. Jabir manages through two rare strokes of luck: he's got a coveted subsidized apartment and a girlfriend who works full-time and is willing to cover most of the bills. Men who can claim to be "all man"—at least by their own lights—often take real pride in this fact.

Second, a good provider must dedicate a reasonable proportion of what is left over to the needs of those in the household he's living in at the time.[4] Prioritizing these needs can also mean diverting resources away from biological children who live elsewhere. Lacey, for example, devotes far more of his excess cash to his youngest daughter, Amani, and his girlfriend's child, Tasha, both of whom live with him, than to his son, Michael, or his older daughter, Angela, who seldom get anything at all. Notice, though, that providing for those in one's household may require devoting resources to the children men happen to live with, even if the child is not their own. Lacey's fiancée's child provides an example.

Surprisingly, few try to shirk the implicit responsibility of doing for a child they live with but is not theirs biologically; they'll usually try to contribute at least something, especially if that child's father doesn't "do" for the child. Indeed, men often embrace the opportunity. As Elliot Liebow observed four decades ago in a slum in Washington, DC, providing for a child who is not one's own offers marginal men a rare opportunity to look good.[5] This is no less true today in the struggling neighborhoods of Philadelphia and Camden.

Patrick Murphy's story shows how "playing daddy" to another man's child works its magic. If, out of the goodness of his heart, this part-time caterer who lives with the family of his girlfriend, Deena, in Pennsport, spends a hundred dollars on her son Kevin Jr., this contribution is judged as a hundred dollars more than he is obligated to pay. For Deena, who badly needs the help because Kevin Sr., the boy's father, does nothing, this represents an act of valor. Ironically, the less that the boy's own father provides, the better Patrick's efforts appear by contrast; a deadbeat dad is, in many ways, the perfect foil for a new man who comes along and wishes to win points with a woman who has a child. This is not to say that the pseudoparental bonds that result are not genuine; our own observation of Patrick's behavior toward Kevin Jr. is enough to convince us that the boy is the apple of Patrick's eye.[6]

Patrick's situation right now is something of a win-win; the young family's very low living expenses—Deena's aunt and uncle charge them no rent—and his relatively high hourly wage, albeit at a part-time job, allow him to do for both his infant daughter and Kevin Jr. The largess he bestows on Deena's son by another man is laudable, and his contributions toward his infant's needs—Pampers, formula, infant sleepers, and onesies—can just about cover the modest cost of her care. Patrick's penchant for wandering into the toy store around the corner each time he gets paid and—"boom!"—wandering out again with some toy for Kevin Jr. tucked under his arm wins him even more points with Deena. But once Patrick moves his family of four out of the front room of Deena's family's home off Two Street and into the tiny unit in Girard Estates he is planning to rent—where he will be suddenly forced to assume the full cost of the family's care—it is unclear whether Patrick's ability to "do" will continue to inspire Deena's enthusiastic regard.

In sharp contrast, if Lacey Jones chooses to put a hundred dollars into the hands of his seventeen-year-old son's mother, the woman he says he likes best out of the three he's had a child with, she might rightly point out that this is but a drop in the ocean. The value of his contribution, coming on the heels of seventeen years of neglect, is calibrated to the amount she thinks he was obligated to provide all those years. Thus, if it's gratitude or admiration he's seeking, better to spend the money on "little girl things" for Tasha, his fiancée's child.

This dynamic is perhaps an additional reason why fathers are hesitant to put money in the hands of their children's mothers and why

Photos were taken in the Camden and Philadelphia neighborhoods we studied. Due to
confidentiality concerns, however, none of the fathers or children pictured are in the study.

DREW HOOD

DREW HOOD

TIMOTHY NELSON

DREW HOOD

most prefer the "as needed" approach. Especially valued are the disposable diapers and formula—the two vital elements of a baby's existence—and pricey sneakers—the prized "extra" that has such currency among children in low-income neighborhoods.[7] In particular, fathers can point to the "sneaks," or "Jordans"—which are nearly always on public display—as their special contribution, no matter how much value the mother assigns to their support.

The high salience of such items speaks volumes about what fathers are trying to purchase when they choose to "provide."[8] When children are young, Pampers and sneaks are a public statement that a man seeks to "do the right thing" with regard to his child.[9] Even highly impractical items, like the Lugz boots that forty-year-old Marty Holmes, an African American father of three who lives in a halfway house, has just purchased for his three-year-old son, serve this function, so their importance should not be discounted. But as children age, the kids themselves become the audience for the performance rather than the mother or the community at large. By purchasing the little extras that a child might especially desire, a man can ensure that his new audience is appreciative. In this way, he can strengthen the father-child bond, a theme we'll return to in the next chapter. He may also secure more rights to ongoing contact, for if the child values his visits the mother will have a harder time denying him access. The downside, of course, is that this practice diminishes men's interest in whether the mother's rent or utilities get paid.

Clearly, though nearly all men say that "the dollar is paramount," few feel the obligation to serve as the primary provider or—in truth—even to come up with 50 percent of what is needed to raise their child. The fundamental assumption is that the primary responsibility for the child's care and keep rests with the mother, a perspective echoed in attitudes toward contraception and the decision about whether to take a pregnancy to term. Lee, the out-of-work optical technician, tells us his goal in life was always to "be able to provide for *me*. And if a woman was in my life, I would hope that she could provide for herself. I tell my woman to be independent. Don't be dependent to nobody. Then, if necessary, you can take care of the kids on your own." And Maurice, a black father of three who cooks at the Hyatt, says, "I always tell they mother, that is the reason that I choose you to be my kids' mother—because you are strong enough, you are a strong independent black woman that you can raise these kids by yourself if you had to."

Another conspicuous way in which words—namely, espousing the 50 percent ideal—and deeds do not match up is in the role many men assign themselves in relation to the child. Most mentally label the mother as the "primary" financial provider—some even declare this outright—and deem themselves as her "helper," responsible only for "doing the best I can."[10] As we've said before, Will is an exception to this rule—this dynamic plays out more fully in the story of the other fathers profiled.

When men find themselves in Will's or Lacey's situation and are able to live with their children at least part of the time, they are much more willing to aspire to the 50 percent ideal or even, in rare cases, provide all the support, as Lacey does now for Amani. But the commonly voiced fears of women's mercenary nature—discussed in chapter 3—hint at another critical fact: these men are seldom interested in serving as mere paychecks, adding funds to the mother's till. In their view an expectation of support without a corresponding extension of rights reduces fatherhood to little more than a debtor's prison. Most expect the right to at least some slice of fatherhood in return.

As evidence of this, there are two main exceptions to the norm that good fathers ought to do at least *something* to financially provide for a child. If they have no contact with the child, particularly if they view the lack of contact as the fault of the mother or even the child, their perceived obligation to provide is usually negated in their own minds; the mother does not necessarily share this point of view. And where there is some doubt about the child's paternity, there is usually no felt obligation either. Think back to the story of John Carr in chapter 2, whose girlfriend, Rayann, ran off to the Jersey Shore five months into her pregnancy and then named another man as the father of his child. Here, it was only the positive paternity test, which John paid for himself when his daughter turned two, that kick-started his sense of financial obligation.

On the underside of the urban labor market, men who wish to "do"—to provide—face a central dilemma: they seldom have the means to meet 50 percent of their children's needs. Deploying a definition of financial provision that can be summed up as "doing the best I can... with what is left over" could, on the one hand, be seen as shirking of paternal responsibility; this is no doubt the case some of the time. But it is also a profound admission of weakness, an expression of vulnerability that is somewhat surprising for young men who are often known for their public displays of crude masculinity. And often it is expressed against a particularly poignant backdrop; their portrayal of the mothers of their children, even those whom they may despise, as admirably "strong" and "independent." The surprising implication is that these fathers view women as inherently stronger than men.

Thus, though the iconic image of Ward Cleaver and his latter-day sitcom cousin, Bill Cosby, arose repeatedly in our conversations with fathers, "doing the best I can" is a plea of "no contest"—a middle ground between innocence and guilt—to the charge that they've failed to provide for the offspring they have produced. While it's true that they are far from the stalwarts of suburban Mayfield, they're not complete moral degenerates either, they insist; after all, most do try to make sure they don't leave *everything* up to the mother.

When the "good provider" is redefined as the man who is "doing the best I can," a father's self-esteem is bolstered at the same time that his perceived financial obligation to his offspring is diminished. The theme of self-sacrifice for the sake of the child, so evident in the accounts of the mothers of these children, is often less strongly articulated and sometimes even absent in the narratives of their male partners, except in the abstract.[11] Not surprisingly, redefining the provider role from "50 percent responsible" to "doing the best I can" wins few points in the eyes of their child's mother. She, after all, has no choice but to make whatever sacrifices it takes to ensure the well-being of her child. For her, 100 percent of the child's need is the only denominator that could possibly count, for this is the only way to avoid the unthinkable—losing custody of her children.

But there may be an upside to this ethos as well. Changing the equation so that "providing" is clearly doable may serve to keep fathers involved, rather than to prompt an all-or-nothing response. Holding men accountable to the fifty-fifty norm they give lip service to might accomplish little more than inciting guilt, which may, in turn, act as a powerful barrier to fathers' ongoing involvement with their children, a theme we'll return to in chapter 6. Some mothers, like Ahmad's girlfriend, Leticia, are sensitive to this dynamic and, in an effort to ensure his involvement, are careful not to demand too much from the father, at least for a time.

Meeting the traditional demands of fatherhood involves more than money of course. Think back to Will Donnelly, who tells us that finances are far from his biggest problem. Will says that the primary challenge is serving as a good role model. "If you are just a normal person," Will says, "with no kids or nothing, you don't have to try to put an example out for anybody." But Will is not a "normal person"; he is a father. Not only must he provide, he must also dispense discipline and protection, offer wisdom and advice, and serve as a moral guide. In sum, he is responsible for keeping his children on "the right path." Nearly all men agree that this is best done by "actions" and not by "lectures," in one father's words.

Because of Will's checkered past, as well as his challenging present situation, he is quite critical of his own parenting. He believes that if he were a truly good father, he would be married to the mother of his children, have a full-time job, and have gotten his girlfriend, Lori, help with her heroin addiction rather than merely "throwing her away." This exchange reveals a second dimension to the "doing the best I can" ethic.

Few men have the requisite biographical resources to serve as good role models, something they are often painfully aware of.

Many fathers with unsavory pasts find a way to at least partially resolve this dilemma; they turn their sordid life story into a morality tale, one that richly illustrates the perils of the path they do not want their children to follow. Take the case of Dave Jones, a gregarious, wiry white man of medium height who has spent all thirty-two of his years living in Whitman, a tight-knit Irish and Italian community in the far southeast corner of the city. Weekday mornings, he catches a 5:30 ride to make his 6:00 shift at Penn Warehouse and Distribution, on South Columbus Boulevard, one of the dozens of low-slung warehouses that hug the banks of the Delaware River in South Philly, though few are still going concerns. He could walk the route if he had to, making his way east through the corridor of boarded-up warehouses and weed-ridden parking lots until he hits the back of the massive IKEA store that, along with an outsize Lowes and a Target, sits on a former warehouse site. Crossing South Columbus, he's there—at the southwest entrance to a red brick structure located strategically alongside an aging terra-cotta clad pier. The mothballed USS *United States,* a 1950s luxury liner that was once the fastest ship afloat, is moored alongside of the structure and, at a length of nearly a thousand feet, is so large that even the huge box stores that dot the boulevard are dwarfed.

Dave strolls back into the house around 3:00 or 3:30 p.m., has a snack, showers, catches a little R&R, and sits down to dinner with Dee and the kids around 5:00. Then, depending on the season, he either heads to the softball field at the Murphy Recreation Center just a few blocks away or up Front Street a mile to the Ralph Rizzo Hockey Rink, named after the late Philadelphia mayor Frank Rizzo's father. Dee's three kids, ages eleven, thirteen, and fourteen, and his own eleven-year-old daughter, Cassandra, who lives with her mother, Marlene, just a few blocks away, play in leagues at these venues as well, along with so many other kids in Whitman.

Encased in the microworld of Whitman, most people's lives are pretty much the same; the tiny two bedroom row homes have been expanded over the years, but are modest, with extended second floors that jut out over the deep porches. Streets without a speck of foliage are relieved by city parks like Mifflin Square, which hugs the western boundary of the neighborhood, and the field at the Murphy Rec. Children's K–8 years are spent at Our Lady of Mount Carmel Parish School if the family has any money to spare. On summer weekends Dave's family hitches a ride with his parents over to Wildwood, on the South Jersey Shore, where the former longshoreman and career house-wife have rented a house for the summer, alongside many of their South Philadelphia neighbors. Wildwood on summer weekends is a Whitman tradition for those who can afford it.

Young Whitman fathers these days typically struggle to maintain employment at unskilled or semiskilled jobs and earn only a fraction of the wages their fathers and grandfathers once pulled in on the docks, in the adjacent warehouses, or at the U.S. naval shipyard that, at its peak, employed roughly fifty thousand workers. Young Whitman mothers work too as cashiers and waitresses and the like. Weeknights are spent playing at the "Rec." or the hockey rink or socializing on the stoop or in the corner bar. Nearly everything of importance is within walking dis-tance. "Oh yeah," Dave agrees, "Everybody knows each other here. Everybody looks out for each other. Whatever you need—watch the house, take care of the dog—they actually leave you a key or whatever. Yeah, it's like everybody is all a big family here. I mean, you got some enemies and neighbors that are assholes and shit like that. That's any-where you go. Just don't bother them, that's all. You know what I mean?"

Dave and his girlfriend, Dee, pay six hundred in rent for what he calls a "piece of shit" tiny three bedroom row that is just around the corner from where Dave grew up, on Lee and Ritner, where his parents still live today. Dave's rental is dirt cheap because it is, quite literally, sinking into the landfill beneath—in the back bedroom the molding has pulled entirely away from one wall. The house sits near the corner of

Ritner and Front, once the center of operations for the Lee Street gang, a group of local boys who ruled this territory, serving mostly as guardians of the neighborhood's ethnic purity and heckling any blacks or Hispanics who happened to venture there. "We all stuck together. The little corner gangs had fights against each other here and there, you know, but it was more about everybody sticking together. We just didn't want minorities coming in here."

Dave's daily routine provides the opportunity to interact with his daughter—as well as Dee's children—at every turn. "All four of our kids play hardball down at the Rec so I see them all the time. In fact, we just ran into Cassandra last night, she was going to McDonald's to get a hamburger. My daughter, I get her anytime I want. Like I could call Marlene right now and say 'Mar, what's the baby doing? Put the baby on. You want to come with Daddy?' School nights she'll usually come over for like a Tuesday and Wednesday night."

Why does Dave, a seemingly model father, need to repair the past? Dave got expelled from Neumann Catholic High in twelfth grade for cutting class and immediately found work "driving a jack, an electric jack, working at a produce place." "How did you find that job?" we ask. "Couple of my friends were working there." He stayed at that job until he turned twenty and then quit, wanting a break. "Where did I go from there? I don't think I went to anywhere. I think I just fell in a corner for a little while," Dave says, glossing over the start of what became a multiyear alcohol and drug binge.

At about that time, Dave met Marlene, who hung five blocks over from where Dave and his friends ruled their corner. "She hung up at Fifth Street I think, or somewhere along that line. But then when I first met her and told her to come around Lee Street, we all hung together." How did the two become parents? "Yeah, well, I started dating her and went out with her for a while and decided to get married. Well, we set the *plan* to get married and then worked on getting kids, yeah."

Dave and Marlene's plan—to "work on the kids" once marriage was part of the conversation—shows a level of forethought that is rare. And it was successful: the wedding at Our Lady of Mount Carmel was shotgun, with Marlene two months pregnant. But by then Dave had fallen even more deeply "into a corner," spending nearly all his leisure time tending to his addiction to alcohol and exploring the allure of recreational drugs. Because of these "personal issues," the marriage fizzled within just a few months. Once Dave moved out of Marlene's parents' home, where the two had been living, Marlene was left raising Cassandra largely on her own. "From a baby on to maybe about six, seven maybe, like I was there, but I wasn't, you know? You follow what I'm saying? Like I was there, I was always around, but *being there* for them, stuff like that and shit, I wasn't. I was tied up in other shit, shit that I shouldn't have been." Finally, when Cassandra turned seven, Dave became desperate enough to seek help at the Jefferson Intensive Outpatient program, also in South Philly and just a mile or so from his home. Sixteen weeks later he was sober.

Ever since, Dave has done a lot to try and redeem the past. He's worked a variety of warehouse jobs like the one he has now, all based on referrals from neighborhood friends. He drives a jack or a crank or, if he's lucky, a forklift. These kinds of jobs should pay better than what he's making, but so far he has only found work under the table or at nonunion shops. And given declines in the industry, the work isn't plentiful. Sometimes, he fills spells of unemployment by working as a general laborer for a buddy who is a "construction guy," doing everything from mixing cement to hanging sheet rock. "It's not what you know, it's who you know," he says, explaining the power of his neighborhood connections for securing work in an era where many of the neighborhood's traditional employers—the warehouses, docks, and shipyards—are now sitting half-empty or closed. "Yeah, I know a lot of people, a whole lot of people." Dave's job-rich network is a resource typically limited to whites; only one black father we spoke to was able to draw as extensively on his network for legal employment.

Dave and Marlene are "still close friends. She comes over here, or we got a place down at the shore, and she's four or five blocks away 'cause her parents have a place there too. I mean, her family and mine are all good friends. We still keep in touch. Anything she needs, she's got it if I have it. I mean, if I don't have it I can't do nothing about that. But we're all good friends." When we express surprise over the ease of this arrangement, Dave says, "Sure. It's good for Cassie. That way, I keep ties with my daughter." Dave is the rare man who trusts his ex-partner with the money, and each week he puts forty dollars—the amount they've informally agreed on—into Marlene's hands. This constitutes about a tenth of his earnings when he's working full-time, though lately he's getting only thirty hours a week at the warehouse. He also pays nearly a thousand dollars annually toward Cassandra's tuition at Mount Carmel Parish School—his 50 percent share of what she doesn't receive in financial aid. And at the beginning and end of each school year, Marlene puts the needed seasonal items—clothing and shoes—on layaway, paying half of the bill and informing Dave that he can retrieve the items and present them to Cassandra when he pays off his share—these trips to the layaway counter totaled about six hundred dollars last year. Little odds and ends come up too, and Dave contributes what he can. All in all, Dave now devotes about four thousand dollars each year to Cassandra's care, far less than half of what it takes to raise her. Still, Dave thinks he's going above and beyond, perhaps because he also pays some of the bills over at Dee's house.

But for Dave, like Will Donnelly, the financial aspect of fatherhood isn't the most challenging. We ask what future he envisions for Cassandra, and his response boils down to the following: be nothing like I was. "Well, I'd love for her to do what her father didn't: complete high school, go to college, become something of her life. I think she may be a basketball player. And as for me I could have became a major league baseball player. I know for a fact that I would be in the major leagues today if I didn't take a turn for the worse, decided to do things that I shouldn't have." Cassandra, he says, can "learn from my mistake. What I did is what I just want Cassie *not* to do."

How does Dave think he can help his child avoid the mistakes that he made? "You know, just to be there for Cassie financially, which I am, and teach her what's right from wrong." Instilling morality usually requires a certain level of moral authority. Ward Cleaver drew this authority from his own biography; the way he lived his life served as a model for his progeny. But Dave is no role model. Like so many others we spoke with, trying to be a good father in these nonfinancial, yet quite traditional, dimensions of the role presents a thorny dilemma—how is he going to deal with the shortfall in the biographical resources he needs to fulfill these critical aspects of a father's job?

Men like Dave typically try to resolve this dilemma by attempting to make a silk purse out of a sow's ear. By redefining his checkered past as a set of priceless "life lessons," he turns "the shit I shouldn't have been into" into an asset. After all, the "shit" gives him a certain sort of expertise and authenticity: "I've been there," he can say, "and believe me, you don't want to follow that path." "Like I told Cassie, 'When you get a little bit older Daddy's going to explain his life and what he did.' And I'm going to be honest with her—I'm going to be very honest with her and tell her exactly what I did that screwed my life up. I told her, 'When you get a little bit older, I'm going to sit you down and explain everything to you, Cassie.' I'm going to spill my guts to her."

By spilling their guts to their children, men like Dave Jones believe that they can fulfill the critical role of moral guide. "Like I throw in now, 'I'd better not catch you smoking, drinking, drugs. The life that you're doing now, Cassie, is the one you need to pass in school. You're doing real good. You're playing sports. You're keeping active. You're not doing what other kids are doing.'" Ultimately, though, the authority behind these words lies not in the fact that his past offers Cassie an example to follow, but that he's been to hell and back and still suffers from the consequences. His own life is offered up as a cautionary tale: "Yeah, I'm just going to sit her down, probably when she's about thirteen, when she'll really understand it, you know, my mistakes."

Back in Fairhill, the North Philadelphia neighborhood that shows all the scars of an industrial base that has long since fled—a possible harbinger of the future of declining white working-class enclaves like Dave's Whitman neighborhood—we ask Will Donnelly what a father can do to ensure his child has a good future. His narrative features the same list of qualities as that of Dave Jones. "Discipline," he says. "If you let the kid run wild and do what he wants, you don't know how he'll turn out." Will is especially concerned about Will Jr. "He's got a bad temper; he's violent. He like hits people with toys and stuff and gets mad. It's not good. Mom said that's how I was when I was little. Bad temper. In fact, my mom always told me I was going to be a murderer and end up in prison the rest of my life." Will and his five brothers got almost no discipline when they were growing up—his mother spent two decades snorting cocaine while his stepfather drank, so neither one offered much structure. Taking the opposite tack, Will too has concluded that discipline is key to making sure his kids end up being "nothing like me."

Closely allied to the fatherly task of discipline is that of protection, since it also involves imposing rules, setting boundaries, and monitoring children's activities. Will says parenting in North Philadelphia is "insane, trying to keep them away from the drug dealers and all the shit that's going on. You have to keep them in. When you take them out like you have to keep them underneath your shirt." But Lori, the children's mother, might pose an equal danger. "She could be out riding around in a car doing drugs with my kids in the back."

Will's career aspirations now center on being the kind of moral force in the community that he feels kids like his desperately need. "I want to be a cop. I want to be able to do something for kids," he tells us. "'Cause I always have kids on my mind. Like, I walk around, I see kids being mistreated by their parents. I tell them, 'Hey, why don't you treat your kid just a little bit better.' 'Oh fuck you,' one lady started cursing at me. I said, 'I don't mind, lady, forget it. You'll learn.' It makes me sick." When he is not contemplating becoming a cop, he imagines other occupations that would allow him to touch kids' lives: "Maybe be like a child therapist, or like a guidance counselor or a social worker. Something like that. Because the generation of kids now, I want to see them do something better than I seen when I was little."

This exchange leads to a conversation about ways Will feels he serves as a moral guide to his oldest, Will Jr., already, despite the fact that Will is not quite the man he aspires to be. "I get him just by himself. I take him for a walk around the block, and I let him look at all the drug dealers, all the people buying drugs, and I just take him back home and explain to him, there's the kind of people you shouldn't be. You don't want to be a crackhead running around the street begging for two dollars or a drug dealer putting a gun to somebody's head." Just recently, an old neighborhood friend has provided the perfect example. "I know this one girl, she's twenty-two. She was gorgeous three years ago. Now she looks—oh God—she looks like somebody beat her with a bat. It's disgusting. Like three years ago, when I first met her, she was the type of person you would like to marry. She was gorgeous. But now she's the type of person you'd like to shoot like a sick horse. She's falling apart."

Most fathers like Will recognize that dispensing discipline and protection, offering wisdom and advice, and serving as a moral guide requires some level of role modeling. This is why having children has slowed Will down so much—at some level, he knows he has to "show" not just "tell" his kids the right path. To be effective in this task, Will feels he should be able to point to his own life as an example of how to rise above the many temptations of the Fairhill streets—drugs, early sexual activity, skipping school or dropping out altogether, and petty criminality and violence. Unfortunately, he does not have the biographical resources to do so. Like Dave, Will's own history prominently features the very activities that he wants his children to abstain from. So in the short run, Will simply "does the best he can," organizing fatherhood around making sure his children grow up to be "nothing like me." While Will, Dave, and the other men we've featured realize that this is not exactly the best way to proceed, it's the best they can do for now.

More than a decade ago—just after we moved to Camden—Maureen Waller engaged several dozen disadvantaged, unmarried fathers in Trenton, New Jersey, in a set of extensive conversations. Her work with these men offered researchers a critical insight: that such men are working to redefine fatherhood, emphasizing the nontraditional aspects of the role—especially emotional involvement—over traditional roles such as those we've discussed in this chapter. At about the same time, Jennifer Hamer drew on interviews with fathers in similar straits across the South and Midwest and made the same observation.[12]

Yet most men we spoke to say that living up to these "traditional" roles remains vital. How do fathers without much in the way of either financial or biographical resources deal with the failure to consistently live up to their own standards? We have shown that in contexts like Will's bottomed-out Fairhill neighborhood, or Dave's declining Whitman enclave, both of which produce a steady supply of young men who are becoming fathers in circumstances that are far from ideal, what it means to be a provider and a role model are also undergoing a profound redefinition. The "doing the best I can" ethos is a powerful short-term tool for reducing men's cognitive dissonance—the gap between their stated values and behaviors. But a critical question remains: how effective is this strategy in the long run, especially when fathers' views come head to head with those of their children's mothers, the demands of the state, and even the expectations of the children themselves?

# FIVE

# *Sesame Street* Mornings

As the Schuylkill River winds south from the leafy green preserves of Fairmount Park and enters the traffic, clamor, and concrete of Center City Philadelphia, it takes one last, brief look at nature in Bartram's Garden before flowing into the barren industrial landscape of Southwest Philadelphia and meeting its end at the Delaware River. Founded almost three hundred years ago by John Bartram, this botanical oasis is the nation's oldest surviving public garden. Seen from the air it is a defiant wedge of green lodged in the surrounding gray of the Kingsessing neighborhood, which presses in on three sides. Originally a collection of small villages and farms, this part of the city didn't have a truly urban feel until the 1920s, when developers seized on its proximity to the burgeoning neighborhoods of West Philadelphia. It became home to white working- and lower middle-class families along with a smattering of the expanding professional class. But in the 1960s rapid racial turnover completely changed the neighborhood's complexion and its economic mix. Home values have since fallen steadily, and as the neighborhood's population has plummeted, its vacancy rate has climbed.

On many of Kingsessing's blocks, there is a gap-toothed look—a well-tended property accented with a colorful garden might be nestled between two units with boarded up windows and weed-choked lawns.

Yet the prewar two- and three-story twins, some plain while others sport gingerbread trim, have survived mostly intact. The commercial activity clustered along Woodland Avenue is limited to strictly low-rent businesses: discount stores, a few auto body shops, storefronts offering check-cashing services and payday loans, beauty salons and barber shops, and a few hole-in-the-wall ethnic restaurants, chicken shacks, and bars. The residential streets here were among the first in the city designed to accommodate automobiles. Both the streets and row homes are wider than in Dave Jones's Whitman or Bear Mallory's Kensington.

Bartram High School opened its doors in the late 1930s to relieve crowding at West Philadelphia High and successfully educated generations of upwardly mobile Philadelphia youth, including Wilson Goode (the first black mayor of Philadelphia) and Patricia Holt (better known by her stage name, Patti LaBelle), while the neighborhood was still largely white. But like the area around it, Bartram High had taken a sharp downward turn by the time Ernest Williams entered its doors as a freshman.[1] Poverty rates were fairly high when Ernest was coming of age—around three in ten residents lived below the poverty line. This was poorer than the city average of about 20 percent, and during his teen years, Kingsessing became notorious for its violent crime.[2] As Ernest entered adulthood Southwest Philadelphia briefly became a mecca for auto theft, with some of the highest rates of stolen and recovered vehicles in the city. Not coincidentally, stealing cars became Ernest's primary vice and the crime that has earned him his felony convictions.

Ernest spent less than a year at Bartram High before a juvenile court judge convicted him for car theft and sent him to the Brandywine School, a disciplinary facility in the southeast corner of the state ("My lifestyle as a child was, it's not really pretty," Ernest explains).[3] Ironically, Ernest remembers his time at Brandywine as a highlight of his younger years. He loved the impressive red brick Victorian buildings with copper cupolas set amid well-tended grounds, the collegelike campus with a backdrop of hills picturesque enough to inspire the artist Andrew Wyeth. The school provides a myriad of excellent vocational training opportunities as well as some badly needed structure and discipline for the boys in its care.

After serving a two-year sentence at Brandywine, Ernest entered a transitional living program back in the city and was able to secure his own apartment and first job. His work as a house-to-house carpet cleaner appealed to his need to stay physically active, and an apartment of his own was ideal for pursuing the one activity he'd missed most while at Brandywine: hooking up with women. "I had a lot of different women in my life coming over," Ernest laughs. "One woman would be leaving out, one would be waiting in the car, hiding her face like, 'Oh my God.' But she would sit in the car and be patient enough till I walk this one to the car. I'm not going to lie. I was a real player, man. I was a real player."

Lynn was a girl that Ernest had met at a party back in his Bartram High days. As he recalls the relationship, Ernest admits that he wasn't taking it too seriously. "It was just a sex thing. 'Cause I had lots of women, and she was just one. She happened to be the one that kept coming to me so much. Every time I turn around, she calling on the phone. Every time I come outside she was standing there, or she coming up the block or she going down the block. And so she always kept being there." This constant proximity proved to have longer-term consequences: "That's when I made him," Ernest says, referring to his twelve-year-old son, Christian.

Lynn was a "house girl" and not a street girl—a virgin before Ernest met her—and yet the news of her pregnancy prompted him to panic and deny responsibility, egged on by his mother who was convinced by the vehemence of his insistence that the child couldn't possibly be his. This continued until his mother paid a visit to the maternity ward. "When my mom came back from that hospital, she looked at me and said, 'It's your baby.'" When asked how he felt at that moment—when his paternity could no longer be denied—Ernest replies that it "made me feel great!" as if the months of vociferous denials had never occurred. "Sure, I was nervous. I was excited. I was a lot of things all at one time. I didn't know what to do, what to feel. But one thing that I did know for sure, that it was mine. And if you seen him today, right now, it look like he came out my asshole! He looks so much like me, man, he got all this, my eyebrows, lips, everything. That's my son. And that's the only one that I have in the world."

By the time Lynn brought the baby home from the hospital, she and Ernest were definitely together, although he stayed in his apartment while she remained with her mother. Ernest might well have gone straight at this point except for his drinking, a habit he'd picked up sneaking hard liquor with cousins at family reunions. Just after Christian was born, in fact, Ernest recalls an epic drinking binge fueled by the festivities over his new baby boy: "It was all the congratulations that made me start drinking more . Every time I turn around, she rocking the baby telling me where to go or what to do, you know? And that was kind of bugging me out, because I'm still with the congratulations. I want to hang out. I don't want to stay in and take care of a child. She said, 'Come on, be a father. I had it—I gave him to you—now you do what you got to do!' But this is not the way that I am thinking, being intoxicated."

Predictably, his nearly constant inebriation soon interfered with his carpet-cleaning job: "I started drinking so bad to where I could not even go back one day. I ain't even go back to get my paycheck," he recalls. One night, in need of cash for another few rounds, he reverted to the routine he had perfected in his preteen years: he stole a car. But the alcohol had dulled his instincts, and he was caught in the act and convicted. "The only time when they really ever caught me is when I was drunk, when I be high. 'Cause I'm not thinking right. I'm not doing my regular procedure," Ernest explains. Over the next twelve years, this pattern repeated itself sixteen more times—upon release from prison or jail, he would find a legitimate job of one kind or another, start drinking, stop going to work, steal a car, and get locked up again.

Ernest claims he's occupied every jail in the city, old and new, and he's also been "upstate and back."

Finally, at age thirty-one, Ernest had a breakthrough. After thirty-six arrests and seventeen spells in lockup, he still managed to land a delivery job for a discount furniture store on Woodland Avenue. He also succeeded in staying off the bottle and getting back with Lynn, who left the man she had just married (the father of her six-year-old daughter, Casey) when she heard Ernest was finally willing to "do what I need to be doing." This reconciliation with Lynn led to his reconnection with his son and to the renewed faith of his own mother, who allowed him to move into her Kingsessing home, drive her car, and even use her bank card. After only six months, however, Ernest "messed up real bad," landed on the streets, and took to "living like a savage," and that ended his contact with his loved ones.

Here's how Ernest recounts this terrible time: "I came home from jail, and I built up so much things back into my life—the trust, the money, the material things, the good jobs, the women—everything just came back. And it was like one day I took a drink, and I just messed up real, real bad. And I felt so ashamed and dirty on the inside that I wanted to end it. I grabbed a .45 revolver and I loaded it up, and I was in the mirror actually talking to myself, crying like a little chump, like a water faucet, crying. I'll never forget it. I had the gun to my head, my finger on the trigger, hammer cocked back, and I was just ready to do it. But a thought came to my mind. 'You never had a father. You always said to yourself if you have a son, how you would be there for him. If you kill yourself, he'll always say "my father was a quitter." Only thing he know you as is a alcoholic, a loser.' And it held me back from doing it."

In the dead of winter and desperate for help, Ernest sought out a North Philadelphia rehab center and filled out the paperwork. But while waiting for the admitting physician to see him, the urge for another drink lured him right out the door and back to the streets. He repeated this pattern twice more in the ensuing weeks, much to the increasing frustration and antipathy of the facility's receptionist. His fourth visit occurred on a frigid February morning. This time a new woman was working intake and handed Ernest the paperwork with a smile. Buoyed by her friendly demeanor, he relaxed and fell asleep in his chair and was only awakened by the sound of his name being called; the doctor was ready to see him.

After nine days in detox, Ernest began a six-month stay at the 131-bed Salvation Army Adult Rehabilitation Center in the Roxborough section of Northwest Philadelphia. Now, the anachronistic sound of a cowbell at 6:00, not just the urge for a drink, marks the start of each day. At 6:30 breakfast is served; then at 7:15 it's time to go to chapel, which, unlike breakfast, is not optional. By 7:30 all residents are in the sorting room, pulling bags out of the trucks, separating men's, women's, and children's clothing and placing them on hangers. Then it's time to climb aboard a white truck with the red Salvation Army shield on the side and collect more donations.

When we first interview Ernest in late May, that cold February morning seems like a lifetime ago. With four months of "work therapy" under his belt, Ernest has entered phase 3 of the program, which means that he can leave the facility overnight on the weekends. Lynn now lives in Reading, about an hour west of Philadelphia, where her steady job has enabled her to purchase a modest home and car—and given his phase 3 status, Ernest can finally make the trip on the Trailways bus to visit without having to worry about making it back to "the Sally" before the ten o'clock curfew. The nineteen-dollar round-trip ticket takes all but one dollar of his weekly spending money allotted by the program, but the benefits of spending "quality time" with his son far exceed the cost to his wallet.

He recalls his most recent two-day stay in Reading with Lynn and Christian as "a beautiful time." Lynn is considering taking him back for the umpteenth time, and Ernest swears privately that he'll give up the three other women he's seeing if she'll only follow through. "Through-out the years I have attached to her. I love this woman, let me tell you. Right now, she's saying, 'I'm going to give you some time. I want to see if you stay out here and do what you're supposed to do.' So in the meantime, to be honest, I am going to continue having three or four different women down here. But when she tell me, 'Come on, let's live together,' I'm dropping all them women at a drop of a dime."

More important, he's managed to have several heart-to-heart conversations with Christian—the first that they've shared in over a year. Ernest believes these father-son talks play a critical role in his son's life, especially now. Christian is on the cusp of adolescence, at the age that Ernest's own delinquent behavior began. "Every time he see me, he do be having questions, and I answer them truthfully. Our last conversation was about sex; I told him about his penis and everything. I told him about diseases, how he got to use condoms. He's only twelve, but these are conversations that he's not having with nobody else, 'cause no man is in his life."

When asked to identify the key qualities of a good father, Ernest draws on his own childhood experiences. Ernest worships his mother, who spent Ernest's early years toiling at the Whitman Chocolate Factory, a Philadelphia landmark employing seven hundred workers before it closed down. She has held too many jobs since for Ernest to remember.[4] He blames himself for going astray but does admit that she "was very hard on me. She was a good mother, but every time I done something wrong, it was always hollering at me, it was always the belt. She was a beautiful mother, but it was always the belt, point blank."

This painful example forms the first principle of good fatherhood in Ernest's mind: to show his son love. "With my son I wanted to be different. I want him to grow up the way I would have liked to grow up, you understand?" The next aspect of good fatherhood he identifies is also drawn from what Ernest felt he lacked. "I'm not saying my mother done nothing wrong, 'cause she beautiful, but I never really had no man near that I could say, 'Hey man, what's up, man? How do a woman feel in the inside? How do you have sex?' Or I might want to ask him about whatever, a gun, things that be on my mind. Or ask him about school or college." Ernest believes that one's kids ought to feel comfortable talking about anything with their father—from sex to guns to college—just like a good friend. "I think a good father is somebody that can break yourself—your attitude, your mind, your way of thinking—down to the child's level, to where he can come up to you and say some things that maybe are even shocking." Having an open line of communication to one's father is particularly vital for sons, he says. "They need the man side, you know. They need that realness because they're men, so they feel a lot more comfortable kicking it with you if you keep it real, if you be honest. His mother asked my son, 'How come you don't want to talk to me about sex?' He told her straight up, 'I don't feel comfortable with you, mom.'"

Fathers often believe they have another advantage over mothers, as we alluded to in chapter 4. "My son, I tell him about jail, how it is. I tell him about school, education, how it's important and how I wish I could have been there and got more of it. I just share stuff to him that I know for a fact that his mother has not experienced." Lynn, a high school graduate with no criminal record, no substance abuse problem, and a steady record of employment is, in Ernest's view, a bit hampered in this role by too much clean living. "I am not grateful or blessed that I've been in jail or been living in the street, you know. But since I have, I had the experience. I can sit there, and I can tell him. I can tell him about how jail is. I can tell him about how breaking the law is not right, how drugs and alcohol is just crazy, smoking cigarettes. And when I do be serious about my experience with him, my past—I be checking him out—he do be sitting there and his mouth just drop open like, 'Dad, you did what?'" But above all, Ernest believes, children need "quality time." "A good father is somebody who is always there. You talk about an event that you have in school. Oh my God, you don't know what that means to a child. Just to come to a ballgame if you win or lose, break or leg or whatever happens. As long as you are there."

Ernest didn't learn the identity of his own father, who he calls a "crooked dude," until he turned twelve, despite the fact that the man was living only one block away. At thirteen, Ernest mustered the courage to knock on his father's door and introduce himself, but the two made no real connection. His father then moved away, but once a year thereafter, the man would roll through the neighborhood in a fancy car and, if he happened upon Ernest in the street, would open the window and hand Ernest a five dollar bill. "He pop up and tell me, 'Look, I'm sorry that I wasn't doing you right, but we can try to be friends.' So I am like, 'Yeah, OK.' So he give me five dollars and he pull off. He just kept disappearing and popping up every year with the same old announcement." Four years ago Ernest's father drove up in a Lexus and asked him if he would like to go for a ride. "I am like twenty-seven years old. He pop up in this nice car talking about 'Come on, I want you to take a ride with me.' OK, you know. I'm older now, I'm mature. Pop want to get into my life, what the hell, you know? Let's try something! You got to start somewhere," Ernest explains. His father took him to meet various family members (who had no idea he existed) and transported him to his new, comfortable home in central New Jersey, where he introduced Ernest to a shocked wife and young daughter. He then charged his son with the task of helping him put in a backyard patio, assuring him this joint activity would help to cement their father-son bond. That was the last Ernest saw of him, though his mother heard through the Kingsessing grapevine that the man now lives in Florida and has a lucrative business flipping foreclosed properties.

Given his own experience, it is no wonder Ernest says a good father is one who is "always there," a hallmark of good fathering so many of our men espouse. But few in Ernest's straits are able to meet that standard—Ernest included—and thus the emphasis on "quality" over "quantity" time. Ernest doesn't see his son every day, or even every week, though he has spoken to the boy fairly regularly by phone when he was sober and not in a lockup. In fact, given his repeated spells of incarceration, heavy drinking, and, more recently, the curfew restrictions imposed by the Salvation Army, months and even years have gone by without any face-to-face interaction. Yet Ernest does not shrink from claiming he plays a vital role. "Every time that I do come around, his mom lets me know how excited he be, how he do good for two weeks. And then when I'm not around it's like the bad behavior comes back. As soon as he sees me again, he's happy, you know." Right now, Ernest is trying to convince Lynn that she should let him move in with her and Christian so as to stave off more "bad behavior." He is envisioning the joyful family reunion that will occur when Lynn picks him up in her car once his time at the Sally is over, in a few months' time.

Peter Lewinski is a white twenty-five-year-old native of New Jersey who moved to Philadelphia after dropping out of Stockton State College in his sophomore year. He works evenings at a tattoo parlor on South Street, sings lead vocal in a friend's heavy metal band, and has aspirations of becoming a professional gambler in Atlantic City. Peter met Shawna, who is seven years older, just after moving to the city. When Shawna told Peter that she was pregnant, he, unlike most of his peers, felt an impending sense of doom and tried to persuade her to have an abortion. Shawna refused to listen, and after three months of arguing, Peter resigned himself to the fact that Shawna wasn't going to budge; he was about to become a father. With this realization came another—he had to grow up and take life more seriously. He began asking his supervisor for more responsibility, but the boss—apparently unimpressed with Peter's work ethic—rebuffed him. Peter left that job, in a used CD store, to work the front desk at the tattoo parlor. Slowly, his relationship with Shawna began to improve as he made peace with his fate, but their tenuous relationship was mortally wounded the night his daughter, Erin, was born. Shawna demanded his presence in the delivery room, but Peter pleaded that he couldn't handle seeing the pain and the blood.

Erin is now seventeen months old, and while Shawna and Peter still live together in a large one-bedroom apartment in Pennsport, they are no more than roommates. They split the bills down the middle and take shifts with Erin, passing like two ships in the night. On weekends he makes sure he stays out of her way—he's either in Atlantic City (to further his gambling career) or out singing with his friend's band. Still, things are tense and Shawna is beginning to pressure Peter to move out. But while Peter's relationship with Shawna has withered, his bond with Erin—the child he was so set against having—has flourished. To keep peace, he suggests partitioning the apartment with a curtain to create two separate living spaces.

Peter cherishes the routine he and his daughter have established— their *Sesame Street* mornings, their outings to Independence Park, the afternoon naps together on the couch—so much that he refuses to let anyone else take care of her if Shawna cannot. Recently, he turned down a chance to fly out west for a friend's bachelor party; Shawna had other plans and he wouldn't entrust Erin to his mother. "I'd rather stay home than be in Las Vegas whooping it up. If something happened to her, you know, I'd never be able to live with myself." When we ask him if he wants any more children, Peter shakes his head. "No. I mean," he pauses and looks over at Erin playing quietly on the rug before adding, "I really don't think I could do any better than her." Although Peter's definition of what a good father does is broad, it is clear that the heart of it is the "quality time" he spends with Erin.

"Most men I know, they're daddies but not fathers," says Michael, the forty-one-year-old African American father of a four-month-old daughter and a twenty-two-year-old son.[5] "Their kids call them 'daddy' but it's not the same as being a father." What's the difference between a daddy and a father, we ask? "When they go to work, come home, and their kids want to do this or that with them, and they're like, 'I'm too tired.' That's just being a dad, to me. But being father, I don't care how tired you are man, you're going to get up and make that effort to be with your child and do something with your child.[6] "What about financially? Do you need to be earning?" we ask. "You have to be giving something," he says, but mostly it's about "quality time."

When asked about their fatherhood *ideals,* men emphasized the importance of investing time in one's children more frequently than any other single aspect of good fathering. Paul, a thirty-five-year-old African American father of a four-year-old son, works at a microfilm company photographing legal documents. For the moment, he has temporary custody of his boy while his ex-girlfriend completes drug rehab. "I think the most important thing about being a good father is just being there and spending quality time," he says. "I think that most kids, that is all they want. I know with my son, I think he is just happy when he is with me. He don't care what we are doing or where we are going, even if it is just like to the playground, as long as he is with me."

The importance of quality time was often raised as part of men's critique of the traditional father—one who simply goes to work and brings home a paycheck but doesn't spend time with his children. Antonio, a thirty-six-year-old black father of three from East Camden who moves between factory jobs and hotel housekeeping, says, "The father's job is to come home and spend time with his kids so that they won't say, 'Well, my dad, all he do is work. He don't never spend no time with us.'" John, the twenty-four-year-old white father of a five-year-old girl who is from Fishtown, and was featured in chapter 2, offers a similar view: "You shouldn't have a job to where you're never home. Like, you can be a high-powered lawyer making two million dollars a year, but if you don't have time for your children you can't be a good father. So, I mean, you have to spend time with your kids."

These critiques are quite general, but often men's negative appraisals take a very personal turn. Roger, a white forty-six-year-old father of four ranging in age from six to thirteen, who has a nursing degree but currently works at a thrift store, says, "I think interaction with the kids is important and being involved in their lives. When I grew up I thought that my dad was not a good father because he was a workaholic, very definitely a workaholic." Larry, a forty-year-old college-educated black father of two teens, fourteen and fifteen, who works as a counselor in a recreation program for at-risk children in Kensington, said, "My father was a provider, and he did the things that a provider should do, but in terms of talking and going out and doing things, no. I was athletic.

I played ball after school. He would drop me off. He was a great man as a matter of fact, but in terms of somebody there to talk to me and see which way I was headed to, to tell me to slow up, that I was doing the wrong thing; it was trial and error for me. It don't have to be trial and error for my kids because I am there now."

Men with older children sometimes turned this critique on themselves. Joe, a white carriage driver with four children (twenty-one, nineteen, sixteen years, and thirteen months) has some regrets about how he raised his older kids. "If I had to do it over again, I wouldn't work as much as I did. I would have spent time with my kids instead of working. But then I figured they needed this, needed that. If I had to do it over again, I would do without a few things. Instead of two days down at the shore, I could have taken a week. They need time. Kids need their parents."

In their critiques of the traditional father role, some singled out not only the preoccupation with work but the emphasis on financial provision. The clear message here is that spending money on children is nowhere near as important as spending time, building a relationship, and showing love and affection. In an interesting and significant twist, Ernest Williams casts the father who provides things for his child— even substantial things like a college tuition—in an almost selfish light as one who spoils his child simply to feel good about himself. Meanwhile, he describes the ideal parental relationship as one in which the child feels comfortable in talking about anything, just like a good friend. "A good father is not a person that gives the child everything they want. I mean, don't get me wrong, it feels good, and it's a good thing to get a child a bicycle, it feels good to put your kid through college. But at the same time, the good father is somebody like your friend. You put your son on a school bus and don't you know, your son will sit next to his friend and talk about things and be open and have fun just by talking to his little buddy. I think a good father is somebody like that."

Fathers and sons carving an entry for the pinewood derby, setting up the Lionel Train underneath the Christmas tree, playing catch in the backyard and basketball games in the driveway, pitching a tent, or fishing together are the iconic images of American boyhood and family life. The inner-city correlate, quality time, can take many forms, from the simple act of watching *Sesame Street* together, like Peter Lewinski and his daughter Erin, to more elaborate adventures, like Will Donnelly's visit with his four children to Penn's Landing. Maurice, a thirty-eight-year-old black father of three, uses the summer months to engage his youngest daughter in an ongoing quest to find "the perfect water ice," a famous Philly treat, and Amin Jenkins delights in impromptu celebrations of his child's first word and first step. Logging hours in even simple activities like watching a Phillies game together or the mutual enjoyment of a bowl of cereal is the embodiment of what fathers mean when they say they want the "whole fatherhood experience." Unlike old-school fathers, who believed children should be respectful and relegated to the background, Tony, a twenty-six-year-old white food-service worker with a toddler, says, "What is great is just being able to play, to roll around in the dirt and totally involve yourself with everything that she's doing."

While fathers do love to simply spend time with their children, these "precious moments" also serve a more important purpose, especially when the children are still young. As the men know all too well, a father may have access to his child for the time being, but life has a way of intervening. When their baby's mother kicks them out of the house, a drug addiction or prison sentence interferes with visitation, one parent or the other moves away, or mom gets a new boyfriend who tries to play daddy to the kids while shutting out the biological father, these father-child experiences can create a store of relational capital that can sustain a child—and a father—through the periods of absence. Though the future is uncertain and fathers know that much of what happens is beyond their control, spending quality time now is a good investment. It creates a stock of memories that they and their children can draw on when things get tough.

But what about the more traditional aspects of fathering we discussed in the previous chapter, particularly the hallmark breadwinning role? When we ask Ernest to identify the hardest part about being a father, he is quick to respond, "Not being able to provide." Yet he doesn't really feel badly about his failure in this area. As he sees it, this lapse is not a matter of weak paternal commitment but merely one of unfortunate circumstances. "It's not like I don't *want* to. I don't have no problem taking care of my son. But I just never really been in the *position* to." What kind of a situation might prompt him to pay his court-ordered child support? "Now if I got out and I got me a steady job, and I'm out doing what I'm supposed to do—months going by, months going by— and if they notify me and find out where I'm at, sure I go in my pocket and do what I got to do. But man, ever since they have been asking me, I never been working or nothing."

Ernest credits his willingness to pay—if the Bureau of Child Support Enforcement "happens" to catch up with him and if he "happens" to be working steady at the time—as an adequate substitute for actual provision for the time being, given his "position." An outside observer (or his son's mother) might point out that it has been Ernest's own behavior—stealing cars and drinking—that has kept him from being "in the position" to provide, not some mysterious circumstance beyond his control. When Ernest's son is a bit older, he may also come to view Ernest's frequent and lengthy absences and his meager financial contributions with the same bitterness many of the men expressed about their own fathers. At this point, however, Christian is still young enough and hungry enough for his father's attention not to hold this against him. According to Ernest, the boy understands his situation. "He know that I don't have much money now, you know? But he do like my company. He love my company."

## FATHERHOOD AS FRIENDSHIP

Most fathers share Ernest's views; while they attest to the importance of the more traditional aspects of fatherhood such as financial provision and moral guidance, the essence of fatherhood is really about the relational aspects—showing love, maintaining open communication, and spending quality time. Ultimately, according to these men, a good father is a friend. This image of father as friend finds significant support in the wider culture, where new notions of fatherhood have permeated the middle class, at least in word if not fully in deed.[7] The traditional image of the father—as provider, disciplinarian, and moral guide—has tended to imply emotional distance and a more authoritarian stance toward children. By contrast, the new model projects an image of paternal warmth and implies a more open and egalitarian relationship.

Adopting this view turns the tables on what it means to be a good dad. No matter how well a father performs in the traditional aspects of the role, he is still missing the mark if there isn't emotional closeness. Lavelle, the African American father of five-year-old Little Toya, had the quintessential old-school dad—a landscaper who worked long hours to provide for his thirteen children. Yet the man seldom took time just to "be there" with his children. Lavelle set out to be different: "Instead of just being a dad, you can also be a friend," he says. Embracing the role of father as friend implies a relationship, not just the fulfillment of a set of responsibilities. More broadly, it implies an internal emotional state and not mere external compliance to a set of "oughts." While a good provider might earn some respect, he is still a mere daddy if he hasn't also accomplished the "fatherhood aspects" of his role. These center on caring, not paying; communicating, not disciplining; just spending time and enjoying one's children rather than serving as a font of wisdom or a moral guide.

This emphasis on friendship has its problems, for there is real tension between adopting this approach to fatherhood and the goal of fulfilling the more traditional roles of disciplinarian and moral guide. By its nature, friendship is egalitarian and not hierarchical, and fathers determined to be their children's friends must cede critical authority over them. Even worse from the point of view of the mother, celebrating the soft side of fatherhood often means relegating all the difficult jobs—paying the bills, setting the limits, providing the good example—to her. Perhaps this is precisely why Ernest characterizes his own mother as being so "hard." Nonetheless, the other fathers we spoke with agree strongly about the absolute primacy of the soft side of fatherhood.

The primacy of the emotional bond is everywhere in men's narratives. Forty-one-year-old Michael, for example, is a long-time maintenance worker for the Philadelphia Housing Authority, now on SSI disability due to the debilitating effects of colon cancer. He hustles odd jobs in his North Central Philadelphia neighborhood to supplement his income. He asserts that "to be a father is to be really nurturing and caring." Fatherhood involves a relationship; it's a "loving thing," not just a financial obligation. Nowhere is this more evident than when we ask whether his own dad was a good father. "Not to me," Michael says, despite the fact that his father held a good city job and was able to provide a middle-class life for Michael and his siblings. "He was there for us financially and everything, but the love wasn't. You got to be there with the love and understanding. He was more of a hollerer and screamer."

"Show him that you care about him and that you'll be there for him," admonishes Will Donnelly, when we ask for his advice about how to be a good father. "If you don't act like you love your child, he might turn out to be a serial killer or something." Will's statement is not pure hyperbole. As we indicated earlier, Will Jr., age five, already shows signs of a conduct disorder according to the boy's school counselor, prompting Will to spend as many mornings as he can volunteering in his son's kindergarten classroom.

Bernie; his fiancée, Laurie; his ex-wife, Rose; and his two daughters, age seven and eight (one from each relationship), are currently doubled up—or tripled up, one might say—with Bernie's sister and her two children in her two bedroom home in the Mantua section of West Philadelphia. This African American father is proud of the fact that he is openly nurturing of his children, both of whom have developmental delays. "I've tried to look at myself as like a modern father," he says, "not being afraid to show my emotions." This thirty-five-year-old African American has been deaf since birth, an SSI recipient since the age of six, and a street performer—he's a mime and a juggler—since he left college at the end of his sophomore year.

Readers might assume that it is only natural that our fathers put such emphasis on love. Yet there is often a special poignancy to their insistence that love is a critical ingredient of fatherhood, for even though most were raised with very limited financial means, love and not money is what they say they missed most from their own fathers. In fact, many were subjected to abuse at the hands of their dads or stepdads. For Michael, for example, things looked unusually good on the surface when he was coming up. He is the product of a stable two-parent family—his parents have been married for more than fifty years and his father held that good city job, advancing to middle management by the time he retired. But Michael's emphasis on nurture and care stem from the fact that his father also was a brutal alcoholic who arrived home roaring drunk and in a rage every payday. "I seen a lot of abuse," Michael says.

Similarly, Will regrets he never had a chance to witness demonstrations of love from any male parent, as his biological father left the scene before Will was even born and his stepfather was too busy drinking to offer much affection. By contrast, Will tries to lavish love on his four kids whenever he can, and he attributes most of the problems he sees with the youth in his neighborhood to a lack of parental affection. To ensure his brother's daughter gets enough love—her mother is deceased and her father is in prison—he's taken her in while his brother serves out his sentence. "I love her to death" he says.

Bernie also grew up in what he calls a "dysfunctional family," though his mother was the more proximate cause of his trauma than his absent dad. "My father, he was not with us. I have two sisters, both younger than me. We all three had different fathers and only my one sister— she's my youngest—ever got to know her father. My father, he's still living, but I first met him when I was thirty-one." More troubling than the ever-shifting cast of men in Bernie's barmaid mother's life was her inability to cope with three children. Bernie doesn't specify the cause, but he was removed from her home and placed with his grandmother when he was ten. Ties to family were further attenuated by the fact that he was required to board at the Philadelphia School for the Deaf and visited his grandmother only on occasion during the school year. No wonder Bernie is so committed to letting his emotions show in his relationship with his daughter Angelique.

When thirty-one-year-old J. J. was a baby his father threw him hard against a wall, an incident he blames for the frequent seizures that keep him on disability. J.J. also recounts that when he was older, his father "pulled guns out on me; he pulled knives out on me. I was five or six when I seen him stab my mom up about five times." The man stopped his abuse only when J.J. was an adolescent, and he and his younger brother got hold of gun and threatened to kill their father if he displayed any more physical aggression. The near obsession J.J. now shows in his desire to demonstrate love to his daughter, who has a mild form of cerebral palsy, is in strong contrast to his own father, who despised the symptoms of J.J.'s disability and still shuns him.

Paternal love is a critical element to healthy child development, according to the credo of these fathers. Showing love can shield a child from the proverbial wrong path. The story men tell of their own histories often reveals that their father's absence, coldness, abuse, or rejection was the source of their own rebellion. Even if an unloved child doesn't become a serial killer—as Will Donnelly fears—he can still be easily pulled into the streets and away from the positive activities that lead to a good life. Particularly for those with unsavory pasts, demonstrating love is a strategy they employ to ensure that their child ends up being "nothing like me."

The need to be loved back—a more selfish motive—is no doubt often in the background, but this is a need felt by parents across the class divide. Beyond the simple human desire to love and be loved in return is the aspiration to provide the foundation on which a child can build the critical inner resources of self-worth and efficacy. This foundation is something fathers think they are in a unique position to provide. After all, despite the often-strong mothers whom many revere, most have never gotten over the neglect or abuse they suffered at the hands of their fathers.

When we asked the fathers we spoke with to describe the critical ingredients of a good romantic relationship, communication, honesty, and trust were by far the most frequently mentioned qualities. Similarly, communication is a core part of the father-as-friend triumvirate of "love, communication, and quality time." In fact, the importance of good communication in the family domain is emphasized with astounding frequency in these men's narratives. Although all parents probably prize this quality, maintaining an open line of communication is especially vital for those whose children are being raised in troubled neighborhood environments. Good communication, many feel, is the best early warning system when a child (or a partner) starts to wander off the path. And fathers who act as authority figures rather than friends may cut off communication by instilling fear in their children. They may also inadvertently encourage deceit, driving deviant behavior and pernicious influences underground where they can't be identified and dealt with. For many men, this conviction that fear instills deceit stems from firsthand experience, as this is how many of them reacted to the harsh discipline of their own more traditional parents.

Better a friend who is trusted and confided in, men often reason, than an authority figure who is feared but easily deceived. Charles, for example, is a white thirty-seven-year-old father who collects SSI for his diabetes and mental-health problems. He works under the table as a landscaper for his stepfather in the summers and has four children ranging in age from four to eleven. He says a good father is one who "sits and talks with [his] kids, and understands them, and listens." Charles's protective instinct is strong. His own father sexually abused him between the ages of eight and sixteen, when Charles was finally able to "step up for myself." Charles's older sister was also a victim; she eventually committed suicide. Naturally, this abusive behavior didn't inspire the trust necessary for Charles to confide in his father; in fact, he hasn't seen his dad more than once or twice in the last ten years. Without proper paternal guidance, Charles acted out, "doing anything to get in trouble; seeking attention because I wasn't getting it at home. All I was getting was negative attention. I guess that's what I thrived on. It was better than getting none. My mom did what she could. But I was a really bad kid. I would rob houses, I stole, I was in detention centers, I was in disciplinary schools, I was in jail, and I think a lot of it was because of the way my father was."

When Charles hit adulthood, "I met a girl in Fishtown and had four kids with her. I started selling cocaine, making money to support them. When I broke up with my girlfriend, I went out with a go-go dancer from Happy Days, and she was on heroin. I didn't like it the first few times, but then I got physically hooked on it. And I was hooked on it for about five or six years. I think if I had the right guidance and the right kind of love, I would have might not turned out the way I turned out to be."

A sharp tension can emerge between creating enough openness so that children will be comfortable enough to share everything and preserving enough authority to correct any risky behavior that does come to light. Sam, a thirty-two-year-old African American father of a twelve-year-old daughter, is walking a fine line in this regard. "I think it's important for fathers to try to open up a channel of communication so that a child knows that they can come to him about anything. Be open and honest and let them know that they won't be punished for trying to be honest. They'll be corrected in a firm but understanding way. 'That was wrong, this is why it's wrong and I'm glad you came to me.' I'm not punishing them hard because I would want the child to come to me and talk to me, versus feeling like, 'Well I can't go to Daddy because he's going to beat me or he's going to yell at me.' So then they hide it and do it again, and it snowballs. So I think the man's job is just to be, well, understanding."

Ernest Williams also struggles to maintain the balance between communication and discipline. When Lynn called to tell him that Christian had skipped school, Ernest caught the Trailways bus out to their home in Reading the next weekend. "I didn't run over there and grab the belt and try to knock his head off, which I could have. But you know what I did? I said, 'Come here, man.' I took him into his room. I grabbed something he probably really liked, and I am just playing with it—it might be a racing car or his joystick to his PlayStation—and I might ask something about whatever it is. Then I will smile with him and make a joke—I am trying to play a little psychiatry on him. And then I kick it to him: 'Why you stay home? Oh man, let me tell you before you tell me: there was one time that I stayed home when I was a kid. I hid under the bed.' I tell him my experience or what I done. What he just did, I tell him how I used to do that when I was a kid. And I give him the detail and tell him how it was. And then I tell him how it wasn't right. And then I get to him, 'So how come you do it?' I guess I go through all that other stuff to get him to open up, 'cause I want him to trust me. I want him to be comfortable. I want him to be able to tell me anything—'Dad, I didn't feel like going to school today'—so I can get into his world and let him know, you know, 'Look, you got to.' And I wind up giving him a good speech."

In this chapter we've examined why men are so eager to "redefine fatherhood," to use sociologist Maureen Waller's term, so that the more relational aspects of fatherhood are given clear primacy over the traditional elements of the role.[8] The most obvious reason, of course, is that these are the parts of fatherhood that these men feel most able to accomplish successfully. As we see in the case of Ernest Williams, these are not viewed as a set of obligations to fulfill but as the embodiment of a relationship most are eager to build and maintain.

Each element of the father-child relationship has a distinct and critical purpose. Showing love is about making children stronger. It is the foundation on which kids can build efficacy and self-esteem. Resisting the streets will be hard, fathers say, and only a kid with a strong sense of purpose and internal resolve will survive. Communication is about keeping children safe. With so many pitfalls in the immediate environment—where kids more often fall prey than rise above—an early warning system through honest talk is absolutely essential. Better that kids view their father as a trusted friend than an authority figure. Quality time, though, is the most vital ingredient of all. It builds a store of capital that can be drawn on in the future, when times might get tough, and, like the "as needed" approach to financial provision, purchases the right to ongoing access. Bill is white and thirty-eight, a drug addict who deeply regrets that he didn't get to put in that quality time when his two daughters, now ten and eight, were younger. "You want to show up on the porch and be father of the year," he says, "but it don't work like that."

Fathers' golden moments with children—engaging in play, watching television together, attending a softball game or a school event—are an insurance policy for an uncertain future. For Ernest the little bit of quality time he has managed to spend with his son in the past is key to the boy's willingness to open up to him now. And the time invested now—since he's reached phase 3 at "the Sally", Ernest is on that Trailways bus to Reading as often as he can—is, to offer another metaphor, a line of credit that he can draw on in case things don't work out with Lynn. Ernest's goal is to find a way to build on the relationship he now has with his son—one that already goes far beyond the annual disbursement of a five dollar bill.

While ordinary times—the *Sesame Street* mornings, regular forays out into the neighborhood to find the perfect water ice, or the walks to Independence Park—are viewed as critical, special times are vital too. This is why it is so important to "have the paper," so they can treat their child to something memorable when they visit, and why visits to the Please Touch Museum in Center City, the Sesame Place amusement park north of Philadelphia off U.S. 95, Penn's Landing, and even the venerable Franklin Institute on the Ben Franklin Parkway feature so prominently in men's descriptions of how they spend—or would like to spend—that quality time.

At some level, of course, these fathers know that reducing the traditional responsibilities to provide and act as a moral guide to merely "doing the best I can" is, in the end, unsatisfactory. They realize they've fallen critically short in these important domains, even if they're not total deadbeats, as we'll see in the next chapter. Emphasizing the relational aspects of fatherhood over those that have traditionally defined the role offers a more flexible and forgiving way to proceed. Here, the content and intent of a given interaction matters more than the frequency of contact between a father and child. As Ernest's story shows, love, communication, and quality time can be extended in a hundred different ways: a phone call, a letter or gift in the mail (Ernest is always borrowing cash from his mother to send his son "little gifts," along with something for Lynn's daughter, Casey), or even a prayer. And fathers are betting that these are gestures their children will deem important, even if their mothers bad mouth them for failing in other domains.

According to Erik Erikson (1958), the central psychological crisis of middle adulthood—the stage Ernest Williams is in—pits generativity against stagnation: "Will I produce something of real value?" is the question a mature adult must reckon with.[9] Among other things, generativity involves caring for and guiding the next generation. Interestingly, the men that we spoke with often feel compelled to be generative at very early ages, perhaps because so many have experienced so much in such a short time or because they sense their lifespan may be truncated. Importantly, younger men are at least as likely to express this compulsion as those who are older, so this is not just an artifact of interpreting one's youthful actions from the point of view of middle adulthood. Simply producing a child—being a daddy—is not generative in itself, and our fathers clearly recognize this. That is why most reserve the term "father" for men who accomplish fatherhood's relational aspects. If their children are to advance to adulthood in better shape than their fathers, the kids will need the strength and the sustenance that a dad's generative activity can provide.[10]

This chapter and the previous one have focused on men's ideals of fatherhood. How do these ideals square with reality? And when word and deed don't exactly match up, how do fathers cope with the dissonance? In the next chapter we explore how the men that we spoke with enact the father role, what factors undergird their efforts to be good dads by their own lights, and what prevents them from fathering in the ways that they wish they could.

# SIX

# Fight or Flight

Knowing what inner-city men think fatherhood ought to look like doesn't tell us much about how they live it day to day, or why they don't live it in exactly the way they think they should. This is especially so for those whose lives have taken extraordinarily difficult turns. More than most, Ritchie Weber knows what it is like to hit rock bottom. Just two years ago he was spending nights huddled on the slide in Tacony Park on Torresdale Avenue, a small city park with a playground attached to a baseball diamond, or, when it rained or turned cold, in the storage trailer of the construction company where he worked. Heroin and child support consumed nearly all his earnings—he had to scrounge dumpsters for food, sometimes subsisting on as little as a single dough-nut a day—but no matter how bad it got, he never missed a day of work. And he didn't let a week go by without seeing his nine-year-old boy.

Now, though, this thirty-four-year-old white father's life has com-pletely turned around; "I'm living my dream," he says. In fact, just the other day, Ritchie was over in New Jersey with his new girlfriend, Mary, the two of them perusing real estate—just for fun—and fanta-sizing about the possibility of one day owning a single-family home with two bathrooms and off-street parking. Mary, who he says is his soul mate, makes good money as a nurse at Jefferson Hospital in Center

City. Though he's still at the same job he held while homeless—which pays eight dollars per hour—the two plan to pool their resources to secure a rental in the Jersey suburbs. When asked to account for such a dramatic change in his fortunes, Ritchie is ready with an answer. "My son," he says matter-of-factly. "My son is my savior. No matter what I went through, the boy stuck by me. He never got mad at me, everything was always OK, and that is why today I can't do enough for him."

Ritchie never gave up on himself either and credits his perseverance to the "big, close-knit" loving family who enfolded him when he was growing up in Port Richmond, a largely white community just northeast of less reputable Kensington. Ritchie is the youngest of five brothers, their mixed heritage of German, Polish, and French reflecting the neighborhood's long-standing history as a melting pot of Catholic immigrants from all parts of Europe. Though solidly working-class, Port Richmond's slightly larger row houses (sixteen feet wide versus the twelve-foot standard) attracted those whose salaries were a cut above the average Kensingtonian's—plant foremen and skilled craftsmen a bit higher on the pay scale than those who worked the factory floor. When Ritchie was coming of age, the neighborhood was populated by families who took pains to appear respectable, including the ultimate local show of decency: sweeping the sidewalks fronting their homes clean each morning. Ritchie still engages in this ritual and believes it has brought him good luck.

Port Richmond parents also did their best to provide each of their children with thirteen years of Catholic education. Ritchie was sent to Saint Anne's on Lehigh, and then to North Catholic, the all-boys school that served the parish, but in tenth grade he "wound up with the wrong crowd" and was expelled.[1] He spent only about a year in public school before dropping out to take a job as an unskilled laborer at a construction site. Never one to set his sights too high, Ritchie says he "ended up" five years later in what he calls a "corner marriage" with Kate, a girl he knew from the local neighborhood set. "We all hung out together," he explains, "and eventually everybody paired off."

However haphazard their origins, corner marriages had formed the bedrock of the Port Richmond community for generations; typically, they had lasted a lifetime, but this was less true in Ritchie's generation. Even the birth of their son, Ritchie Jr., about two years into their marriage couldn't save this volatile union. Just after their son turned two, Ritchie and Kate split for good. Afterward, Ritchie was as faithful to his son as he had always been to his job, visiting nearly every day. But "whenever there was a dispute between me and her, somehow it always got back to where she would keep Ritchie Jr. from me." While Ritchie had gloried in the prospect of fatherhood, the couple's mutual antipathy made enacting the father role very hard. "Kate and I hated each other for a long time. We didn't get along at all. We didn't want nothing to do with one another."

Up to this point in his life, Ritchie had displayed remarkably little ambition—a lack of drive is why he had worked the same job at the same lousy pay for a decade, never really aspiring to anything more. And neither marriage nor parenthood—critical life events that had shifted the trajectories of generations of Port Richmond men—had provided that magic turning point for Ritchie.[2] But suddenly, Kate's attempt to play gatekeeper sparked a steely determination he never knew he had. "She would try to keep him from me, but I was not that type of guy to allow that. I got the police, and I went down there and banged on that door," he recalls. He also says he took Kate to court dozens of times in the early years to ensure his right to visitation.

Still, this wasn't enough to turn Ritchie's life around. In fact, for a brief time, beginning when Ritchie Jr. was five, it seemed as if heroin might win out over Ritchie's paternal commitment. "It was a time in my life when drugs were so important to me that that is all I concerned myself about. I wound up owing five thousand to six thousand dollars in back child support. I wound up to the point where I was living on the street." But even then Ritchie kept stopping by to see his son. "I had long hair and was unbathed for days at a time, and I remember crying to my son, telling him how I was sorry. And I remember my son hugging me, saying it was OK, as long as I just came to see him. That Christmas I didn't have anything for him. He said me just being there was all the present he needed."

The turning point finally came when a friend tried to convince Ritchie that to conquer his addiction he needed a change of scenery; the friend had a contact in Florida who had agreed to set Ritchie up with a job and an apartment. Initially, Ritchie thought he should grasp at this lifeline, but the thought of leaving his young son instilled a strong conviction that he couldn't simply flee from his problems. "It was the thought of never seeing him again that ripped through me. I remember that night; instinctively I knew that I had to break down and face everything that I caused in order to keep my son in my life." Accordingly, Ritchie started attending AA and NA meetings, determined to reclaim his sobriety. Being homeless while sober was the hardest thing he had done. "I was homeless sober, stone cold sober as a matter of fact. But I was the AA group representative, had keys to two clubhouses. AA was the only place that I had any respect besides my son."

Just as his new resolve and his responsibilities with AA were beginning to resuscitate his self-esteem, Ritchie's boss discovered that he was sleeping in the trailer's storage room and offered him an efficiency apartment he owned in neighboring Harrogate, left vacant because it was located on a run-down street that included two crack houses. With a place of his own, Ritchie was able to petition the court to set a visitation schedule that included overnights. Even though Kate was dead set against it—due to Ritchie's past—Ritchie began taking his son every other weekend when he could afford to feed him—the child support and the payments on his substantial child-support arrears ate into his meager earnings. "We ate spaghetti and we ate beans and franks, but I could get my son, and he loved that place. It was a two-room efficiency, and he loved it because me and him were together and that is what it was all about."

Then, about a year ago Ritchie had one other stroke of good luck. Through the matchmaking efforts of his brother and sister-in-law, he reconnected with a woman named Mary, another one of the corner girls from his youth whose marriage had also failed and who was raising her daughter, Kayla, on her own. "We are actually best friends and soul mates before anything," Ritchie says. He explains the unexpected success of his relationship with Mary in this way: "We know each other from the corner, so it is not like I could be somebody that I am not. I am who I am and she is who she is, and we just really click together." Mary accepts Ritchie as he is and is extraordinarily supportive of his relationship with his son; just last month she purchased a PlayStation for Ritchie Jr.'s birthday but put Ritchie's name on the card instead of her own, knowing he couldn't afford to buy his son the coveted toy.

Every Monday morning Ritchie is up at 5:00 a.m. to finish off a pot of coffee and a cigarette before the thirty-minute walk to the pickup point, where he catches a ride from his boss, an "Italian guy from the old school who is going to push me like the mule that I am." They travel to the day's construction site, where Ritchie and two other laborers "bullwork all day long."[3] For eight hours' hard labor, Ritchie accrues sixty-four dollars in cash; "It's all I know how to do." Then it's the ride back to the office, the walk home, and a quick shower before he's out again to stop by Kate's place on his way to pay a visit to Mary.

Now Ritchie is more than satisfied with his lot: "Life is good. I strive, work, and do everything that I do just for this moment, not for some futuristic thing that is never going to happen to me. If a great big house on the hill comes along, then great. In the meantime I will be happy with what I got. My son says to me, 'Dad I love you,' and that is the most rewarding thing. He makes me be a parent whether I like it or not, just like I make him use his manners whether he likes it or not. We need each other. We are good for each other. We deserve each other."

Even Kate has responded to Ritchie's turnaround, allowing Ritchie Jr. to stay over on some days not on the visitation schedule. This fall he was with Ritchie for a two-week period, while Kate sorted out a "personal problem."[4] Ritchie views this as a particular triumph, which he attributes to his persistence in demanding the right to see his son. "I was always there for that boy. He was my heart and soul. And because I never gave up, because I believed in *me and him,* everybody else finally backed down. I fought for our rights because nobody could fight for him but me."

Just recently, there has been even more good news in Ritchie's life. Mary's six-year-old daughter, Kayla, has asked her mother whether Ritchie would mind if she called him daddy—her own father doesn't visit and she feels the lack of a dad. When Mary came to him with Kayla's request, "Tears came to my eyes," Ritchie says. "Apparently she sees more in me than I do."

Holloway Middleton is not on this upward trajectory, yet he can also recall a time when he thought he was on top of the world, with a steady relationship, a roof over his head, and a night job cleaning office buildings. Through hard work and reliability, Holloway had risen from the minimum wage up to almost nine dollars an hour at the cleaning company, with regular opportunities for overtime at double pay. Not bad, he thought, for a black man without a high school diploma. And he had just moved in with his first real girlfriend, Katrina, whom he had met at a Center City dance club. Katrina was raising her sons, aged eight and ten, in a row house on Gratz Street in North Philadelphia's Nicetown section—a thoroughfare of two story rows with awnings encased in a rainbow of colored aluminum—a bright spot in the otherwise drab streetscapes of North Philadelphia. She had acquired the home, one among miles of cramped prewar two-bedroom units, from a recently deceased relative. The neighborhood sits a stone's throw from the decrepit, yawning campuses of two former industrial giants that used to employ thousands of the neighborhood's residents—the mighty Midvale Steel, where the father of scientific management, Frederick Winslow Taylor, began his time-and-motion studies, and the Budd Company, the legendary manufacturer of railway cars—and close by the neighborhood icon, the aromatic Tastycake production facility on Fox Street.

When Holloway met Katrina, there was no other man in the picture—one of her son's fathers was dead from a bullet and the other from a drug overdose—so Holloway had taken on the role of surrogate dad. With a steady job, a ready-made family, and a decent home over their heads, Holloway felt as though he was living the Nicetown version of the American Dream. "It was like I was the man of the house, bringing in my little pay and stuff like that. It was a family, and she made me feel like I was the boss."

Holloway had grown up just next door to Nicetown in the Fairhill section of the city, the son of a brick mason and stay-at-home mom. His parents provided him with a stable home life, and his father was a good provider. But then Friday night came. "On weekends, man, he used to drink. Ooh man, when he drank my father used to go crazy. Half of the time we had to leave on the weekend. He hit my mom, hit her a lot of times. I mean he used to really give it to her, you know? Sometimes he took it out on us too." Things got so bad that Holloway landed in foster care for a while. Troubles at home were mirrored by troubles at school; Holloway dropped out of high school in the eleventh grade because he simply couldn't keep up with the work. "I was kind of slow. My teachers, they tried to help me, but I just felt bad. You feel bad when you can't do what the other students do." He tried to learn bricklaying from his father, but he failed at that as well. "I never really could catch on. He would get mad at me too, 'cause I never could just take this ruler with this fluid in the middle of it [the level], stick it down on the ground, measure it. I could never do it."

Desperate to learn a trade, Holloway signed up for Job Corps at seventeen and was sent to a facility in Gary, Indiana. But Job Corps turned out to be more like prison than school. "I had to hang with the guys from Philly, 'cause if I didn't there was no protection for me. People would be like stabbed, beat up real bad." Holloway was thrown out of the program along with another kid after a big brawl between the Philly boys and other boys from another city. He joined the National Guard but quit after just a few weeks. "I got problems with finishing stuff," Holloway admits. "I'm messed up like that."

Finally, at twenty-three he thought he had found his golden ticket—the janitorial job. He had just gotten a raise when he met Katrina. For some time after that things were "perfect." Then, after two years of unprotected sex, Katrina got pregnant. They started talking marriage and Holloway even put down money on an engagement ring. But before he had time to think much more about their future together, the bottom began to fall out.

The first blow was when the company Holloway worked for was bought out by a larger building-maintenance firm. The new management proceeded to fire him and all the longtime employees—those commanding the highest wages. He collected unemployment while looking for another job, keenly feeling the pressure now that a baby was on the way. Then, desperate for cash, he began to seek work through a temporary agency that paid just a little better than the minimum wage. He brought all his earnings home but could see that Katrina was beginning to lose respect for him.

One day Katrina was entertaining friends in the front room while Holloway was back in the kitchen making himself a sandwich out of their sight. What he overheard, he says, cut him like a knife. "How much he make an hour?" one friend asked. "What he give you yesterday?" another insisted. "Fifty dollars," he heard Katrina say in a dismissive tone, followed by derisive laughter from the whole group. Katrina's friends responded, "Come on!" "He can do better than that!" "He's a loser!" Burning with embarrassment and shame, Holloway slinked up the stairs to the bedroom, resolving once again to find a better job. But despite years of solid performance at the cleaning company, and the lack of any obvious impediments like a criminal record or an addiction, he did not succeed.

Soon thereafter tragedy occurred. One night Holloway awoke to the smell of smoke and rushed downstairs to find the row house's kitchen engulfed in flames. He ran back upstairs and shouted for everyone to get out. While Katrina grabbed the boys and, with the help of firefighters, fled out the front second-story window, Holloway escaped out the back door. When they met up in the front of the house, Holloway was relieved to see that everyone was accounted for. Yet something was wrong; Katrina was hysterical, screaming that he had to go back in the house, that there was someone still inside. Holloway assumed that she had become confused by inhaling the smoke and assured her that everyone was safe. By this time the structure was too far gone for anyone to enter. Paramedics rushed Katrina, Holloway, and the boys to the hospital to treat them for smoke inhalation and burns. But later on firefighters discovered the body of a four-year-old boy—a cousin—who had suffocated in an upstairs closet; Holloway hadn't realized that the child had been sleeping over that night.

In the aftermath of this event, Katrina's family turned against Holloway, whom they blamed for not rescuing the boy. Her kin had never really liked him and the loss of his janitorial job had been further proof of his worthlessness. In their view their young relative's death in the fire was yet another reason to convince Katrina to get rid of Holloway, which she did. Holloway's daughter, Christine, was born soon after. Holloway's father was dead and his mother had moved to New York, so he moved in with his brother, the only member of his immediate family who lived in the area and was not behind bars—a welder who had once worked for the Budd Company and owned a house around the corner.

Six years later Holloway is still showing up at the day-labor agency six days a week at 6:00 a.m. He says he manages to get work only about two-thirds of the time and still makes just over the minimum wage. He makes valiant attempts to stay connected to Christine and comes by to visit almost daily—whenever he has enough left in his paycheck to buy her a treat or to go shopping for something she needs. Katrina initiates contact only when she fears that her daughter is getting out of hand. Recently, she called and told Holloway that the six-year-old had been hanging around some older girls and had run off with them on several occasions, leaving her to search the streets for hours. Alarmed, Holloway gave Christine a stern warning. "So I told her, I said, 'the next time you run off, I'm gonna beat you!'" But Christine had just looked defiantly up at him, put her hands on her hips, and declared, "No, you ain't!"

At first he was taken aback by her insolence, but he has come to view such incidents like these philosophically. "It seems like when you don't have custody of your kids and stuff like that, not being there all the time, they don't really give you that respect." Right now Holloway can't take the child overnight or on weekends because his wages consign him to living with his brother, who was once accused of raping his girlfriend's daughter. Never mind that the charge was later dropped; Katrina won't hear of Christine even entering the brother's home, much less staying there all night. Resigned, Holloway concludes, "I don't blame Christine for her behavior, man. It's just that her mother don't let me be around her enough. If only I could be around her more, like when I get a better paycheck and get a little place of my own, so she could stay over, you know, she wouldn't act that way."

Recently, when Katrina started seeing another man, she told Holloway he couldn't come by the house to visit anymore. What worries Holloway is that Katrina's new boyfriend "seems like he's trying to take my daughter from me." Lately, the only time Holloway sees his daughter is through a chance encounter. In fact, trying to orchestrate such encounters has become a near fixation. "I'm always snooping around the corner. Katrina say I be spying on them. But I don't be spying on them. I am just trying to see my daughter."

Just the other day, when Holloway had been lurking around in hopes of encountering Christine, he happened to witness the new man buying ice cream for his daughter. The rapport between the two was apparent. Holloway tears up when relating this memory: "I wanted to pull him to the side and say, 'Look man, she's my daughter. You don't really gotta buy her ice cream. You know, I *do* work sometimes. And this guy she's with, he got kids somewhere else. He lost his family, so he gotta take mine.'" He then shrugs and says, "Well, he has the power to do that because he has a good job. He's like a big shot." Though Holloway, like many other men, rejects the notion that finances are paramount in the fatherhood realm, the power that money affords still figures prominently in his story.

Despite considerable adversity, Holloway is still determined to stay in Christine's life. "My brother, he talking about don't go see my daughter or nothing, leave them alone. But see, I got a problem with that. I don't want to abandon her." "I ain't much," Holloway concludes, "but at least my daughter knows that she has a father."

### THE FRAGILE FATHER

Ritchie and Holloway are both well into their thirties. Neither of them finished high school, which is a large part of why they work manual-labor jobs paying at or just above the legal minimum, have no health insurance or paid vacation, and must rely on others to make ends meet. Ritchie's brother and his girlfriend, Mary, have both taken their turns helping him out with his rent, while Holloway's brother has the good welding job that puts a roof over both their heads. Looking at their situations, we might be tempted to agree with Holloway that these men "ain't much." But there is one attribute that both possess, one that is actually fairly rare in these surroundings, even among men in somewhat better circumstances: they have been able to enjoy uninterrupted relationships with their children, consistently seeing them several times each week.

Neither Ritchie nor Holloway conform to the image of the "deadbeat dad"—a man simply too lazy to try. Indeed, a remarkable degree of commitment and perseverance has been required for each of them to stay involved. Until recently Ritchie had to fight tooth and nail to block Kate's attempts to deny him visitation. He is still thousands of dollars behind on his child support, and paying back the debt plus keeping up with his ongoing support obligation takes up a considerable portion of his income. Holloway has to deal with Katrina's contempt as well as her new boyfriend's money—not to mention Christine's belligerence and disrespect. Perhaps the most profound obstacle, however, is that over time a father's performance scorecard often becomes so littered with disappointment. What kind of father is an addict who sleeps on a slide and has no gift for his son at Christmas? What kind of a dad has such a rotten job that he can't even afford to treat his daughter to ice cream? Sometimes the failures are due to the hard living that many fail to shake when their children are born—take Ritchie for example. At other times, just plain hard luck is the cause—this is Holloway's problem. To persevere in the face of these obstacles, poor inner-city dads who try to stay involved with their children after their relationships with the mother have crumbled must have considerable grit. While men expressed the key quality required in different ways ("responsibility," "prioritizing the kids," "being there," "sacrifice"), this quality is perhaps best expressed by the word "commitment." When the child's mother tries to restrict access, when they don't have ready cash for even an ice cream cone, when their own sense of shame wrought by the lack of a decent paycheck, an addiction, or a felony conviction is telling them that their kids might be better off without them, are they willing to do what they have to do to "make the kids number one," as one father said, or are they going to put fatherhood on hold until some unspecified time when things might get easier?

As partnerships fall by the wayside and children grow older, a father's path often gets steeper and more unpredictable. Despite widespread agreement that paternal commitment ought to be unshakable— a good dad ought to "be there"—our fathers' relationships with their children were remarkably varied (see table 6 in the appendix). At one extreme are children who see their father face-to-face several times a month. Some of these children live with both parents outside of a marital bond, but others have fathers who manage to build in visits as a regular part of their weekly or biweekly routine, like Ritchie and Holloway—a pattern we call "intensive involvement." Then there are children whose fathers have in-person contact at least once a month, but the contact is not part of a regular routine; we describe this as "moderate involvement." Children whose fathers have had some contact within the past six months, but on a more sporadic and haphazard basis and not always in person, fall in the "somewhat involved" category. Finally, there are children whose fathers are "not involved" —there has been no contact during the past six months.[5]

Among the men we spoke with, the black fathers are somewhat more involved with their children than white fathers are, especially when their children are younger. For those with children under two, all black fathers have been at least somewhat involved with that child in the past six months, and nine in ten report intensive involvement—routine in-person contact with their children several times a month. Intensive involvement characterizes only two-thirds of black fathers with children between two and five, however; just half of children between six and ten; and only a third of all children older than ten. In short, though men's rhetoric might indicate otherwise, a father's engagement with his children fades rather markedly over time.[6]

The white fathers we spoke with have had less contact with their children no matter what the children's age. Though nine in ten of white fathers with children under two said they were at least somewhat involved with their child in the past six months, only slightly more than half were intensively involved with their children at this age. These figures don't differ appreciably for white men with two- to five-year-olds, or among those with kids ages six to ten, where just over 40 percent of dads are still intensively involved. But only a quarter of those white fathers with children over ten have in-person contact several times each month.

These figures are roughly consistent with national data, which show very high levels of involvement for young children with a large falloff over time.[7] Survey data also show greater involvement for blacks than whites, when all else is equal.[8] Readers should keep in mind that we are relying on fathers' reports here, which might paint a somewhat more positive picture than what mothers might say.[9] But mothers' estimates of father involvement should not be taken as gospel; some ex-partners would almost certainly underestimate their children's father's involvement because it occurs surreptitiously or through an intermediary. Nonetheless, even based on fathers' own claims, this portrait is far from rosy from a child's point of view. How can we reconcile the gulf between men's ideals with regard to paternal involvement—where commitment triumphs over all—and the reality that they often spend long periods absent from a given child's life?

To explore this conundrum, we asked fathers to identify the barriers that kept them from being as involved as they would like to be with each of their children (see appendix table 7). Most often, fathers' own limitations and behaviors are the obstacle: the problems that occur when the transition to parenthood fails to turn a young man's troubled trajectory around.[10] While Ritchie is clearly an exception to this rule, men struggling with drug addictions or those for whom prison has become a revolving door often deliberately distance themselves from their offspring, as they are too ashamed to let their children see them in such humiliating circumstances. The "rippin' and runnin'" that typically lead to these problems begin in men's midteens but can extend into their late twenties or early thirties until they are willing and able to "settle down." By then, they've lost precious time with their progeny. The critical point here is that early father-child bonding may be interrupted by a drug or alcohol problem or a prison spell, and this has long-term consequences for fathers who wish to remain connected or reestablish a connection with their children later on.[11]

Barriers due purely to finances usually accrue only to those who are at the very bottom—those working for minimum wage, like Holloway, or at low-end entrepreneurial trades (take Jabir Rose, the neighborhood handyman or David Williams, the guy selling newspapers at the foot of the Ben Franklin Bridge). A father who doesn't even have the wherewithal to treat his child to ice cream or purchase a pair of sneakers will often feel that he has no business coming around. Holloway comes around a little less often than he might for that reason, though it is worth noting that having no "funds" to offer didn't deter Ritchie at all: at one point, Ritchie was so poor that his own son felt compelled to offer him the change from his pocket—which he says was the all-time low in his life.

While it is men's own problems that interfere most often, maintaining contact with one's child is not simply up to the father alone; mothers are capable of throwing up significant barriers too. Of course, his problems and her efforts to keep him away—often called gatekeeping—are often related, but virtually any misbehavior on the father's part can be used by a child's mother as justification for a forced separation. According to Ritchie, Kate has used any number of excuses to try and keep him from his son—his drug use, missed child-support payments, his failure to relent in an argument—while Katrina has had only one excuse to draw on: Holloway's meager financial contributions. It must be said here that gatekeeping is sometimes clearly justified; an ex-partner who is frequently violent or high can pose unacceptable risks for a woman who is trying to shield her child from harm. But such dangers are by no means ubiquitous, and many women who engage in gatekeeping don't, in fact, truly face these risks.

Gatekeeping is often sparked by the denominator problem—the mismatch between what a man feels he ought to provide financially—a sense of obligation that has been sharply curtailed by the "doing the best I can...with what is left over" ethos we write of in earlier chapters—and the true cost of raising a child. Mothers like Katrina can easily grow tired of having to figure out how to cover the bills, and in the midst of her frustration it can be tempting to conclude that a father like Holloway is not worth bothering with. Another common precursor to gatekeeping is when the child's mother forges a relationship with a new partner, as Katrina did.[12] Because of the rampant lack of trust between women and men in low-income communities, particularly in the sexual domain, a new paramour can often become jealous when an old lover keeps stopping by.[13] To keep the peace and maintain the new union, mothers may feel that the best course is to try to simulate the nuclear family, isolating old partners while giving the new man the title of daddy, as Mary has done with Ritchie and what Katrina seems to want to do as well. Often, the daddy title is given as a reward for his voluntary contributions to her child, which makes the biological father's meager contributions appear even more paltry by comparison.[14] When a new man comes on the scene and plays daddy, dads' visits can provoke rivalry over the child as well. Andre Green's brother was shot dead by the father of his girlfriend's baby after the man witnessed Andre's brother playing daddy to his child. Whatever the cause, when contact almost inevitably leads to conflict, it is even easier for a woman already frustrated by a father's low monetary value to convince herself that she and the child would be better off without the nuisance of his visits.[15]

Conversely, sometimes a birthday card or a once-in-a-blue-moon visit are the sum total of men's attempts to stay connected, if that, and a lack of involvement seems largely due to an absence of desire. Few men admitted to lack of desire outright; thus our assessment of how frequently lack of interest is a barrier is based on our own judgment drawn from men's larger narratives and behaviors. From that information we determine a lack of interest to be a significant barrier for 7 percent of the father-child relationships we observed. This is no doubt an underestimate, as men who have lost, or never had, a desire to enact the father role are presumably less likely to engage in a study like ours or are more likely to lie to save face.

We also took stock of those factors that enabled ongoing involvement by fathers. One of the most important is the attitude of the child's mother and the degree to which she regards her child's father as dispensable or replaceable. A man with the good fortune to have a cooperative ex-partner who values the role he can play in his child's life has an enormous advantage; not only does this ease involvement, it also improves the child's attitude toward the father and enhances men's self-regard.

At the moment Ritchie enjoys this advantage; Kate can no longer judge him for his failings because she has developed a "little problem" of her own—in early September Ritchie Jr. called his father, upset that Kate hadn't registered him for school. When Ritchie stopped by to see what was going on, Kate appeared strung out; "it looked like she was high on crack," he says. Alarmed, he announced he was taking the boy until she got herself together. She offered no objection, and he kept Ritchie Jr. for two weeks. This incident must have convinced her of Ritchie's competence, because she has been letting the boy stay over more and more.

Forty-year-old Giovanni, a white father who has been back and forth to prison for much of his adult life, has a shaky relationship with his sixteen-year-old daughter, Nicole, whom he sees only every other month or so. He isn't even sure he deserves the title of father, so he tells her, "Don't call me your dad right now. Talk to me as you would talk somebody on the street corner." But even this tenuous relationship would not have been possible, he says, without Nicole's mother, who "never bad-mouthed me to my daughter" and allowed her to stay with him on the weekends during a three-year period several years earlier, when he was on the outside and working steadily as a bartender. In contrast, every time twenty-nine-year-old Montay, a black father of a nine-year-old boy who lives with his mother and two younger half siblings in Florida, calls his son on the phone—the boy's mother slams the receiver down on the counter and says, "Hey, it's your deadbeat dad who ain't shit—he's on the phone."

When a breakup causes hard feelings and animosity, the availability of an intermediary can prove invaluable. Debbie is angry that her children's father, forty-five-year-old Bruce, the white father of twins, has taken up with new flame Peggy so quickly after breaking up with her and that his cash contributions to the family are suddenly way down. His longtime boss just retired and closed the construction business, so for now Bruce is subsisting on $205 a month in General Assistance plus proceeds from selling blood. In retaliation Debbie only grudgingly allows him an occasional visit and only when the twins are at her brother's house while she attends evening classes for a nursing degree; that way, she doesn't have to see him. "But," Bruce gleefully reveals, suddenly animated, "I see them more than she thinks I see them. Between me and you and that tape recorder, I see them maybe twice a week at her brother's house—me and her brother is all right. But if she would ever catch me over there, there would really be a big argument over that."

More commonly, a father's own mother or sister plays this intermediary role. Twenty-one-year-old Kervan, the black father of a one-year-old child, is prohibited from coming by his baby's mother's house by a restraining order.[16] Yet the child's mother is a friend of his own mother—they even go to the same church—and she babysits their child, meaning that Kervan can see his baby at his mother's house without dealing with his baby's mother at all.

Go-betweens mute the animosity and tension that can accompany visitation. In addition, intermediaries sometimes advocate for the father's involvement and work to diminish the mother's resistance. But as children grow older, cooperative mothers or intermediaries become less important, as fathers can forge a relationship with their child directly, without any third party. Marty Holmes's oldest child, Nikka, now lives on her own, which means this forty-year-old African American doesn't have to face his ex-girlfriend Clarissa to maintain contact. Donald, a thirty-seven-year-old African American father of a fourteen-year-old child, has circumvented the efforts of his daughter's mother to keep him out of his child's life by surreptitiously arranging to meet her after school for a quick outing to McDonald's before sending her home on the bus. The daughter's willingness to go along with this scheme is probably due to the connection Donald was able to build with her earlier, when she was young and he was enjoying a period of sobriety before falling off the wagon again, underlining once again the importance of periods of paternal bonding during the child's earlier years.

Fathers are also offered a greater opportunity to be involved when mothers' alcohol or drug use or other behaviors threaten their ability to perform their roles as primary caregivers adequately, as Ritchie's story shows. A more dramatic example comes from Andre Green, from chapter 2, who convinces his own mother to seek custody when his ex-girlfriend is charged with neglect. Similarly, Lacey Jones gains custody of his nine-year-old when her mother is judged mentally incompetent. Indeed, Will Donnelly, from chapter 5, may be well on his way to taking on the primary caregiver role for his four children due to Lori's heroin addiction. A particularly dramatic story comes from Kevin, the thirty-five-year-old black father of a seven-year-old boy and three young daughters, who took custody of his son when the boy's mother fell into drugs so heavily that she became a prostitute. When we inquire further, he says, "I'd rather not talk about her because I'd rather shoot her in the fucking head." It is usually only in these extreme circumstances such as these that a mother's inability or unwillingness to parent gives fathers an opportunity to take a leading role, but only if he is in a position to take on the responsibility. If he is not able—and this is often the case—then other parties step in, usually the mother's kin, but occasionally the father's. In cases where no family member is in a position to help, the state takes custody and the father may have trouble maintaining any relationship at all.

It should be apparent by now that despite men's best efforts to reject the traditional package deal and establish a direct relationship with their children, their ability to father is still powerfully influenced by their relationships with their children's mothers. When a couple has a child and then splits up, each party's story continues to unfold. Men may get and lose jobs, find new partners, have more children, be evicted from their homes, move to another city, get sick, go to prison for a spell, and then return. Each of these changes has consequences, often pro-found ones, for their ability to perform the father role. Meanwhile, mothers experience transitions as well, some of which may influence their ability or willingness to facilitate fathers' access to a child. Kate's change of heart toward Ritchie, prompted by both his transformation and her "little problems" is an example. Then there are the children, whose openness and trust may also vary over time—contrast Ritchie's son to Holloway's daughter. To understand shifting levels of father involvement then, it is not enough simply to examine fathers' charac-teristics or behaviors. One must also plot the evolution of the mothers' and children's situations and how these correspond to where the fathers are. It is the *alignment* between men's, women's, and children's lives at a given point in time that is the crucial factor.

## RISING ABOVE

That there are significant obstacles to nonresident father involvement, particularly among inner-city men without much in the way of education or earnings, should come as a surprise to no one. Yet we came across as many fathers who have prevailed despite these difficulties as have been crushed by them; this is why the stories of Ritchie Weber and Holloway Middleton are so important. How can we understand why some of these father-child relationships remain relatively strong while others atrophy or experience periods of disruption, sometimes for years? One clear prerequisite for achieving the standards men articulate for good fatherhood is the single-minded commitment displayed by Ritchie and Holloway. Like any distribution across a population, our men's commitment to the father role varies; as we show in the next chapter it may even vary from child to child as fathers' maturity and conditions change.

Beyond commitment, though, persistence in the face of mounting barriers to father involvement requires significant emotional muscle. Men must have reserves of self-esteem, optimism, and sheer tenacity to rise above the formidable challenges they face in staying connected to their children. Given their often-difficult pasts and challenging present circumstances though, many are as deficient in these reserves of inner strength—what we call psychological resources—as they are in the economic and biographical resources we spoke of in earlier chapters. When one considers that men's families of origin are more often sources of continuing trauma than emotional sustenance, that their own histories are so frequently punctuated with a series of failures—at school, at the workplace, in relationships, in repeated attempts to get clean or stay sober—and that they constantly are made to feel superfluous in a society that rewards attributes that are the opposite of theirs, it is no surprise that the strength to "rise above," both as partners and as parents, is sometimes in short supply.

An often neglected factor in understanding father-child relationships over time is how fathers' psychological resources may be either shored up or diminished by the attitudes and responses of their children, particularly as the kids get older. Ritchie Weber provides the clearest positive example of this dynamic. It was the loving and respectful response of his son, who was always glad to see him even when he was homeless, penniless, and filthy, that gave him the inner strength to turn his life around, and why Ritchie refers to his son as his "savior." This unconditional acceptance is not offered by Holloway's daughter, Christine, who is tendering defiance and disrespect.[17] Christine's attitude is not likely to improve if her mother's gatekeeping continues to reduce him to a shadow lurking around the corner hoping for a chance encounter, or if her mother's new boyfriend—the big shot with the better job—continues to compete for the father role. Here we do not mean to blame the children, as many may have good reason for losing faith in their fathers. It is reasonable for children to ask how long their father will be able to sustain his resolve to stay involved.

Maurice, a thirty-eight-year-old African American father, offers a story about his own childhood that serves as a poignant illustration of the power of children to rob or imbue fathers of the emotional strength to stay involved. When Maurice was sixteen, he stopped going to school and began to hang around with the wrong crowd. Maurice's mother asked his father to come over and set him straight, but Maurice was burning with resentment over his father's spotty presence during his younger years. "I'll never forget this. I told him, I said, 'I don't need you.' He looked at me and said, 'You don't need me?' and I said, 'No, I don't need you.' I was just a sixteen-year-old kid, and he looked at my thirteen-year-old brother, and he asked my brother, 'What about you, do you need me?' My brother said no because he listened to what I was saying. My father left that day, it was in the summer—like July or August, and that was the last time I ever saw my father."

Maurice has three children—a sixteen-year-old son and two daughters, ages fourteen and ten—by one woman. He was out of their lives for many years, first because of a drug addiction and then because of a move to central Pennsylvania, a relocation aimed at facilitating his recovery. He's been back in Philadelphia and "in the picture" with his kids for two years and sees them twice during the week and again on weekends. He is determined to remain involved, but his middle child is beginning to show the same kind of attitude that drove away Maurice's own father. What happened to him is not going to happen to his kids, he says. "They are growing up to be real good kids, and I plan on being there every step of the way, no matter what comes down the pike. My youngest daughter, we got this thing where we are going around to find the perfect water ice. I will pick her up and be like 'We be back, we are going to get our water ice.' And we go out and get our water ice and we talk and everything." His relationship with his son is even more gratifying: "a lot of days he spends the whole day with me. He wants to be close to his dad, and I like him close to me. He is in the choir at church, a devoted Christian. I back him with whatever he does."

It would be hard to overstate the sense of renewed worth Maurice's relationship with these children has given him. In fact, his unexpected success in resuming his fatherhood role, particularly his ability to deter his teenage son from "going the wrong way," has sparked a desire in Maurice to work with troubled kids. He just resigned from his job as a cook at the Hyatt Hotel and will train for a job as a counselor at an Outward Bound program. "I am looking forward to an exciting job, new adventure, new career. And maybe I can make a difference in some kids' lives."

But Maurice's middle child refuses to come on outings or stay over at his apartment, claiming it is boring and that she would rather be with her friends. Her attitude has sharply curtailed the role he can play—he now can function only as a watchdog. The last time she refused to come over with her siblings, he told her, "OK, you be with your friends and remember I don't want you hanging on the corner in front of no stores, and I don't want to see you out there like that." Still, Maurice refuses to be completely deterred; "I am keeping a close eye on her," he insists.

Our aim here has been to offer insight into some well-known facts: fathers like ours express high hopes at the time that their children are born—nearly all say they plan to stay involved in their children's lives. And in the first year or so, most live out this pledge; but this is easy to do because most are in a romantic relationship with the mother at first—about 80 percent—and half are still with her a year later, when the baby turns one.[18] As parents break up, however, father involvement drops off quite dramatically. In short, when unmarried couples' rough imitation of the old-fashioned package deal is in play, where the mother-father relationship is intact, father involvement is very high— what could be easier? But when men try to enact the new package deal we spoke of in chapter 3, where it's all about the baby and the mother is peripheral, good intentions are often derailed by complex realities.

We devoted the first part of this chapter to detailing common barriers to father involvement, as well as the factors that facilitate dads' ability to stay involved. These factors are dynamic and multifaceted; at any given time it is the alignment between the father's and the mother's circumstances and attitudes, as well as the child's, that often makes or breaks his ability to be involved. But while understanding these barriers and facilitators may be necessary, it is not sufficient. Some, like Ritchie and Holloway, manage to rise above in the face of tremendous difficulties, while others' good intentions are easily thwarted. We've argued here for the importance of fathers' commitment and their psychological resources—by the latter we mean the emotional mettle to carry on when staying involved becomes difficult and even painful. We've shown that most fathers voice considerable commitment, though this can vary across children and over time, but not all have the emotional strength to persist when things get tough, particularly when two other critical resources, economic and biographical, are also lacking.

Men vary in their assessments of how good of a father they are to any given child. Yet the next chapter shows that over time, these assessments become less important to them than whether they are satisfying their fathering desire. When a man can't perform as well as he'd like to, he can still say he's doing his best if he's engaged in fathering at least one child or set of children. In fact, we show that if he chooses to selectively parent, which having children by multiple partners allows, he can marshal all his meager resources in service of performing the father role well with one child—as Amin Jenkins, the four-time-father-failure David Williams, Marty Holmes, Lacey Jones, and Ray Picardi, whom we meet in the next chapter, have done.

# SEVEN

# Try, Try Again

Ray Picardi is a thirty-six-year-old clean-shaven Irish American of average weight and height. He lives in Fishtown, next door to his mother in a small row home filled with carefully preserved furnishings he inherited from his grandmother. The neighborhood has been solidly white and working class since the American Revolution, but its residents' fortunes have changed quite dramatically over time.

Ray is the son of a machinist who pulled down quite a decent family wage when Ray was a boy. But by the time Ray came of age, only a trickle of young Fishtown males could follow their fathers into semi-skilled labor on the factory floor. These days virtually the only employers willing to hire men like Ray are filling slots in low-skilled, low-paying occupations. A decade prior to our conversation—at about the time his son Johnny was conceived—Ray was camped out in an abandoned Kensington row home that his uncle owned, handy because it was right next to the vacant lot where the construction company that employed him parked its trucks. It wasn't as bad as it sounds—he had made the place habitable by stocking each room with a kerosene heater and by hooking up the electricity and water illegally, valuable know-how in a neighborhood where 25 percent of the real estate lies abandoned, a haven for squatters.[1]

Ray had met Jill on New Year's Eve when she was tending bar at Dempsey's and he was there celebrating with friends. Jill had asked to go back to his place that night, but because his quarters weren't quite suitable for company, "I came over to her apartment, and I just stayed over." When we ask Ray to reflect on how an overnight encounter led so quickly to the conception and birth of a child, he shrugs. "You know, shit happens."

Johnny is now nine, and Ray pays his share of the boy's keep out of the ninety-six dollars a day he makes as an under-the-table roofer when the weather is OK for outdoor work. Jill is still working at the bar, keeping the neighborhood drunks at bay, but she also spends much of her free time there, which poses a problem. Seven years sober, Ray is "done with the bar scene" and while the two still "talk," Ray says they aren't really together. In fact, Jill maintains her own apartment and Johnny lives mostly with Ray. Jill, whose bar-scene lifestyle leaves little time for parenting, has more or less surrendered Johnny to his care, though since the two never married, Jill holds legal custody.

Like a reenactment of the classic 1979 movie *Kramer vs. Kramer*, Johnny has become Ray's world since Jill has begun to fade from the scene, and being a father consumes nearly all his free time. Each morning he wakes the boy at 5:00 a.m., gets him dressed, and deposits him next door to eat breakfast with his grandmother while Ray catches a 6:00 a.m. ride to the construction site. After school Johnny knows to go straight to Grandma's, where he plays with his cousins—Ray's sister and her two children live with his mother—until Ray comes home from work. Father and son nearly always eat in, and after washing the dishes Ray takes the radio outside to sit on the stoop and unwind while he supervises his son's play. Then it's homework, a bath, and early bedtime.

But Ray is still not quite the father that Ritchie Weber and Holloway Middleton have proven to be. He has an older child he hasn't seen for years. We ask Ray to recall his time at Kensington's Mastbaum High, where he met that child's mother, Regina Walker, in their junior year.

Ray says it was not exactly love that brought them together. He describes her as "one of the school hos" and says he was just one of the boys who "got laid in the abandoned building across the street from the school," thanks to Regina. When this extracurricular activity resulted in the birth of their son, David, Ray says he decided to "do the right thing": drop out of school, find a job, and move in with Regina and her family. "I was living with her and her mother and her brothers and two dogs," he recalls, "all in a small row house in Fishtown."

Ray found a job with his uncle's roofing business and proved to be a quick study; however, he not only deftly aced the skills of the roofing trade but also quickly mastered the lifestyle. "We'd go to work, go bang a roof out, coat it, and go home—go home and get drunk!" It was this last part of the daily ritual that eventually got him in trouble. By the time David turned four, "Regina and I were battling all the time because I would be drinking. I was still roofing and still staying with her, but one night I drank a whole bottle of blackberry brandy, and I got pretty rowdy and radical with her. Her brother threw me out."

After the blackberry brandy mayhem brought an end to the relationship with Regina, Ray came by occasionally to see his son, but the visits always managed to end in discord. He recalls one visit in particular: "I drove by her house and David—who was five at the time—was outside, and I stopped to talk to him. Regina got pretty indignant and upset about one thing or another. I still remember leaving because driving away brought tears to my eyes." Why does this day stand out in his memory? Ray says simply, "That is the last day I seen him."

Now David is just about to turn eighteen. To excuse the fact that he hasn't seen his son for more than a decade, Ray says, "Regina moved out of the area and until this day I still don't know where they moved to. I try to think what David looks like now. Somebody seen him and said he is about six foot two and that he weighs about three hundred pounds. They say he is a big bad boy." It is fairly clear from our conversation, however, that Ray could have found David if he had tried—after all, Regina's family still lives in the area, and the "somebody" who tells Ray he's seen the boy is a local. Does Ray simply lack the desire? Does he find the prospect of confronting Regina's strident tongue just too overwhelming? Or is his own past behavior—the drinking and mayhem that led to the breakup—simply too humiliating to recall? In circumstances like these, the path of perseverance can seem long.

Let's turn to another serial dad, Marty Holmes, the black father of three. He sits at the table in the always-chaotic McDonald's on Lehigh Avenue as he recounts his past in a calm and deliberate way, his contemplative manner out of sync with the scratchy, insistent pop music in the air and the nearby commotion of scraping chairs and overexcited children. When we ask about his own family background, his tone hardens. "I came from a dysfunctional family," he says tersely. "My mom used drugs. My dad wasn't around—he died of cirrhosis of the liver when I was fifteen." Marty then quickly adds, "But it really didn't have no effect on me because he was not around in my life. So I really didn't know him.... But I always wanted a father figure."

Marty seems fixated on resurrecting his role as a father figure to Rahmere, his two-year-old son by Michelle—a role he had involuntarily abdicated by landing in prison just before the boy was born. Marty is in a halfway house at present, serving out the remainder of a sentence for yet another parole violation. As part of the program, he spends part of each day searching for work, and he plans to use his first paychecks to secure an apartment where he, Rahmere, Michelle, and her two older boys can live together; "then I can see my son every day."

To explain what went wrong with his two older kids, Marty takes us back to his own childhood and tells us that his mother was only fifteen when she had him. Due to her age the two stayed with his grandmother in Tasker Homes, the predominately black housing project marooned in the middle of white Grays Ferry. Though Marty's parents parted when he was an infant, his mother found a steady boyfriend a few years later, and Marty looked up to the man as a role model until he succumbed to drugs and Marty "lost all respect for him."

Despite struggles at home, Marty enjoyed school and graduated on time from Bok Vocational High, where he had taken up welding. He found his first job through the school counselor, a minimum-wage position in maintenance at the Philadelphia airport. But Marty soon realized that the slow money from the legal labor market wouldn't be enough to get him what he really desired: the wardrobe that many other young men in the neighborhood were displaying. "Everybody in my neighborhood was dressed nice, and I wanted to be dressed nice too. I knew there was two ways of getting it: either you work for it or you stole for it. I did both; I worked and I stole."

While Marty was working both "jobs," he met Clarissa. "My best friend was dealing with a young lady, and I went with them one evening. We went to her house, and she had a sister—a nice looking, dark-skinned girl. I liked her and started talking to her, and we hit it off. As time went on she eventually got pregnant." But when he and a friend were caught in the act of committing a burglary, Marty was sentenced to four and a half years in jail. His daughter Nikka was born while he was locked up, but he was able to spend a little bit of time with her and her mother after his release when she was four years old. By the time she turned six, just after Marty and Clarissa conceived their second child, Marty was charged with violating his parole—he couldn't keep his urine clean—and was locked up again. After that, repeat parole violations made prison a revolving door. "I have an issue with authority," he explains.

Marty was incarcerated again when Clarissa gave birth to Sterling, and it is the history of his relationship with this son that shames him the most. By the time the boy was in grade school, Marty was so deep into drugs that he had taken to living on the street and had broken off all contact with his children. One day, by chance, "my son seen me out there like that. That was a hurting thing. He said, 'Dad, what you see in that stuff? Why would you mess with that stuff, Dad? I know that you better than that.' I didn't want my son to see me like that because I seen my mom use drugs. She used to shoot drugs intravenously."

When we meet Marty he is forty and already a grandfather—Nikka, who now lives on her own, has recently had a baby, but he hasn't seen the child yet. Since his release Marty has been attempting to mend his relationship with his daughter—his status as the grandfather has given him the courage to try and claim a role in her life—but she has made it clear that he has a lot of history to overcome. "In the beginning we were close, but after me keep getting myself in trouble going back and forth to prison, I guess she kind of gave up on me. I was never around, and I guess it hurted her. We just recently had a conversation on the phone, and I had to explain to her that I loved her dearly, and we had a little rapport. She cried and she explained why she feel that she didn't have no dad."

"It hurted me to hear that, but it was the truth. I don't blame her in a way because I wasn't there," Marty continues. "I have been trying to incorporate myself into her life again and in her daughter's life. She is coming around now; she is coming to accept me more. But I don't think she is putting her all in it, because she maybe feels as though she don't know if I am going to disappear again." Marty has also just gotten in touch with Nikka's eleven-year-old brother, Sterling, and last weekend the two saw each other face-to-face and spent "a little quality time." But overall his efforts with Sterling have been tentative. Marty says this is because he is determined not to make any more promises that he can't keep. And the boy seems uncertain too; just the other day on the phone, Sterling told his father, "losers make promises, winners make commitments."

Marty says he deeply regrets the years away from both of his older children, especially since he had made a vow never to abandon them like his own father did. "Growing up, I was wondering what it was like to always have your dad around. I always told myself that I would be around for them. But I found myself doing to them what happened to me by me being incarcerated and not there for other reasons in the years when they were growing up and their little personality starting to develop."

Marty's current privileges allow him to leave the halfway house campus from 8:00 a.m. to 4:00 p.m. on Saturdays and Sundays. He spends most of this time on outings with Michelle and their two-year-old—they can't go over to Michelle's mother's house because she doesn't want her daughter associating with Marty.[2] But Rahmere isn't responding the way Marty thinks he should. The boy is shy around him and treats him as if he is a visitor, not a dad. Michelle tells Marty to be patient, as he is still a virtual stranger to his son—yet he finds the situation deeply distressing. He blames Rahmere's behavior on the fact that "I am not there all the time, though I want to be, and it hurts me and it upsets me."

Marty's efforts with Rahmere may be admirable, but what about his relationship with Nikka, whom he's called only a couple of times, and then only recently, or with Sterling, who he has seen only once since the chance encounter on the street about four years ago? Our story is based on fathers, and not on their partners or children.[3] But one might wonder what children like Ray's son, David, and Marty's children think about the situations their fathers subject them to. While we cannot answer this question in full, Marty's phone call with Nikka hints at the devastation that father absence can cause in a child's life. When Marty first contacted Sterling by phone, the boy told him, "Dad, I don't want your money. I just want a little of your time." Yet shortly after offering this touching statement, he made it clear he wanted a commitment, and not a mere promise, from his dad. Two-year-old Rahmere's reluctance to treat Marty as more than a visitor, even after four months of spending weekends together, suggests hesitation as well. Is it safe to put one's trust in a father like Marty Holmes?

What men say about the absence of their own fathers, a story we've told in other chapters, offers additional clues to how fatherless children may feel. These accounts can be summed up quite simply—few discount the pain of their own father's absence and, in fact, often cite this as the source of their own father thirst. They often see unplanned pregnancy as an opportunity to take the first step toward repairing the past, vowing to become the father they wished their own had been. Marty is one of many who swore that he wouldn't be like his own absent dad and yet has still managed to replicate his behavior.

Ray and Marty are only two of many of the fathers we met who have failed with an older child but have then tried again. Amin Jenkins, from chapter 1, welcomed the news of his oldest son's conception, only to deny paternity once the child was born—a fateful act that led to years of separation. By the time the boy's mother had relented and let him see his son it was too late; by then the boy was too unruly to listen to his fatherly wisdom and seemed unwilling to bond. But we might wonder how hard Amin really tried, given the potent distraction of another son—Antoine, the baby boy he had just had with his coworker Antoinette. Could it be that beyond the barriers listed in the last chapter, a new baby—with a new woman—crowds out men's sense of obligation to the kids he already has? And even if such a man wants to perform the fatherhood role equally well with all of his children, would his limited resources allow it?

One consequence of the high rate of partner churning among disadvantaged urban men is that they are at high risk of what social scientists call "multiple partner fertility." In fact, for couples having children outside of marriage, children by multiple partners is now the statistical norm.[4] Yet almost no father in our study spread his time or financial resources equally across his kids unless they all lived in the same household.

Recall from prior chapters that men's father thirst is strong and that they ultimately seem to want the "whole fatherhood experience"—to live with a child, observe the developmental milestones firsthand, and have a strong hand in their upbringing—rather than the part-time fatherhood, or the attenuated father-child relationships, that often result from their initial efforts. It is this unfulfilled desire that puts them at risk of repeating the series of nondecisions that will bring yet another child into the world with a new partner. But once a father gets another try at "real" fatherhood, how much time, energy, and finances will he have to devote to that new role? How much will be left over for the kids he already has, when he's desperately trying to fulfill all the mandates of the new familylike relationship that has suddenly come into being? For a serial dad, is it better to be a great dad to one kid, particularly one he hasn't failed yet, rather than a so-so dad to all of his kids?

For David Williams, whom we met at the end of chapter 1, the choice is clear. He is a four-time failure as a father by the time he conceives his fifth child: he has lost contact completely with his two middle children, both sons, and is now making no effort to reconnect. He only occasionally sees his daughters, now in their late teens. But he is clearly over the moon about his youngest, Julian, the boy who comes out of Winnie's womb "spinning like a bullet."[5] The story is the same for Lacey Jones. In his youth he conceived two children just a few months apart by two different women who lived on his block: "It was back and forth. I'd mess with her for a minute. I'd go mess with the other one for a minute." He was barely involved in the lives of his son and daughter, now seventeen and eighteen, when they were growing up, though since leaving prison last year he has managed to make a fairly strong connection with both. But he devotes nearly all of his time, energy, and financial resources to his nine-year-old, who is his heart. Now that he is living with that child, he says she has given him the precious gift of "seeing at least one of my children grow up." "Now I'm trying to do the right things, like a law-abiding citizen."

In light of David's and Lacey's stories the reader might be asking whether one, two, or even four failures aren't enough; why are men willing to risk failure again and again, especially since unqualified success is so unlikely? But men at the bottom believe they have little to lose by playing the Russian roulette of unprotected sex once again, because even for those who will ultimately fail utterly at fatherhood and end up having no enduring connection to any biological child, the mere act of procreation ensures they will still come out ahead. Trevor, the son of a convicted bank robber and a heroin addict, is a seemingly hopeless addict himself by the age of twenty-four. This white cab driver hasn't seen his one-year-old daughter in three months. Yet he tells us that by fathering a child, "I have done something good for the first time ever." It is hard to imagine a life so devoid of good news that an unplanned pregnancy and the birth of a baby—a child one can't possibly support—is viewed as a blessing, but that is precisely Trevor's claim. Albert, a twenty-three-year-old black father of a seven-year-old child whom he finds himself visiting less and less often, sees an even greater benefit—he plans to live through his child, and in this way achieve a vicarious form of upward mobility: "My child is a better image of me, you know. What I accomplished I feel she could do twice as better. Fatherhood is like making a duplicate of yourself but just making it better."[6] Thirty-four-year-old Edwin, of black and Latino descent, has spent much of his adulthood in prison and forcibly separated from his children but now sees them occasionally. He says child-bearing offers immortality. "When I first found out I was going to be a father I felt very special. I was really happy that I had something I could leave behind when I leave this planet."[7]

At minimum, then, fathering a child is still proof that one can accomplish something of value; it still offers the opportunity to see one's potential expressed in another, less damaged individual. And even those who see their children rarely can still usually say they are better than the "deadbeat" who has simply walked away from his children and—most important—doesn't seem to care. Even among those who have had no contact with their kids for some time, the fact that they have not disengaged emotionally can allow them to salvage some measure of self-regard. Apple, a twenty-seven-year-old African American father of four who does janitorial work and cuts meat at the famed Pat's Steaks in South Philly, hasn't seen his three older children for almost four months, yet he still considers himself to be a good dad, "because I care, and I'm still willing to try."

Yet it is vital to note that most fathers who have grown disconnected from their children are seldom satisfied with the scrap ends of fatherhood. For most, the desire to father actively—and claim the "whole father experience"—is strong. Apple, in fact, went on to father a fourth child with a new partner when the mother of his older children suddenly married another man and then began to push Apple out of the kids' lives. Apple is not alone in his determination to engage in fatherhood in some way, even if he ends up fulfilling his goal through another child in a new relationship.

This is not to say that Apple—or hardly any man that we spoke with—*intended* to conceive a new child to replace the old; one does not need to be intentional to end up as a serial father. What requires intent is the feat of *not* producing a subsequent child in a new relationship; given the allure of children, men in Apple's straits often seem unable to muster the willpower to do what it takes to avoid another accidental conception. And once that conception results in a birth, a new set of dynamics is set in motion that may considerably weaken a father's commitment to prior children.

In 2009 sociologist Andrew Cherlin coined the term "marriage-go-round" to connote the predilection among Americans to marry, divorce, and remarry at such high rates.[8] Men at the bottom are less likely to get married, but they are far more likely than those in the middle class to have children across multiple partnerships.[9] These men are on a family-go-round, where good fatherhood is accomplished by moving from one child to another—by trying and trying again. As fathers fail in one romantic relationship, they usually move quickly to a new one.[10] Then they find that maintaining a strong connection with children from a previous partnership is remarkably hard. When the new liaison produces a pregnancy—often "unplanned"—there is an easier option at hand and an opportunity to snatch victory from the jaws of defeat.

Starting in 1979 a national random sample interviewed male youth ages fourteen to twenty-two and has followed them ever since. This study, the National Longitudinal Survey of Youth, gave social scientists the first reliable, representative data on the family formation behaviors of young unwed men. Economist Robert Lerman and his collaborators were the first to seize on the value of this study for exploring the lives of young unwed fathers. Lerman and Elaine Sorensen asked a particularly interesting question of these data that other scholars had not: for men in the prime family-building years who have ever had a nonmarital birth, what proportion are involved with *at least one* of their nonmarital children at any given time? This question was of interest to us because it represents the perspective our men take when assessing their success as fathers—they focus less on whether all their children have an engaged father and more on whether they are successfully accomplishing fatherhood in some manner with any child at a given time. In fact, it may be that the only way many can truly feel successful as fathers is to marshal nearly all their scarce resources in service of the relationship with their youngest child, especially if they are still in a relationship with the child's mother and must also perform the role of romantic partner and sustain a household together. While fathers do circle back to reestablish relationships with older children sometimes— take Marty Holmes as an example—they seldom redeploy their financial resources in service of the restored bond, though they may devote time.

Unlike studies using children's experiences as the denominator, which show rapidly declining rates of involvement as a child grows older (such as the figures we provided in chapter 6), a measure of what Lerman and Sorensen called "maximum involvement" revealed that for men who had ever had a nonmarital birth and were in their late twenties and early thirties (twenty-seven to thirty-four) at the time they were surveyed, fully two-thirds were seeing at least one of their nonmarital children at least weekly, while nearly three-quarters were visiting at least once a month, if not more. A substantial proportion—about half of the remaining quarter—were married and living with a child who had been born within the marriage.[11]

Still, these data offer only a snapshot of father involvement, which our narratives show is, in fact, highly dynamic. Longitudinal surveys should allow us to calculate what portion of time a man spends actively engaged in parenting each of his children. Yet we know of no analysis of this kind. Nor are the data that Lerman and Sorensen cite very current—their analysis ends in the early 1990s. We aren't aware of any study that updates their figures, but there is evidence that as unwed childbearing has become more common, unmarried fathers' rates of engagement have increased.[12] The information we do have gives weight to our observation that among unmarried, disadvantaged fathers living in inner-city communities, many spend a significant portion of their family-building years actively engaged in some form of fatherhood activity.

The way Lerman and Sorensen posed their question thus turns out to be vital, since it shows that disadvantaged men's desire to father can be satisfied, at least in part, through selective fathering, even though most children still spend much of their childhood without a father actively engaged in their lives. And it is the mismatch between these two points of view—the child's versus the father's—that reveals the answer to the central question that we pose in this chapter: when their good intentions aren't fully realized, how do fathers cope with failure, and how do so many still manage to conceive of themselves as good fathers nonetheless?

Recall that Ray's ongoing contact with Regina produced nothing but conflict—which proved too much for Ray to handle; he didn't have the psychological resources to cope with her anger. But while Ray almost casually abandoned any attempt to stay connected with his older child, his bond with his nine-year-old is strong. As we've said, echoes of Ray's story are repeated again and again in this book—with Amin Jenkins, David Williams, Lacey Jones, and Marty Holmes, to name just a few. All essentially shrug off their obligations to their older children while forging a close connection to a younger child.

This behavior is possible only because the mother is the presumed custodial parent of the child in all but the most extreme cases. Unless they utterly fail in the mother role—by becoming a drug addict, for example—women accumulate all the children they bear. The men can be more discriminating regarding which children they actively parent, but only because they have these children serially, across multiple partners. Each new partner offers a man a tantalizing opportunity for a do-over, a fresh start. The physical distance from children of past relationships is precisely what allows the "out of sight, out of mind" mentality necessary to optimistically seize the opportunity to father again, with a new partner. Why expose oneself to the trials and tribulations that Ritchie and Holloway have subjected themselves to when one can still manage to enjoy the thrill of fatherhood with a clean slate by focusing one's efforts on a new child?

We have little direct evidence that unfulfilled father thirst prompts a conscious desire for more children with a new partner. More likely, a mere continuation of past practices—relationships that move at lightning speed, where forgoing contraception is a signal of commitment—is the cause. When fathers can't satisfy their desire to be a fully engaged father to one child their motivation to *avoid* fathering another child with a new partner may be diminished. What we can show, however, is that fathers who enter into new partnerships and have more children are subsequently less likely to marshal their time and money in service of older children, a pattern also documented in analysis of longitudinal representative survey data.[13] As we have noted, for men with limited means, adequate role performance in one father-child relationship seems to virtually require placing all of one's eggs in a single basket.

It is also true that men need not have failed with one child to feel a strong pull for another. Even a relatively good relationship with a child might not fully satisfy a man's desire for "the whole fatherhood experience." It might be that he doesn't get to live with his child—for some men, even regular visitation isn't enough, and they want a 24–7 experience. It might be that they have a child of one gender but want a child of another—especially a boy. Given the conventional wisdom, one of this study's biggest surprises is how many low-income, inner-city men seem to find children immensely attractive, and how eagerly many embrace new opportunities to father—either socially, biologically, or both, even when they already have close ties to another child.

To illustrate this point, we turn to the story of Mark Brooks. We first ran across this well-muscled sandwich maker at the Three Sisters Grocery in the Fairmount section of the city. Mark treats every hoagie he makes for his customers—mostly kids from Vaux High—as a work of art. "This is my profession right now; this is an art to me," he says. "I am going to take pride in what I do." The convenience store inhabits the first floor of a three-story brick building on the corner of Master and Twenty-Fifth, in a rougher part of the neighborhood. There is only a hint of graffiti tarnishing its exterior—probably because of the fresh coat of lime-green paint that envelops the bricks on the exterior of the ground floor. Mark works there each day from 8:00 to 1:00. After that he heads over to Center City to work out and play basketball—he plays point guard and swing guard in a local sports league. Fridays he coaches for the Sonny Hill Community Involvement League, founded by former star player, TV commentator, and radio personality Sonny Hill, who in 2010 was named Pennsylvania's official "Mr. Basketball." Hill founded the legendary youth league in the sixties to curb gang warfare in the city's streets.

Mark has held much better jobs than this one in the past—in fact, just ten months ago he resigned from a position as assistant athletic director at Girard College, a residential school for disadvantaged children not far from Three Sisters. But the $125 a week he draws tax free from the deli, plus weekend painting jobs that bring in an additional $50 to $200, is enough for now.

Currently, three things in Mark's life bring him joy. Basketball is obviously one. Another is his daughter, Stefanie, age eleven, the child he sacrificed college and perhaps a basketball career for. The third is Dexter, a four-year-old boy who lives down in Chester, Pennsylvania, about thirty minutes away. He is the son of a female "friend," whom

Mark has been "talking to" for a while. "There is a little boy that I call my son," he explains. "Biologically he is not mine, but I take care of him financially, and I go see him on the weekends that I don't have my daughter."

There is no hint of street in this fast-talker with a pleasant smile and an open face, though he was raised in a pretty tough neighborhood— West Kensington. His mother was strict, he says, so much so that she beat Mark and his brother Luke, the two oldest of five boys, on a regular basis. After a particularly bad beating, he relates, "we said to ourselves 'we ain't never going to do this.' My brother said, 'Mark, promise me that you will never hit your kids out of anger.' And I said, 'You promise me that you will never hit your kids out of anger.' We was like twelve and thirteen at that time."

That brother, a high school athlete of some note, was shot and killed in a drug bust when Mark was twenty-one. He's lost a cousin to drug-related violence too. But at the beginning of high school, when he began seeing his friends—older boys—go wrong, Mark decided to go a different way. "I was so scared. I didn't think I was going to make it to twenty-five. My family," he says, referring to a close network of aunts, uncles, and cousins, "was excellent. It was just the surroundings, the neighborhood that I was in." So Mark kept his head down, stayed away from drugs, ruled the basketball court for Kensington High, lived to play summers in the Sonny Hill League, and graduated at nineteen. Then, after seeing him play in a summer league game, a recruiter from Wake Forest University called.

But Mark had gotten a girl pregnant and decided that he needed a job. Rather than head off to North Carolina, Mark donned a McDonald's uniform. He was living in his grandmother's home and his room in an attic space was relatively private, so Desiree moved in. Then he swapped the fast-food job for work cleaning office buildings and started saving so they could move to an apartment of their own. Desiree began collecting welfare and stayed home with the baby, and Mark slept mornings, played basketball in the afternoon, spent time with his family in the evenings and on weekends, and pushed a mop at night. They got the apartment and began collecting furniture, dishes, and pots and pans. Two years into this idyll, the apartment building burned to the ground.

Losing everything broke Mark's resolve. He quit the janitorial job and for the next twenty-two days, he dealt drugs. "Why I started selling was because of my daughter—that is an excuse, true, but my daughter didn't have nothing for that Christmas. I didn't buy my daughter nothing for that Christmas and it sent something inside and it just totally blew my mind. If a dad loves his kids, and if he can't get them stuff for that special occasion, it sends something through him. That is why we see a lot of murders and robberies during the time of Christmas and holidays because you got a lot of people out there acting on impulse, and it is very emotional."

On day twenty-three Mark was arrested and found himself facing a surprisingly stiff sentence, twelve to twenty-four months. He served just over a year. Desiree and Mark were still together, or at least he thought so, and he assumed that when he returned home he could pick up where he left off. He also began to fantasize about what it would be like to surprise her with an engagement ring and then plan a wedding. The future looked so bright. But he was home only for a few days when the rumors started; someone claimed to have seen her "creeping around" with another guy while he was away. Mark asked Desiree straight out if this was so, and she vehemently denied it. But then she discovered that she was pregnant—a little too pregnant. Mark says he tried to stick it out "for the sake of my daughter," but the sting of Desiree's betrayal was too biting, even though he believes his decision to sell drugs was ultimately to blame for the termination of their union. "If I wouldn't have got locked up I would have still been with her, since then it would have never happened. She would have never meet no one else, so I can't say that the blame was hers. The blame was me and myself. I put myself in that situation."

Mark has abided by the law in the seven years since he served his sentence. Upon release he took a job with his cousin, who painted apartments in the huge Jacobean-style Alden Park Manor complex in the Germantown section of the city. When a basketball injury prevented him from climbing a ladder, Mark was able to get a job in Alden Park's security department, monitoring entry to the campus. Then, he wanted to spread his wings, and through a fellow league player he was able to secure an assistant manager's job at a jazz club. When the club lost its lease, a referral from a fellow coach in the Sonny Hill League yielded an invitation to apply for the position of assistant recreation director at Girard, the boarding school for disadvantaged youth, where he worked his way up to $8.49 an hour. And recently someone else associated with the Sonny Hill League has raised the prospect of a management job with a new nursing home he is opening in about a year. Meanwhile, Mark and his cousin are trying to start their own party-starting business, which they have tentatively named Party Starters, Inc.

But Mark sees fatherhood as his primary job. He sees Stefanie every chance he gets—usually a couple of days each week and every other weekend. But he can manage the weeknight contact only if he catches her after school on her way home. Desiree is now married to the man she was seeing while Mark was in prison, and Mark doesn't like to stop by the house for this reason. He emphasizes that when he and his daughter do meet, they spend "quality time." As Mark shares his views with her about various things, he is careful to show Stefanie respect by treating her as his equal rather than talking down to her. They also do schoolwork; just last week the two headed to the public library, where they worked on a book report together. Mark enjoyed this outing immensely. But he still feels like he doesn't get enough time with his daughter.

Meanwhile, he delights in "taking care of" Dexter as well, buying him gifts, outfits, and other things he needs. We note that Mark refers to the boy repeatedly as "mine" or "my son," though he gives the boy's mother, Kelly, the far less intimate title of "friend." He is obviously enchanted with the boy and raves about Dexter at several points in our conversations: "He is a fun guy! He is very athletic, energetic. We just like doing things together. We get out there and be having a ball together!" he says, grinning. While visiting them down in Chester, he immerses himself in the role of surrogate father. And the four-year-old, who rarely sees his biological dad, has taken to Mark like bread to butter.

Mark is not the only one who was eager to seize the opportunity for second-chance fatherhood via another man's child. Close relationships with social children—as Mark's story illustrates—were quite common. And in a few exceptional cases—which prove the rule—men insisted on claiming children who weren't actually biologically theirs, though they might have initially thought they were. Not even a negative blood test could put to rest these stubborn claims. For example, Kanye, a twenty-eight-year-old African American who is unemployed and looking for work, had his first child when he was sixteen. He says that the girl he was with wanted to have a baby for her own reasons ("just to have something, but *I* wasn't thinking about having one!"). Crystal's birth stoked the impulse to father in Kanye, but he could see his daughter only every once in a while, as her mother lived in Bensalem, a suburb northeast of the city and a fair distance from Hunting Park, where she and Kanye had met.

Several years later, when Kanye needed a place to stay, he moved into a house with Diana, a woman he met through a mutual friend. Kanye and Diana were never "together," as Kanye recalls—"we just lived like roommates." But the two were still "intimate" when one, the other, or both were between relationships. When Diana became pregnant, she named Kanye as the father of the child because he had a steady job and was thus more stable than the drug dealer she was seeing on and off. But when baby Sequoia turned six months old, "Suddenly this dude pop up. He was like, 'Sequoia is mines,' and I am like, 'What? Get out of here!' And he was like, 'Diana, tell him.' And she was like, 'I don't know whose it is.' I was fighting for Sequoia. I was like, 'No! She is mines!' I couldn't believe it, and we went to court and had a blood test done and come to find out she was his. But I been there raising her.

That is why I feel she is mine, and I still see her today." Sequoia is now nine years old and still carries Kanye's last name.

Montay is a black twenty-nine-year-old father of a nine-year-old son with his former girlfriend Quetta. He has spent years trying to convince himself that Quetta's fourteen-year-old son is also his biologically, though he admits he has no recollection of the one-night stand that supposedly produced the boy. Montay first remembers meeting Quetta when he was sixteen and she was eighteen and her oldest son was an infant. Montay was attracted to the pair, and even brought by Pampers for the baby from time to time. After drifting apart Montay saw Quetta at a party two years later and next thing he knew, they had moved in together. This is when she made her claim that Montay was actually responsible for her child. "It was when we started living together, and her baby was two, that's when we started picking up all these back-in-the-back-in-the-back-in-the-days stuff that went on, like when we supposedly had sex that one time."

What is most striking about Montay's story is his eagerness to credit Quetta's claim. "My family kept saying, 'Don't listen to her,' but I was just so happy that I had a kid," he explains. Montay's family refused to believe the story, even after she gave birth to another son who was undisputedly Montay's. Quetta's mother didn't believe it either, but Quetta kept making the claim until she decided to relocate to Florida with the kids last year. Now, she's changed her story. "Now she all telling me that I only have one son and everything." How does Montay respond? "I ignore it 'cause whether he's mines or not, I'm the only father he knew growing up. And you know, Dante, he's still like my son in my heart, whether he is or not."

Each week Montay calls to speak with Dante and to Quetta's middle son, Roy, the child who is definitely his biologically, though Quetta and the kids don't always pick up the phone. "He miss me and everything, and he's telling me his mom talking bad about me. When I call to talk to him, I hear in the background, 'It ain't your damn dad. I don't know why you want to talk to him anyway.' Dante even said, 'Even though you're not my dad, I will always look at you as my daddy.' I'm like, 'You'll always be my son.'"

Once men like Mark, Kanye, and Montay have had a taste of fatherhood, they often fight against relinquishing any subsequent opportunity to play that role. Social fatherhood is the most common form of substitute fatherhood, but the cases of "overclaiming" children—insisting the primacy of tie which they may have thought was biological for a time—are illustrative as well. One reason why these men seem unable to turn their backs on the opportunity to father these additional children is that their relational responsibilities in these circumstances are diminished in much the same way as their financial ones are, as we discussed in chapter 4. That is, they don't *have to* be a father to their girlfriend's kids or to a child whose biological tie has been disproven. Thus, anything they do in this regard—no matter how little—is credited to their moral worth because there is no standard of obligation to measure it against.

But while men are often decidedly keen to be fathers to nonbiological children, they still hold out for an even better outcome—the whole fatherhood experience.[14] A year ago, shortly after they met, Dexter's mother became pregnant by Mark "in her tubes" and eventually miscarried.[15] Mark says the experience almost destroyed him—he couldn't function well on the job and was cited for a number of outbursts of anger. He begged for time off to recover, but his boss refused, so he simply resigned. "She lost the baby and it was really hard because I wanted my boy. Even if it was a girl [I wanted it bad]. Yeah, it was a lot of emotion. Even though I may adopt children," he says, referring to his role as Dexter's father figure, "I see myself having another child in the future. I see my little guy—he is mine." Kanye went on to have another child who is now five years old, and Montay has both a two-year-old son and an infant daughter with his current girlfriend.

Serial fatherhood, in which men bring children into the world across several partnerships, seems to be the almost inevitable conclusion to a story that begins with an accidental pregnancy between two economically disadvantaged young people who are usually merely "together" and not in a "real" relationship at the time. If that relationship fails, there is little to prevent them from repeating this cycle again. And no matter what their intentions, when things get tough with the first child, men find that the new partner and baby, relationships not yet tarnished by his mistakes, offer fewer challenges and more immediate rewards.

Yet even if all these subsequent chances fail, a man will still have gained something of immense value. Like Trevor, men can believe they've done something good just by procreating. Like Albert, they believe they can live vicariously through the "little version of me ... who can do twice as better." Like Edwin, a man who fathers a child has left at least some evidence that he was on the planet. And these benefits accrue to him even if he neither supports nor visits any of his children. Regardless of how challenging their personal circumstances or structural positions, many of our men insist that fatherhood is a no-lose proposition, and this is why. And it must be said that doing something—anything at all—is always better than zero; no one expects much of him anyway. Of course, the proposition is almost certainly no-win from the point of view of the child, the child's mother, and society.

But as Lerman and Sorensen show, most can justly claim they are succeeding at some form of fathering during the prime family building years. Serial, selective fathering offers an alternative narrative to that of father failure, but it is a reactive one. It has been shaped by a social structure that increasingly excludes these men, especially those with few skills, families of origin that have often done them harm, their own bad choices, the attitudes and orientations of the women in their lives, and the approbation or contempt that their own children may show them. For men like Ray or Marty, who've failed their older children profoundly, it can seem like the only road to success is embracing the opportunity to try again with someone new—and perhaps to try over and over, as David Williams has done. When the traditional markers of making it in America—home ownership, marriage, and a career—seem hopelessly out of reach, what else is there but children? And what could be better, really? As Peter Lewinski says while gazing down at his little girl, Erin, "I really don't think I could do any better than her."

The processes that lead to multiple partner fertility are not ones that are deliberately chosen. No one we spoke with set out to become a serial father. Instead, nearly all the circumstances these men find themselves in just seem to "happen," with little volition involved. And much of what ends up occurring goes against men's own stated principles—they show widespread adherence to mainstream norms, such as the belief that a man should put off fatherhood until he has a career and is married. If the romance with the baby's mother goes sour, he quickly begins "affiliating" with another woman he happens to meet on the stoop, outside the corner store, or down the block. And when one thing leads to another, he'll likely once again leave the responsibility for birth control to her. He'll fail once more to initiate the conversation that would provide the assurance that she's on the patch or the pill. When "shit happens," he'll again find himself responding to the news of an accidental pregnancy with joy, or at least acceptance—he may even encourage her to have the baby when she is struggling over how to resolve the pregnancy. And if she decides to carry the pregnancy to term, he'll view it as a chance to redeem the past, to accomplish something good. None of this is the right way to go about things, he'll say, but as one father in this situation said, "You've got to make the best of what you've got."[16]

# EIGHT

# The New Package Deal

In repeated conversations with 110 low-income inner-city men parenting outside of marriage, our goal was to understand why so many ultimately fail to be the fathers they aspire to be. Is it that they simply don't care, as Moyers's portrait of Timothy McSeed might suggest? We began by asking how these young urban men—whom observers may deem completely unprepared for parenthood—become fathers in the first place. We introduced Amin Jenkins, from North Philadelphia's Strawberry Mansion neighborhood, who is no paragon of moral virtue but who also can't simply be cast in the role of the stereotypical Casanova who "hits"—gets a woman pregnant—and then runs. Amin's story offers a vivid example of what is actually the typical course of a liaison in the period preceding pregnancy. While few fathers claim to have been in a "real relationship" when their children were conceived, most say they were more or less "together" with their babies' mothers at the time. For Amin and most others like him, it all begins when two people who meet more or less at random begin "socializing."

There is little partner search involved—she walks by his stoop or hangs out at his favorite corner store, just a girl on his block, a friend of a friend, or is even his best friend's "girl." In short, she is often just the one that he happens to be "with" when a pregnancy occurs. Conception rarely stems from an explicit plan, yet once couples achieve a modest level of cohesion, consistent contraception is rarely practiced. And it all tends to happen so quickly. "Affiliation" is the bureaucratic term often used to describe the tie—replacing terms like "love" or "commitment" that typically appear in American courtship stories.

But whatever the label, these relationships usually have moved beyond mere casual encounters when pregnancy occurs. And Amin Jenkins and his cohorts are far from indifferent to the news of the pregnancy. Shotgun marriage may have faded from the American scene, but the shotgun relationship is for real. Suddenly, with the advent of a pregnancy, mere togetherness is transformed into something more—what men call a "real relationship." For Amin and many like him, having a baby is not a symbol of love and commitment; instead, pregnancy and birth are often the relationship's impetus. Amin and his contemporaries work to "get it together for the sake of the baby" but do so almost entirely of their own volition. This is perhaps why surveys show that such an astoundingly high number—eight in ten unmarried mothers and fathers—say they are in a romantic relationship when their baby is born and why such a large majority (73 percent of women and 88 percent of men) predict they'll stay together and perhaps even marry.[1]

The numbers don't begin to suggest the fundamental fault lines that often cause relationships like Amin's and Antoinette's to crumble. Tenuous relationships and a lack of sufficient desire to *avoid* pregnancy typically result in an unplanned conception. Men are drawn in—usually after the fact of conception—by the rare opportunity for a profound connection to another human being, a child of their own. Fathers- and mothers-to-be—young people who often don't know each other that well—usually work fairly hard to forge a stronger bond around the impending birth. The arrival of the baby often supports further efforts, at least for a time. But the conditions under which these conceptions occur make for very long odds of success.

Why are young men who ought to see parenthood as nothing but trouble nonetheless so eager to be fathers? Andre Green is an unbelievably buoyant fifteen-year-old East Camden youth who is happy—even down-right delighted—at the news that he's about to become a father by a girl with a drug problem, from a short-lived relationship he's long since left behind. Sonya's pregnancy is accidental, and Andre's aunt Charlene's announcement—"she pregnant!"—takes him completely by surprise. At first glance one might assume that his delight stems from pleasure that he has proven his virility.

But for Andre joy over the pregnancy is far more than a crude expression of masculinity. Indeed, fatherhood is not merely a desired status but an eagerly embraced role. Fatherhood offers the opportunity to connect with a child—an unsullied version of oneself—in an intensely meaningful way. But fatherhood is also a tool, almost a magic wand that youth like Andre can use to neutralize the "negativity" that surrounds them as they come of age in chaotic and violence-charged neighborhoods like East Camden. Though becoming a father while young and unprepared may not be the ideal, young men who choose to embrace the simple acts of parenting a child—changing a diaper or fashioning twists in a little girl's hair—are accomplishing something positive by their own lights. While columnist George Will once charged that men who have children outside of marriage were a bigger menace to black progress than Bull Connor, Andre seems to think he's a hero, not a villain.

Not only do young men like Andre Green show a surprising desire to parent their kids, most also say they want to make a go of it with the mothers of their children around the time that their children are born. Given these high hopes, why do most relationships end so quickly? Bear Mallory, a resident of Harrogate, near the infamous North Phila-delphia "Badlands," offers a story that illustrates the complex relation-ship dynamics for which sudden pregnancy, a strong underlying desire for children, a palpable mistrust of women, and lofty standards for mar-riage all serve as critical backdrops. Bear and Amber, a young couple who barely knew each other before conception, suddenly discover that they do not share the same values and priorities once the baby is born.

Caring for a baby together triggers certain expectations on her part—suddenly he is supposed to be the straight arrow nine-to-fiver that he never was, and he has to be accountable to her 24–7. Men like Bear know that their baby's mothers expect them to straighten up, keep a job, and arrive home at a regular hour once the baby arrives. But in the end, it becomes hard to make the necessary sacrifices when he didn't choose her; he ended up with her because a baby was on the way. Furthermore, it is the baby, and not her, whom he is really attached to.

It may not be surprising that most fathers we spoke with are deeply cynical about marriage, yet it is striking how many still aspire to it nonetheless. The imagined bride, though, is not just someone to raise the kids and share the bills. Instead, these men say they long for, and must hold out for, a "soul mate" as a marital partner. Problem is, their baby's mothers—the women they are trying to forge a "real relationship" with—are more often viewed as the former than the latter. Thus, high standards for marriage cast the real relationship in a profoundly unflattering light—Plain Jane must suddenly compete with the contender for the Miss America prize.

Marriage, these men say, requires absolute trust and utter commitment that will not waver in the face of real life challenges such as a drug addiction, a prison term, or the loss of a job.[2] Ernest Williams, from the Kingsessing section of Southwest Philadelphia, believes only a "crazy love" can produce this rock-solid, extravagant devotion. Exhibit A is his son's mother, who has stuck with him through thirteen years of substance abuse, prison spells, and a multitude of infidelities—the evidence necessary to prove her love. Juxtaposing these ideals with the deep conviction that most women, at their core, are heartless mercenaries who won't continue to love if a man doesn't continue to "do" creates very low rates of marriage, at least in the prime family-building years.

The old-fashioned "package deal"—where the adult relationship takes priority and men's relationships with the children come second—has been flipped. The fact that it's now mainly about the baby and the mother is seen principally as a conduit to the child is what is at the *their childhoods?* "crazy love extravagant devotion"

heart of the relationship's fragility. When fathers are far more sure of their commitments to a child than to the mother of that child—when they tell themselves, as they so often do, that their relationship with their child ought to have nothing to do with their relationship to that child's mother—they are even less willing to do what it takes to turn their lives around. Though the level and visibility of their deviant activity may decline for a while, most continue to "drink and drug," to remain "out there" with other women and get swept up in criminal activity.

Most noncustodial fathers end up contributing very little to the support of their children over the eighteen-year span for which society holds them responsible. This leads to the question of how these men—who really want the kids—view the obligations that the fatherhood role typically carries. Almost no one among the fathers we spoke with believes that good fathers should "leave everything to the mother." Good fathers, they say, should provide. But the definition of good provider is unexpectedly broad. First, in the terms used by one father, he must be "all man" and provide for himself, not relying too much on his mother or his girlfriend. Though this point may seem obvious, it was often made explicit in our men's accounts, presumably because for many it is no easy feat. Second, he must mollify those in his current household by paying some of the bills. If he is living with a girlfriend, it's some share of the bills plus a little something for her kids now and then. After settling these accounts, he can offer his nonresident children some portion of what remains. This sharply abridged sense of financial responsibility—"doing the best I can . . . with what is left over"—is what drives both men's sense of obligation and their financial behavior.

When asked to name an ideal father, men cited the 1950s television icon Ward Cleaver with surprising frequency, despite the fact that the series ended in 1963, before most of our fathers were born.[3] The hero of *Leave It to Beaver,* Ward, provides the archetype of what good fathers ought to do: serve as a role model and provide. But even with his steady-as-a-rock job, Ward had to draw on more than his financial resources to ably fulfill his responsibilities as a father. He also had to marshal biographical resources—his own fine example—to serve as a role model to Beaver and Wally.

For Will Donnelly, an ex–drug dealer from Fairhill whose past is littered with rich illustrations of what he desperately hopes his kids *won't* be like, biographical resources are in precariously short supply. Men like Will deploy another version of "doing the best I can"; when the moral authority to serve as a model and guide is lacking, they can appropriate an alternative form of authority—"I've been there, and, believe me, you don't want to follow that path." Will offers up the past as a cautionary tale and prays that his kids will take heed of his negative example.

American society tends to assess the unwed father's moral worth with a single question: how much money does he provide? But the men that we interviewed in Philadelphia and Camden vehemently reject the notion that they should be treated as mere paychecks. Instead, they desire, and even demand, at least a slice of the "whole fatherhood experience" in exchange for a portion of their hard-earned cash. When mom acts as gatekeeper or when a child refuses contact, even this relatively weak breadwinner norm can be eroded or nullified. Returning to the story of Ernest Williams reveals that while unwed fathers offer strong lip service to the importance of serving as provider and role model—the more traditional aspects of the fatherhood role—they have radically redefined fatherhood to sharply elevate the softer side of fathering: offering love, preserving an open line of communication, and spending quality time. According to the image of the hit-and-run father, children are mere notches on a belt; fatherhood is just a status and not a job description. We are not claiming that men who take such a cavalier view do not exist—they do, and we interviewed several who fit that description. But treating a child as a mere status symbol is not how Ernest thinks a father should behave; he reviles men who fit this description—men like his own dad, who had tried to renew his father-hood card with a drive-by hello and a five dollar bill once each year.

For Ernest a good father can be described in one word: friend. Men who fail to either pay or engage in the relational side of fatherhood are mere "daddies," and such men are almost universally derided (even by those who fit this description themselves). Then there are the drones that send money but aren't otherwise engaged. They are on a slightly higher plane than a daddy, but certainly haven't earned the rank of "real father." Fatherhood is a relationship, not merely fulfilling the obligation to bring home the bacon or dispense discipline and wisdom from a distant authoritarian pedestal.

Too often though, a father's good intentions aren't fully realized; so our final questions are how it is that these men so often fail, how do they cope with these failures, and how do most nonetheless manage to deem themselves successful fathers. For the Fishtown roofer Ray Picardi, an excess of blackberry brandy and the inevitable eviction from his girlfriend's home—plus the violent fights that his subsequent visits ignite—spell the termination of his relationship with his firstborn son. Dealing with Regina, and her enraged family, becomes too much for Ray to handle. Ray has now clearly shrugged off any sense of responsibility for his older child.

What keeps fathers like Ray from staying involved? Often their own behavior is the cause. Substance abuse, criminal behavior, and a lack of financial wherewithal to even purchase a treat—ice cream, for example—are all common barriers. In these situations, fathers often withdraw from pure shame. But the mother is also often implicated; she may choose to play the role of gatekeeper and prohibit the father from seeing his child, sometimes, but not always, for good reason. And the child's disposition is also important; how much trust is a child willing to extend to a father who may have already failed again and again and broken repeated promises?

That these men face obstacles to father involvement should come as a surprise to no one.[4] Yet these narratives contain as many examples of fathers who have prevailed despite difficulties as have been crushed by them. How can we distinguish between those who manage to persevere and those who do not? Fulfilling the aspiration to father consistently and well requires both commitment and strong emotional mettle—what we call psychological resources.

Holloway Middleton, from Mantua, is crazy about six-year-old Christine and manages to see her nearly every day, at least until recently. But this day laborer feels he can visit only when he has the "funds" to do something special with his child, like buy her ice cream or take her to the corner store for a treat. Some days he just doesn't have the resources to do so. But now, a new and even more potent threat is on the horizon: Christine's mother, Katrina, has found a new man with a steady job, a "big shot" trying to win Christine's affection and push him out of her life. Just the other day, while slinking around the corner in hopes of catching a glimpse of Christine, he observed the new guy treating his daughter to ice cream. It is painful for him even to describe to us the feelings of utter worthlessness and the haunting fear that he just couldn't compete. Yet against these odds, Holloway presses on. Similarly, Ritchie Weber's drug addiction has taken him to hell and back, and even had him sleeping on a slide in the park. Yet he never let a week go by without seeing his son, whom he credits as his "savior."

Like any distribution across a population, our men's commitment to the father role varies. Indeed, in those cases where the children don't have regular contact with their dads, 7 percent of the fathers seem to have failed in the role due to sheer lack of interest. Beyond commitment, though, persistence in the face of mounting barriers to father involvement requires significant emotional strength—the kind that Holloway and Ritchie seem to have. But given the trauma of so many men's childhoods and the tenuousness of their present circumstances, the strength to "rise above" is sometimes simply lacking.

How do they cope? Ultimately, many find that it's easier to start fresh than to persevere. While children usually remain with their mothers throughout childhood, men move from one household to another as relationships fail and then form. It is the physical distance from children from past failed relationships that allows the glittering prospect of a clean slate with a new partner and child. And as the work of Robert Lerman and Elaine Sorensen has revealed, across the nation an astonishing proportion of younger men who have had a child outside of marriage—around 70 percent—do manage to be intensively involved with at least one of their children at any given time.[5] Meanwhile, fathers enjoying their slice of the whole fatherhood experience in do-over fashion can mentally discount, or simply ignore, their earlier failures as fathers. Having children across several partnerships, what we call "serial fatherhood," has an almost dazzling allure—it allows men of very limited resources to successfully lay claim to the title of "good father" one child at a time, but this dynamic leaves scores of fatherless children behind.

## THE MEANING OF FATHERHOOD

Classic ethnographic explorations into the family lives of the working class and poor in the middle of the past century—what many nostalgically view as the "golden age" of American family life—have depicted men as detached from their children even when living with them. According to these portrayals, lower-class men are even quite distant from their wives, living parallel and peer-driven lives. A compelling portrait of 1950s white ethnic family life in Boston is offered by Herbert Gans in the classic book *Urban Villagers,* an in-depth exploration of a working-class Italian community in the city's West End. Here, fathers only rarely even speak to their children, or of them, except when a mother brings some aspect of a child's behavior to a father's attention.[6] A decade later Lee Rainwater's meticulous examination of black family life in a Saint Louis housing project, *Behind Ghetto Walls,* notes "a high degree of conjugal role segregation," where men are expected to provide, but to do little more, especially with regard to the children. Elliot Liebow's incisive portrayal of lower-class black men living in

Washington, DC, in the late sixties, *Tally's Corner*, offers the following characterization: "It is almost as if there is no direct tie between the father and the child, outside the tie between the father and the mother." Fathers in Liebow's book almost never initiate contact with children and are as likely to respond to their progeny with a slap as an embrace.[7]

If we accept these portrayals as typical of their time and contrast them to our own findings, the meaning that lower- and working-class men attach to fatherhood certainly seems to have changed. The question is why. In Kathryn Edin and Maria Kefalas's analysis of 165 in-depth interviews with single mothers in the same Philadelphia and Camden communities from which we drew many of our fathers, the women had little motivation to stave off early childbearing, as young women in these environs see children as their chief source of meaning and identity, and other sources of esteem are in short supply.[8]

We make the same claim about the men who we spoke with, and for the same reason. The roles of son, sibling, and kin are often attenuated when young men choose the wrong road. Successful siblings or relatives may shun a black sheep, and even a mother's love is challenged when a son robs her for drug money, or when he is in and out of prison. "Friend" is a status almost no one can claim—there is simply too little trust to make such relationships work. Instead, "associates," short-term instrumental or casual relationships, must stand in for friends. "Worker" has limited meaning when all one can claim is one "chicken shit" job after another at the bottom of a labor market where companies may shut down, change owners, and shed workers at the drop of a hat. For some residents of these communities, religion offers a powerful source of meaning, but outside of Alcoholics Anonymous or its sister organization, Narcotics Anonymous—both imbued with discourse about the importance of a higher power—ties to organized religion are rare among our men.[9] And since succeeding long term in a romantic relationship seems improbable, if not impossible, why not invest meaning and identity in the one status any man can successfully claim if he desires: that of a father?

One allure of fatherhood for men is that it is a biological fact that cannot be denied. A man who fathers a child has at least someone who, in one man's words, "can't deny me." When ex-partners, like Holloway's ex-girlfriend Katrina, challenge this assumption by letting another man—a new boyfriend—play the daddy role, especially when they give the new guy the "title," men read this as a signal that they've been judged as so worthless that she's willing to nullify their basic rights as dads. It is even worse when children join in the fray. Recall that Jeff Williams, from North Central Philadelphia, says his nearly grown daughter, Jacina, is offering the proverbial slap in the face when she reminds him that her mother's boyfriend "does" for her more than Jeff has done. He asserts, "irregardless, if this person is doing something for you or not, he can't fill my shoes.... If I give you a million dollars or I give you a penny, I'm still your father." But few men try and claim that they're a "father" (rather than a "daddy") based purely on a biological tie.

Two key themes about the meaning of fatherhood emerge from our conversations with these men. First, think back to the seemingly inexplicable rush of enthusiasm Andre Green, at only fifteen, felt when he first learned Sonya was pregnant. There is no evidence that he wanted a child at the time, or that the two planned the pregnancy, yet the prospect of fatherhood was deeply compelling. When surrounded by the "negativity" of a chaotic family and neighborhood environment, young men like Andre often ache to play a positive social role. They long for a chance to be consumed by a set of activities that are good—unsullied—something to take pride in and something that their own fathers didn't manage to accomplish. "I want to be a *real* father to my kids," Andre says. "I want to not only make a baby but I want to take *care* of my baby."

But Andre's youth and his history as a "straight arrow"—no drinking, drugs, or crime and regular church attendance and good grades—make him a standout among the young men we spoke to. Far more common than the desire to merely "counteract the negativity" of one's external situation—one's family and neighborhood—is the yearning to also purge one's own negative past. Amin, the black sheep in Betty Jenkins's fold, had squandered much of his life in disciplinary schools, detention centers, and prison. His son, Antoine, was the "mini me" who might someday achieve what Amin felt he could not. Having a child is a chance at redemption, albeit intergenerationally. Recall Albert Saunders, a line cook at Bennigan's who graduated at the top of his high school class but never went to college. The father of a toddler, he tells us fatherhood is like watching "a better image of me" at work.

## THE DEINSTITUTIONALIZATION OF FATHERHOOD

In 1978 sociologist Andrew Cherlin wrote a seminal paper, "Remarriage as an Incomplete Institution," that attempted to explain why rates of dissolution were higher for remarriages compared to first marriages. He concluded that subsequent marriages did not have the requisite institutional support that offered couples ready-made solutions to common problems such as child discipline. Those who remarried had to make up the rules as they went along, an ad hoc form of family life that rendered second unions significantly more fragile. Twenty-six years later he followed with the essay "The Deinstitutionalization of American Marriage." In it he proposed that even *first marriage* was becoming deinstitutionalized—less bound by widely accepted norms.[10]

Unwed fatherhood is the least institutionalized family role of all, argued David Blankenhorn in his 1995 polemic, *Fatherless America:* "[Unwed fathers] never signed on to anything.... They never agreed to abide by any fatherhood code. They do not have—they have never had—any explicit obligation to either their children or to the mothers of their children."[11] Blankenhorn blames rising rates of fatherlessness—which he views as the critical social problem of our time—on the breakdown in the basic dictate of family life: put the marital relationship first, and then the kids.

The logic behind Blankenhorn's claim is simple: law governs marriage, and the paternity of children born within marriage is assumed.

Divorces are costly to obtain (and they also used to be hard to get) and are adjudicated through courts. They are also still often the source of considerable personal anguish and social shame. And though the role of the father postdivorce may be less clear than in marriage, divorced dads clearly know—it's spelled out on paper—what their responsibilities are, though compliance with the child-support orders that result is far from universal. Furthermore, the court automatically assigns visitation rights when levying child-support obligations.

Now consider the case of the unwed father. When his child is born, if he wants to claim the child he must go to the hospital and sign paper-work to claim paternity. What does he get in return for his voluntary admission that he is the father? Usually nothing but the booby prize: his name is now available to the state's child-support apparatus when his child's mother chooses to make a claim on his resources.[12] Though some jurisdictions employ a presumption of joint custody, most assume that the unmarried mother is the primary custodian. When the child-support enforcement agency levies an unmarried father's financial responsibilities he may merely receive a letter in the mail that assigns a dollar amount based on his earnings or the state's minimum monthly payment standard, whichever is greater.

Visitation agreements are usually not an automatic part of the pro-cess, as they are in divorce. Securing visitation rights usually means taking his child's mother to court. And while the United States spends millions to enforce child-support orders, most states do virtually noth-ing to ensure visitation agreements are honored. Thus, even if he man-ages to get visitation, he may have difficulty seeing his child. In a startling reversal of the way gender typically operates in American society, unwed childbearing seems to offer mom, and not dad, all the power: "it's her way or the highway," in the words of one father.[13]

According to Cherlin's analysis, the problem lies in the fact that the institutions regulating the family have not yet caught up with the sweeping changes in American family life; this certainly seems to be the case with unwed fatherhood. But there is some evidence from our fieldwork that fatherhood outside of marriage is gradually becoming more institutionalized among men in terms of informal norms. There was remarkable agreement among the men we spoke with about how to define the role of father and what the most critical elements of that role are.

This is particularly true for our African American dads, whose descriptions of the ideal father were more richly articulated and uniform than those of their white counterparts. And there is additional evidence for a more institutionalized role for the unwed dad among blacks than among whites as well. Black men seem to have a language whites lack for the not-quite-real relationships that end up making them a dad. And our black fathers are more involved than the white fathers are with their children, especially when the kids are younger. This is not too surprising: when nearly three-quarters of all black children, compared to only about three in ten whites, are born outside of marriage, norms governing this arrangement are almost certain to grow more quickly among African Americans than among whites.[14]

What is perplexing, however, is why views among women—black or white—haven't seemed to change as well and why the battle between the sexes is so bitter.[15] "I'm not just a paycheck! I'm a father!" he attempts to assert. "What have you done for us lately?" she retorts, rubbing the invisible missing lucre between her index finger and thumb. The traditional nature of the legal system, our child-support bureaucracies, and policy makers at both the state and federal level who have created "deadbeat dad" laws with requirements the courts have no choice but to enforce might be stoking this battle.[16] Virtually every legal and institutional arrangement governing these father's lives tells them that they are a paycheck and nothing more. Unless he has a visitation order, no institution will help to ensure that a father will even be able to see his child. At least in practice, a mother like Antoinette can simply abscond with a child without offering a forwarding address, leaving a father like Amin utterly powerless. Nor is there any guarantee that the unwed dad who doesn't live with his child can have any influence over his children's upbringing. At every turn an unmarried man who seeks to be a father, not just a daddy, is rebuffed by a system that pushes him aside with one hand while reaching into his pocket with the other. Even unwed dads who live with their children and pay a share of the bills are still technically subject to child support in many jurisdictions.[17]


## A REDEFINITION OF FATHERHOOD

Allow us to recap very briefly the history of the family scholars typically tell.[18] When most of America's families lived on farms—41 percent of workers were employed in agriculture in 1900, 16 percent by the end of World War I, but only 4 percent by 1970—fathers had wide-ranging influence over the family.[19] Since the family itself was the basis of production, men's work, like women's, was "inside the home." Fathers didn't disappear for hours each day, returning at dusk with the proverbial bacon; instead, the whole family was engaged in raising, tending, and then slaughtering the hog, curing or otherwise preserving the meat, and cooking and consuming it at breakfast time. Fathers were their children's vocational instructors—especially their sons'—charged with training their offspring to take their place in the productive order. And while this period in American family life was no picnic, fathers could hardly be distant, at least physically, from their children.

But when the glories—and higher wages—of the assembly line began to entice more and more white men from the family farm, a father's role in family life diminished. The history of black men is somewhat different, of course; when the boll weevil and the cotton gin put a merciful end to the sharecropping system of farming, black families traded rural life for the dubious joys first of the southern industrial town and then of large northern cities, where they were consigned to a liminal existence working in the shadow of the manufacturing economy.[20] In either case fathers in the industrial age were increasingly relegated to a single task—breadwinning. And it was a weighty job, taking fathers out of the home eight or more hours each day.[21] Throughout the war years and beyond, the rewards to at least one form of low-skilled employment—manufacturing—grew considerably.

Then came a force powerful enough to tear apart the burly working-class neighborhoods of Greater Kensington and North Philadelphia; the humble hardworking pockets of the South, West, and Southwest sections of the city; plus virtually all of the once-pulsing Camden: an unprecedented decline in the wages of the non–college educated. Any number of powerful social forces have been blamed for this drop in pay—supply-side factors, deindustrialization, a demand for skills driven by technology, waning union strength, and a stagnant minimum wage.[22] The Philadelphia metropolitan area felt the groundswell of one source of this change—the decline in manufacturing—much earlier and much more deeply than the nation as a whole.

Neighborhoods like Whitman, where Dave Jones's longshoreman father once worked long hours but brought home an ample family wage, offer powerful testimony of this change. Falling wages and rising home prices mean that it now takes two solid earners just to stay in Dave's modest row home—never mind the summer weekends he spent as a child on the Jersey Shore, courtesy of his father's ample overtime on the docks. Meanwhile, even men raised in the city's poorest predominately white neighborhood, like Kensington-born Will Donnelly, often find they must cross the color line of Kensington Avenue and venture into the black and Puerto Rican neighborhoods to the west, the location of the city's most dangerous, and highest poverty, tracts, if they wish to live in a modest home like the one they grew up in. Byron Jones, from Mantua, and Amin Jenkins, who grew up in Grays Ferry, both had mothers who toiled all their working lives as housekeepers for wealthy West Philadelphia Jewish families, sure that their labors would bring prosperity for the next generation, yet their sons have certainly not reaped the promised rewards.

About the time that breadwinning became more difficult for men at the bottom, marriages began failing in droves—among those married in the late 1980s and early 1990s, divorce rates were roughly twice as high for those without a college degree as for those holding a college diploma. Increasingly, these men stopped marrying altogether, at least during the prime family-building years.[23] And their rate of nonmarital childbearing exploded. Meanwhile, Murphy Brown notwithstanding, hardly any in the middle class are now bearing children outside of marriage, and since 1980 fewer and fewer have been divorcing.[24]

Consider the strong correlation between earnings and marriage rates. For those in their thirties and forties in the top 10 percent of annual earnings, a group that saw real earnings increases over the past four decades, 83 percent of men were married in 2010 (down from roughly 95 percent in 1970). For men at the median (whose earnings have declined by about 28 percent), only 64 percent were married by the end of this period (down from 91 percent). For men in the bottom quartile, where earnings have fallen by a whopping 60 percent, only half are married, compared with 86 percent four decades ago. Most of the decline in men's marriage rates over the past forty years is due to the increase in men who have failed to marry—like most of our fathers—and not to those who have divorced. At least some of the rise in nonmarital childbearing is probably due to these changing economic circumstances.[25] But Kathryn Edin and Maria Kefalas have argued that culture—specifically, culture-wide changes in the meaning of marriage—is also a crucial part of the story.[26]

Public intellectuals from the right like Charles Murray tell one version of the culture story, which points to a decline in the adherence to core American values among those at the bottom. In Murray's version the middle class has held firmly to marriage and other vital virtues, while the bottom 30 percent has abandoned them en masse. It is undeniable that the less educated are marrying far less than they used to—we've described the dramatic decline. But is this due to a change in their values vis-à-vis those of the middle class? Indeed, Murray's own data show that those in the bottom 30 percent of thirty- to forty-nine-year-olds in the white distribution—the group his story centers on—reveal that they have retained more, and not less, traditional views about marriage than those in the upper 20 percent, even as the class gap in behavior has widened.[27]

An alternative story, told by Kathryn Edin and Maria Kefalas and based on interviews with low-income single mothers in Camden and Philadelphia, is that poor women have, in fact, embraced a set of astonishingly mainstream norms about marriage and the conditions under which it should occur—they revere it but hold it to an exceedingly high standard. These authors see rich and poor alike responding to a new cultural definition of marriage, one that deemphasizes the instrumental value of the institution but has, at the same time, raised the bar on the level of assets and earning power—not to mention the relationship quality (read: "soul mate")—required. Accordingly, those in the upper-middle class aren't willing to marry until they've launched their careers, they've put childbearing off until their thirties, and they are choosing spouses with the same class credentials as their own. Meanwhile, Edin and Kefalas write, "those at the bottom of the class ladder today believe that a wedding ought to be the icing on the cake of a working-class respectability already achieved."[28] Due to challenging circumstances, however, the less advantaged are less likely to be in relationships that clear the new bar.

We seek to explain fathering, and not marriage behavior, and also invoke culture as a partial cause. Yet for our purposes it is not very illuminating to point to inner-city fathers' deviant values as the primary source of what we've observed, as so many public intellectuals from both sides of the political divide have done. Instead, we direct our attention to a culture-wide shift in the meaning of fatherhood that has accompanied changes in the meaning of marriage—a shift that began in the 1970s and has profoundly affected all Americans. We argue that men on all rungs of the ladder have responded to the shift, but their reactions have been conditioned by their position on the ladder and especially by the growing distance between the bottom and top rungs.

Let's begin with the middle class. Family historian Robert L. Griswold argues that the emergence of the "new father" ideology among the middle-class "gray flannel suits," to use Barbara Ehrenreich's phrase, was a response to a massive shift in the composition of the labor force.[29] The dramatic rise in their wives' employment, writes Griswold, threatened to topple husbands' role and source of authority in the family.[30] Meanwhile, the followers of feminist Betty Friedan were urging and even demanding that husbands do more than merely take out the garbage and conduct the odd tire change—and the compositional shift in employment lent strong legitimacy to their call. Suddenly, these fathers were thrust into the nursery to master the diaper change and were told it was imperative to develop deep, empathic, and expressive relationships with their offspring.[31]

Middle-class men have clearly responded to the call of the new-father ideal. Time-use diaries show that between 1965 and 2003, husbands tripled the amount of time spent caring for their children.[32] But fatherhood's "softer side" has not replaced the more traditional aspects of the role among the middle class. For them new responsibilities have come alongside the old. In 2007 married men still brought home the lion's share—about two-thirds to three-quarters, depending on the husband's education—of the household income.[33] And married women still do the large majority of the housework and child care, though men's relative contributions have grown.[34]

Now let's turn to those near the bottom of the income distribution. Men like ours, both black and white, have responded to new fatherhood in a wildly different set of circumstances than their middle-class counterparts.[35] From the early fifties to the year just preceding the Great Recession of 2007, industrial employment fell from about a third to just 10 percent in the United States as a whole. But this is a mere foreshadowing of what happened in Philadelphia. The year 1953 marked the city's postwar manufacturing height, with more than 350,000 manufacturing jobs employing fully 45 percent of the total labor force. By 2007 only 30,000 of these jobs remained and provided employment for only 5 percent of workers.[36] Wages for the unskilled more generally fell precipitously as well and for a number of reasons, as we've indicated earlier. Economist David Autor writes that this fall in the rewards for work, for such a large portion of the population, is unprecedented in the United States.[37] By the 1970s, when the new-father ideology first came on the scene, the job prospects of those with no credentials beyond a high school diploma, including in Philadelphia and Camden, were already in free fall.

What is most surprising about our story is not that such changes would undermine lower-skilled men's role in the family but that, while those affected by this massive economic shift have been shying away from the role of husband—like the mothers in Edin and Kefalas's story, they hold marriage to such high standards that they often can't manage to achieve it—they haven't fled from the role of father, at least not by their own lights. Instead, if our interviews are any guide, men at the bottom seem to have developed an unbelievably voracious desire to take on the ideals propagated by their middle-class brethren—indeed, given the timing of their labor market woes, the new-father role emerged just in the nick of time to offer an alternative way to engage with their progeny.

But for men at the bottom the tasks associated with the new father have *replaced* and not merely complemented the more traditional aspects of the role. It is their children's mothers who are the chief breadwinners—most men fully expect women to bear the ultimate responsibility for providing for the children. Hyatt-employee Maurice, for example, tells us outright that he explicitly chose a "strong independent black woman" because he believed she could raise his children on her own if she had to. Mothers are also usually the ones who set the good example. The rare woman who behaves like so many of our fathers have done—drinks to excess or does drugs, runs around with several different sexual partners, or sells narcotics—is often scorned by both men and women alike. Will Donnelly depicts one such woman in his neighborhood in very graphic terms, saying, "She's the type of person you'd like to shoot like a sick horse."

For our men, time spent with children, whether skillfully fashioning a daughter's hair (Andre Green) or teaching one's son to pee in the bushes (Bear Mallory), is viewed as priceless and a treasure any man would naturally want to claim. The opportunity to express love and have rich conversations with children is a gift—not just to the children but for the fathers as well. These are the moments, fathers say, that truly make life worth living—not the womanizing or the ripping and running, nor repetitive days of work or the heady risks of crime.

It is almost as if engaging in the softer "relational aspects" of the role is a must-have for men trying to forge meaning and identity in an economic age that has left the unskilled worker behind. Relating to children—not hanging on the corner with peers—is the vital ingredient that adds zest to life.[38] And even in these challenging neighborhood environments, visiting family is what fathers often want to do with their free time. Consider Fairhill's Lacey Jones, for example. Released from prison just one year ago, this African American prep cook with three children by three different mothers—an eighteen-year-old daughter with two children of her own, a seventeen-year-old son, plus a live-in nine-year-old daughter—glories in his present routine. "I go in the restaurant and . . . go through the daily hassles of cooking in a restaurant. Then once I'm off, I . . . generally go home and like to spend some time with my younger daughter or visit my son. I talk to my older daughter on the phone, talk to my grandson on the phone. I try to spend as much time as I can with them. 'Cause there was a time when I couldn't spend it. A good week is when I spend a lot of time with my family."

In sum, declining marriage rates among the less educated, the corresponding rise in nonmarital childbearing, and lower-skilled men's desultory participation in the child-support system all hint that a seismic shift has occurred in lower-skilled men's ability and willingness to shoulder the traditional breadwinning responsibilities of the family. According to our story, at the bottom end of the skills distribution we see not just a withdrawal but a headlong retreat—it is nearly a dead run—from the breadwinner role.

For our men, the Ward Cleaver norm—assuming 100 percent of the financial responsibility—has been replaced by a "doing the best I can" ethos of financial provision. Meanwhile, however, unskilled men's revolt in the breadwinning domain has been matched by an unexpected incursion.[39] Our men's response to the societal condemnation often levied at them is the loud proclamation: "I'm not just a paycheck!"—the "just" implying that they insist on being something more. Just as our fathers are shrugging off much of the obligation to support their children financially, they are trying to lay claim to a new set of roles that in the industrial age were viewed as a mother's exclusive domain: love, communication, and quality time.

These fathers now want roles more like conventional mothers' roles. Meanwhile, mothers have been forced by sheer necessity to take on more of the traditional father's tasks. A cynical interpretation of this attempted role swap is that it excuses the men from financial and moral responsibility—that they're trying to claim a poor man's version of the Disneyland Dad, one that reduces a father to a buddy while skipping the harder tasks of providing financially and setting a good example. While that charge can't be dismissed entirely, a more forgiving interpretation is that rather than backing away from their responsibilities altogether, men are choosing to emphasize those aspects of the father role they can most reasonably fulfill.[40] Whatever interpretation one chooses, one fact is inescapable: men in this segment of society couldn't flee, or even try to flee, from the breadwinner role and attempt to "elect" instead to invest in relational fathering *but for the massive decline in their propensity to live with their children*—an outgrowth of the changes in the meaning of marriage. We can see this in our data; the live-in fathers look much more like their middle-class counterparts—combining breadwinning with nurturing—than their male friends and neighbors who live away from their kids.

Still, the upside of this refashioning of fatherhood is that given their economic and social conditions, which seriously limit their ability to play traditional roles like breadwinner, unwed dads may have hit on a definition of fatherhood that will allow them to find some productive way of contributing to their children's lives despite limited means. Listening to the father-son narratives of Ernest Williams or

Ray Davies—who are far from exemplary parents—it is still hard to imagine that their children are worse off for their fathers' involvement. And if we attend to men's own coming-of-age stories, some contact may be better than none even if the man in question isn't exactly a gem. So many of our fathers claimed they had never recovered from the absence of their biological fathers, even if their mothers had worked hard to compensate for the loss.

Perhaps the greatest benefit of validating men's attempts to engage in the softer side of parenting is not for the children, but for the men themselves. Criminologists who have studied the trajectories of men headed for trouble in their youth point to a variety of life-course events that can serve as turning points: a steady job, entry into the military, marriage, and parenthood.[41] While romantic relationships seem to have little of this transforming power—presumably because of the limited stake that fathers have in them—fatherhood just might.

Readers will probably be surprised by our claim that most men at the bottom—regularly portrayed by the media, as well as some social scientists, as heartless players who merely hit and run—are actually eager to claim fatherhood and to engage in at least some aspects of the role. But one need only note the extraordinarily high rates of voluntary paternity admission at the hospital, despite the specter of child support, to at least give some credence to our claim. And why not? After all, for generations women have found intense meaning and identity in the everyday tasks of parenthood, and society has given them immense social honor for doing so.[42] It is also true that one's children are beguiling, fresh, and hopeful, at least in their younger years. By the time men become fathers—even if they are relatively young—many are already beginning to tire of the "rippin' and runnin'," perhaps because they began to engage in these misdeeds at such a tender age. Many acknowledge that when they extend into adulthood, extreme forms of adolescent male behavior are exhausting at best, life threatening at worst, and ultimately not that fulfilling. While some younger men are not quite sure they are ready to put street life entirely behind them, others are quite eager to try and settle down somewhat, if it offers a chance to establish a meaningful connection with a child.

That said, while nearly every man claims he wants the whole fatherhood experience, the tasks these men actually end up performing in their children's lives are more like those of a favorite uncle—the man who can be counted on to spring for the diapers or tennis shoes when things get tight, show up on the weekends for a visit, attend the birthdays and special events, and dispense earthy wisdom won from his misspent youth.[43] This is especially true when a father no longer lives with his child, or when he comes back into the life of an older child with whom he had lost contact. But the favorite uncle is not the role that any man thinks is ideal—men often level a powerful self critique for not being able to provide the "real family" that they feel their kids ought to have. But what they see as a real family—a lifetime marriage—seems to most an impossible goal, at least in the near term. We ask Montay Smalls, who grew up in East Camden, what marriage involves. This neighborhood handyman replies, "Being a good husband—you don't be with nobody else but your wife.... I'm not saying that therefore you gotta cut your friends loose but as far as having sex with them, yeah, you gotta cut that loose. You and her have to have everything up-to-date as far as bills, financially, you know, with the kids tooken care of and situated." Then he tells us, "But it's impossible; that's an impossibility."[44]

In the end, though, these men's bold attempt to refashion fatherhood often fails because it is too bold and too out of synch with what mothers and the wider culture demand. While middle-class men have moved at least somewhat toward androgyny in the domestic sphere, taking on both traditional and some new-father tasks simultaneously, lower-class fathers have tried to bargain for a wholesale reversal of gender norms, and—ironically—their partners and the wider culture often judge them as "deadbeats" precisely because of it. The combination of "approach" (embracing fatherhood's softer side) and "avoid" (assigning the traditional responsibilities mostly to the mother) is part of what propagates father failure.

The new package deal—which men hold to like religion—is the new-father ideology taken to its extreme. Viewing the world through this lens renders the partner little more than a black-and-white one-dimensional figure, while the child emerges fully 3-D and in living color. The accidental pregnancy is how men must enter the family scene—the vehicle through which those who feel they really can't afford, and might never be able to afford, to do fatherhood in the right way can still enter into this story, and with a noble narrative: "I'm no irresponsible impregnator! I stepped up to the plate though the pregnancy wasn't even planned."

Serial fatherhood—where a man's children are spread across multiple partners—offers more chances to claim the whole fatherhood experience, and it lowers the bar by enabling selective fathering. Eventually, the inner-city father hopes he will manage, through this pricey form of trial and error, to finally father at least one child well. Meanwhile, due to this family-go-round, children are highly likely to lose hold of the time and resources of their biological dads. Subsequently, they may be exposed to the confusion of new parental figures who come and go, and they will likely accumulate half siblings along the way.[45] Kids are amazingly resilient, but the rate of family change among children of unwed fathers has become so rapid, and now leads to such complicated family structures, that kids might have a hard time adjusting.[46] And if children are placed on a father-go-round where no one man is ultimately responsible for their long-term well-being and care, who will make the investment to see them through high school, through college, and beyond? Leaving it all to the mother seems like a poor bargain for American women and children.

Actions speak louder than words. The way in which our social institutions, and the culture at large, treat fathers speaks volumes about the value we ascribe to men's parenting roles. We now take great pains to ensure that fathers fulfill their financial obligations—through a child-support system that attaches wages, strips those in arrears of their tax returns and professional licenses, and even puts nonpayers in jail in some jurisdictions. We do not disagree with the impulse behind these efforts—after all, it is critical to children's well-being that the bills get paid. Yet despite significant toughening up of child support, getting fathers to pay what the state thinks they ought to has still proven enormously difficult. Most children born to unwed parents still receive only a fraction of what is owed to them, and there is probably not much more that policy can do to improve the situation.[47]

The need to address unskilled men's economic woes is obvious. Even the most well-crafted efforts to shift disadvantaged fathers' values with regard to marriage and enhance their relationship skills have not kept many more unmarried fathers in their children's homes—and none have prompted more marriage.[48] When men cannot predict whether they will be employed from one week to the next, they will find it extraordinarily difficult to contemplate marriage. They'll find it hard to set up housekeeping with their child's mother or maintain a common household. Ironically, though, we've argued that this same uncertainty weakens men's motivation to stave off having children until they are economically ready to provide for a child: why muster the effort to avoid pregnancy when being appropriately "situated" is viewed as a contingency that may never occur?

Policy makers and practitioners have put forward any number of "solutions" to economic and behavioral problems of such men—from offering substance-abuse treatment to anger-management courses to more standard approaches such as investing in their human capital or supplementing their wages through substantial tax credits such as those now available to custodial single parents who work.[49] While such efforts are no doubt vital, we call for a broader and more sweeping set of changes.

Perhaps a paradigm shift is in order. Imagine if America's social institutions realigned so that men's parenting efforts were treated as a resource with real potential value. If we truly believe in gender equity, then we must find a way to honor fathers' attempts to build relationships with their children just as we do mothers'—to assign fathers rights along with their responsibilities. While some low-income fathers are violent or potentially harmful to their children, such problems are far from universal, and it is wrong to characterize a whole class of men in this way, particularly when we don't do the same for middle-class, predominately white fathers.

Taking a bold new approach to unmarried fatherhood has risks, but it also has large potential payoffs. It is possible that if men gained greater satisfaction from parenting, they might also find the strength to stay involved even in exceedingly hard times, as Ritchie Weber has done. Ongoing involvement, in turn, might stave off additional childbearing with new partners and leave fewer children on the father-go-round. And perhaps most important, if society helped unwed fathers to build quality, long-term relationships with their children, these bonds might help turn fathers' lives around. How one might implement this approach is still unknown, but in reading these pages, it is hard to conclude that continuing on America's current path is the wisest course.

# APPENDIX

The figures and tables contained in this appendix are referenced throughout the text. Table 1 and map 1 provide demographic data on Camden and on the study neighborhoods in Philadelphia. All were at least 20 percent poor in 2000, though the predominately nonwhite neighborhoods were much higher in poverty than the predominately white neighborhoods of Kensington, Fishtown, Port Richmond, Pennsport, and Whitman.

Table 2 corresponds to the discussion of reactions to pregnancy in chapter 2, while table 3 reports the level of intentionality associated with each pregnancy, also discussed in that chapter. Though ours is a relatively small, nonrepresentative sample, we compare the figures for African Americans to those of whites and find little difference in how black and white men reacted to the news of a pregnancy. We see some differences by race in the degree to which men say the pregnancy was planned, with whites showing somewhat higher levels of intentionality; black men are more likely to say they conceived when they were "just not thinking," while white men were more likely to say a pregnancy was "semiplanned." But there are no large differences in degree to which pregnancies are characterized as "planned" or "accidental." Also following the discussion in chapter 2, table 4 shows that while there is a strong positive relationship between pregnancy intentionality and the relative enthusiasm of men's response for the sample as a whole and for blacks and whites alike, the correspondence is far from perfect. In particular, happy or accepting responses are the modal response category for all levels of intentionality except those actively avoiding pregnancy at the time (those in the "accidental" category). However, blacks who say they conceived when they were "just not thinking" were less happy about the news of pregnancy than whites who were "just not thinking."

Table 5 lists all sources of strain fathers cited in their relationships with their children's mothers, complementing the discussion in chapter 3. We find some quite striking differences by race in this regard. In particular, father's drug use, severe conflict, and—to a lesser degree—domestic violence, pressure from the mother's kin, and mental health issues are more common among whites. African Americans are somewhat more prone than whites to say their relationships were strained because they were not in love. The reader should keep in mind that these figures do not represent the incidence of these factors per se. Rather, they are included only if they are named as sources of relationship strain. For example, Amin Jenkins's extensive incarceration history didn't pose any strain on his relationship with either of his children's mothers because he was not in a relationship with either of them during the years he was in and out of prison or jail.

Table 6 complements the discussion in chapter 7 and compares the levels of involvement that fathers in our study report compared to mothers' reports in the Fragile Families and Child Wellbeing Study (FFCWS), a nationally representative sample of urban births. We draw the FFCWS estimates from Edin, Tach, and Mincy (2009), who restrict the FFCWS sample to parents with black and white nonmarital births at each survey wave, conducted at the time of the birth, and when the children reached approximately one, three, and five years of age. Note that the two studies coded father involvement somewhat differently. We have arrayed the table as a continuum, from lowest to highest rates of involvement, as measured by the questions or coding scheme used.

There were also important demographic differences between our sample and the FFCWS. First, all our fathers had earned less in the formal economy in the prior six months (we didn't count informal wages in our selection criteria) than the poverty threshold for a family of four and lived in neighborhoods of at least moderate poverty, whereas FFCWS had no income cutoff or neighborhood criteria. Second, and relatedly, our respondents were somewhat less likely to live with their noncustodial children than fathers in FFCWS, especially our white respondents. Since our sampling scheme excluded a far greater range of white noncustodial fathers than their black counterparts (who are more likely to earn low wages and live in higher-poverty neighborhoods), these differences probably account for the lower involvement rates of our whites compared to white respondents in FFCWS. The reader should also note that father involvement among blacks in our study is consistently higher than that in the FFCWS, suggesting that our sampling method produced somewhat more highly involved black fathers than one would find in the general population of black men with nonmarital births living in cities.

Table 7 documents barriers to father involvement, as discussed in chapter 6, and finds no large race differences in fathers' reports. Tables 8 and 9 summarize Lerman and Sorensen's work, discussed in chapter 7, on "maximum involvement" among men at various ages who have ever had a nonmarital birth. Table 8 reproduces work by Robert Lerman and Elaine Sorensen, drawn from the 1979 National Longitudinal Survey of Youth for men as they reach various ages, and table 9 contains revised estimates of maximum father involvement using these same data but excluding men married at the time of interview. Since none of the men in our sample were married and living with a spouse (i.e., not separated) at the time we interviewed them, these estimates are more consistent with what one might expect of men like those we interviewed. Limiting the sample in this way yields a somewhat lower estimate of maximum father involvement.

TABLE 1  Demographic characteristics of Camden, New Jersey; Philadelphia, Pennsylvania; and study neighborhoods within Philadelphia

| | Median income | Individuals living in households below poverty line (%) | Non-Hispanic black population (%) | Non-Hispanic white population (%) | Asian population (%) | Population of other races (%) | Hispanic population (%) |
|---|---|---|---|---|---|---|---|
| Camden, NJ | 23,421 | 35.5 | 53.3 | 16.8 | 2.5 | 22.8 | 38.8 |
| Philadelphia, PA | 30,746 | 22.9 | 45.0 | 43.2 | 4.5 | 4.8 | 8.5 |
| Philadelphia Study Neighborhoods | | | | | | | |
| Mantua and Belmont | 15,507 | 41.30 | 95.52 | 1.73 | 0.43 | .37 | 1.36 |
| Elmwood Park | 24,817 | 29.50 | 55.40 | 31.15 | 10.33 | .75 | 2.25 |
| Fairhill | 13,795 | 56.02 | 27.14 | 21.42 | 0.78 | 45.41 | 70.25 |
| Fishtown | 29,940 | 20.97 | 17.38 | 68.34 | 1.50 | 9.01 | 16.68 |
| Grays Ferry | 17,619 | 36.70 | 56.29 | 39.00 | 2.58 | .66 | 1.72 |
| Harrogate | 16,625 | 49.19 | 23.36 | 33.99 | 3.88 | 33.87 | 53.50 |
| Hunting Park | 17,455 | 45.39 | 38.80 | 18.55 | 1.44 | 35.98 | 56.83 |
| Kensington | 25,109 | 32.26 | 4.04 | 79.99 | 6.63 | 6.00 | 11.56 |
| Kingsessing | 23,050 | 30.26 | 95.28 | 1.81 | 0.67 | .49 | 1.12 |

| | | | | | | | |
|---|---|---|---|---|---|---|---|
| Mill Creek | 19,226 | 33.30 | 96.39 | 1.37 | 0.32 | .39 | 0.96 |
| North Central | 13,906 | 44.15 | 93.80 | 3.08 | 0.83 | .81 | 2.07 |
| Pennsport | 32,388 | 22.80 | 16.89 | 70.25 | 8.26 | 1.99 | 5.22 |
| Point Breeze | 19,212 | 34.45 | 78.08 | 8.18 | 10.94 | .72 | 1.83 |
| Port Richmond | 23,399 | 31.05 | 9.73 | 76.55 | 1.38 | 9.01 | 14.65 |
| South Philadelphia and Whitman | 24,400 | 24.90 | 12.68 | 69.70 | 12.89 | 1.58 | 4.33 |
| Strawberry Mansion | 14,775 | 41.03 | 97.58 | 0.55 | 0.24 | .22 | 0.99 |
| Tioga and Nicetown | 21,167 | 30.46 | 92.83 | 3.26 | 1.03 | 1.25 | 2.30 |
| West Kensington | 15,300 | 48.76 | 21.18 | 22.81 | 2.17 | 47.05 | 68.36 |

Source: U.S. Census Bureau (2000). Information on Philadelphia neighborhoods provided by the Philadelphia Neighborhood Indicators Database, University of Pennsylvania (Philadelphia Neighborhood Information System 2012).

Note: Detailed descriptions of specific Camden neighborhoods are not included because all of Camden was included in the study, not selected neighborhoods. Hispanics may be of any race. The percentage of neighborhood residents who are black, white, Asian, or other race, a category provided for those whose racial identification did not fit within the six census–designated race categories, does not equal 100 in all cases because a small portion of residents are Native American or Alaskan Native, Hawaiian or Asian Pacific Islander, or of two or more races.

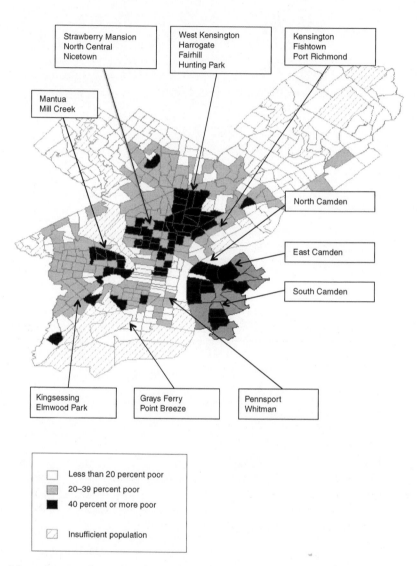

Map 1  Poverty Concentration in Philadelphia, PA, and Camden, NJ, 2000

**TABLE 2**  Reactions to pregnancy (%) for each live birth reported by 110 Philadelphia/Camden fathers (N = 205)

|        | Happy | Accepting | Ambivalent | Rejecting* |
|--------|-------|-----------|------------|-----------|
| All    | 55    | 21        | 10         | 13        |
| Blacks | 55    | 21        | 12         | 13        |
| Whites | 55    | 22        | 9          | 15        |

*Note*: Men reported a total of 218 births. For 13 births we could not establish how fathers reacted to the news of the birth.

*Includes paternity denials.

**TABLE 3**  Level of pregnancy intentionality (%) for each live birth reported by 110 Philadelphia/Camden fathers (N = 205)

|        | Planned | Semiplanned | Just not thinking | Accidental |
|--------|---------|-------------|-------------------|------------|
| All    | 15      | 34          | 37                | 15         |
| Whites | 12      | 44          | 28                | 16         |
| Blacks | 17      | 26          | 43                | 14         |

*Note*: Men reported a total of 218 births. For 13 births we could not establish the degree of intentionality.

**TABLE 4**  Level of pregnancy intentionality (%) by reaction to pregnancy for each pregnancy reported by 110 Philadelphia/Camden fathers (N = 205)

|                   | Happy | Accepting | Ambivalent | Rejecting* |
|-------------------|-------|-----------|------------|-----------|
| **All**           |       |           |            |           |
| Planned           | 100   | 0         | 0          | 0         |
| Semiplanned       | 71    | 25        | 1          | 3         |
| Just not thinking | 39    | 23        | 19         | 19        |
| Accidental        | 10    | 21        | 17         | 52        |
| **Blacks**        |       |           |            |           |
| Planned           | 100   | 0         | 0          | 0         |
| Semiplanned       | 88    | 9         | 0          | 3         |
| Just not thinking | 27    | 31        | 21         | 21        |
| Accidental        | 12    | 24        | 18         | 47        |
| **Whites**        |       |           |            |           |
| Planned           | 100   | 0         | 0          | 0         |
| Semiplanned       | 55    | 39        | 3          | 3         |
| Just not thinking | 56    | 6         | 22         | 17        |
| Accidental        | 8     | 17        | 17         | 58        |

*Note*: Men reported a total of 218 births. For 13 births we could not establish how fathers reacted to the news of the birth or their level of pregnancy intentionality. Discrepancies due to rounding.

*Includes paternity denials.

**TABLE 5** Relationship strains preceding breakup for any partner with whom a father shares a child

| | Drug/alcohol abuse (father) | Severe conflict | Cheating (father) | Cheating (mother) | Incarceration |
|---|---|---|---|---|---|
| Total (N) | 41 | 35 | 32 | 29 | 22 |
| Total (%) | 37 | 32 | 29 | 26 | 20 |
| Black (N) | 17 | 16 | 22 | 16 | 12 |
| Black (%) | 23 | 21 | 29 | 21 | 16 |
| White (N) | 24 | 19 | 10 | 13 | 10 |
| White (%) | 52 | 41 | 22 | 28 | 22 |

| | Money issues | Drug/ alcohol abuse (mother) | Not in love | Domestic violence | Pressure from kin (mother) |
|---|---|---|---|---|---|
| Total (N) | 20 | 19 | 19 | 14 | 13 |
| Total (%) | 18 | 17 | 17 | 12 | 12 |
| Black (N) | 13 | 11 | 15 | 6 | 5 |
| Black (%) | 17 | 15 | 20 | 8 | 7 |
| White (N) | 7 | 8 | 4 | 8 | 8 |
| White (%) | 15 | 17 | 9 | 17 | 17 |

| | Partying (mother) | Too bossy/ greedy (mother) | Crime/gang involvement (father) | Trust issues (father) | Mental-health issues (father) |
|---|---|---|---|---|---|
| Total (N) | 12 | 10 | 8 | 7 | 6 |
| Total (%) | 11 | 9 | 7 | 6 | 5 |
| Black (N) | 9 | 6 | 4 | 6 | 0 |
| Black (%) | 12 | 8 | 5 | 7 | 0 |
| White (N) | 3 | 4 | 4 | 1 | 6 |
| White (%) | 7 | 9 | 9 | 2 | 12 |

*Note*: This is not a count of the incidence of these problems; they are included only if mentioned by the respondent as a source of relationship strain. For example, fathers cheat far more than mothers by their own admission, but when a father learns his partner is cheating, he often cites it as a source of strain—he is not as likely to perceive his own cheating as a problem. To offer another example, blacks are incarcerated far more often than whites, but whites are considerably more likely to note incarceration as a source of strain. Strains noted by less than 5 percent of the sample are excluded.

TABLE 6  Father involvement by race and age of child, Philadelphia/Camden births (N = 218) and the Fragile Families and Child Wellbeing Study (N = 1484)

| | Contact since last survey wave (in person) | Some contact in past six months (not always in person) | Irregular contact within the past month (in person) | Contact at least monthly (in person) | Contact several times monthly (in person) | Contact at least weekly (in person) |
|---|---|---|---|---|---|---|
| P/C: black, aged <2 | | 100 | 89 | | 89 | |
| FFCWS: black, aged ~1 | 96 | | | 83 | | 66 |
| P/C: black, aged 2–5 | | 91 | 78 | | 65 | |
| FFCWS: black, aged ~3 | 87 | | | 71 | | 58 |
| FFCWS: black, aged ~5 | 81 | | | 66 | | 49 |
| P/C: black, aged 6–10 | | 83 | 77 | | 51 | |
| P/C: black, aged >10 | | 79 | 52 | | 33 | |
| P/C: white, aged <2 | | 93 | 62 | | 54 | |
| FFCWS: white, aged ~1 | 96 | | | 83 | | 71 |
| P/C: white, aged 2–5 | | 84 | 58 | | 47 | |
| FFCWS: white, aged ~3 | 86 | | | 76 | | 65 |
| FFCWS: white, aged ~5 | 82 | | | 74 | | 61 |
| P/C: white, aged 6–10 | | 84 | 56 | | 44 | |
| P/C: white, aged >10 | | 78 | 33 | | 24 | |

*Source:* Figures for FFCWS adapted from Edin, Tach, and Mincy (2009).

TABLE 7 Barriers to father involvement for fathers
with at least one barrier

|  | Substance abuse | Conflict with mother | Gatekeeping | Prison |
|---|---|---|---|---|
| Total (N) | 49 | 32 | 31 | 22 |
| Total (%) | 26 | 17 | 17 | 12 |
| Blacks with barriers (N) | 25 | 19 | 15 | 14 |
| Black (%) | 24 | 18 | 14 | 13 |
| Whites with barriers (N) | 24 | 13 | 16 | 8 |
| White (%) | 29 | 16 | 20 | 10 |

|  | Distance | Lacks desire | Economic | Mother relocated |
|---|---|---|---|---|
| Total (N) | 17 | 14 | 9 | 8 |
| Total (%) | 9 | 7 | 5 | 4 |
| Blacks with barriers (N) | 8 | 10 | 8 | 4 |
| Black (%) | 8 | 10 | 8 | 4 |
| Whites with barriers (N) | 9 | 4 | 1 | 4 |
| White (%) | 11 | 5 | 1 | 5 |

*Note*: Excludes barriers that occurred only once.

TABLE 8 Maximum involvement of a father with any child born outside
of marriage by father's age (%)

|  | 1984 (19–26) | 1988 (23–30) | 1992 (27–34) |
|---|---|---|---|
| Did not visit | 11 | 9 | 13 |
| Visited less than once per month | 14 | 12 | 12 |
| Visited one to three times per month | 9 | 9 | 7 |
| Visited at least once per week | 28 | 22 | 20 |
| Lived with child but not mother | 3 | 4 | 5 |
| Not married, lived with child and mother | 11 | 15 | 14 |
| Married, lived with child and mother | 25 | 30 | 29 |

*Source*: Lerman and Sorensen (2000, table 1).

TABLE 9 Maximum involvement of a father with any child born outside of marriage, who did not subsequently marry (%)

| | 1984 (19–26) | 1988 (23–30) | 1992 (27–34) | Average of all ages |
|---|---|---|---|---|
| Did not visit | 14 | 13 | 19 | 16 |
| Visited less than once per month | 18 | 17 | 17 | 17 |
| Visited one to three times per month | 12 | 12 | 9 | 11 |
| Visited at least once per week | 38 | 31 | 28 | 31 |
| Lived with child but not mother | 4 | 6 | 7 | 6 |
| Lived with child and mother | 15 | 21 | 19 | 19 |
| Moderate involvement (once a month or more) | 68 | 70 | 63 | 67 |
| High involvement (visited at least once a week, lived with child but not mother, lived with child and mother) | 56 | 58 | 54 | 56 |

*Source*: Authors' calculations based on Lerman and Sorensen (2000).

# NOTES

## INTRODUCTION

1. Bennett (2001, 93–94).
2. Cosby (2004).
3. Lawrence (2007).
4. Such fathers do exist, and paternity denial, while relatively rare, is more common among very young men who father a child, at least according to our data. Waldo Johnson's in-depth interviews in Chicago and Milwaukee also show that denial of responsibility for a child is fairly rare. See Johnson (2001, 2002) as well as Parke and Brott (1999). For an ethnographic portrait of young men who do deny paternity, see the "Sex Codes" chapter in Anderson (1990).
5. For example, see Corry (1986). Conservative columnist Adam Meyerson (1989) listed the television event as one of the "One Hundred Conservative Victories" during the Reagan years, stating that "conservative wisdom on poverty becomes conventional wisdom as Bill Moyers' report on CBS, 'The Vanishing Family: Crisis in Black America,' blames breakdown of families for persistence of poverty in inner cities."
6. Fuchs, quoted in Carmody (1986).
7. Cohen (1986).
8. Raspberry (1986).
9. Will (1986).
10. The awards include the National Television Reporting Award and the gold baton from the Alfred I. duPont–Columbia University committee for the

greatest contribution to the public's understanding of important issues or news events (Belkin 1987).

11. Landsberg (1986).

12. See Moynihan (1965).

13. See Ellwood and Jencks (2002, figs. 5, 6).

14. See Martin, Hamilton, and Sutton (2010, 8). These trends wouldn't spark the same degree of concern if unwed partnerships were as stable as marriages. Though half of unwed parents are living together at the time their children are born and 80 percent say they are romantically involved, such relationships are exceedingly fragile—far more so than marital ties (McLanahan 2011). By age five, only about a third (34 percent) of those born outside of a marital union will still share a household with their dad, while 85 percent of children born to marital unions will do so (Manning, Smock, and Majumdar 2004).

15. Figures for college-educated women are 2 percent for non-Hispanic whites, 26 percent for Hispanics, and 27 percent for non-Hispanic blacks. Corresponding figures for high school dropouts are 62 percent for whites, 50 percent for Hispanics, and 87 percent for blacks (unpublished calculations performed by Kelly Musick, 2012). Manning, Smock, and Majumdar (2004) show that by age five, the odds of disruption are 14 percent for white, 16 percent for Hispanic, and 25 percent for black children.

16. There are important exceptions to this generalization. Two demonstration projects, one conducted by Public Private Ventures and the other by the Manpower Research Demonstration Corporation, were quite revealing. See Achatz and MacAllum (1994) and Furstenberg, Sherwood, and Sullivan (1992). Excellent recent qualitative studies on the subject portray black inner-city fathers as caring parents desiring involvement with their progeny. See Hamer (2001), Waller (2002), and Young (2004).

17. Some of the earliest statistical portraits of these men appear in a volume by Lerman and Ooms (1993).

18. See Hofferth et al. (2002).

19. Our fieldwork began in 1995; we lived in East Camden for two and a half years. We concluded our interviews in 2002. Between 2002 and 2012 we conducted multiple follow-up visits to each of the neighborhoods in the study.

20. Historical data on Camden is from Phil Cohen's website (2012).

21. See Gillette (2005, 30, 56).

22. See Dorwart (2001).

23. See Gillette (2005, 43).

24. Ibid., 48.

25. Ibid., 84–86.

26. Winker (2007).

27. Gillette (2005, chap. 3).

28. Median income has grown somewhat since 1999, while public assistance receipt has declined. According to the 2000 census, median income in 1999 was just over twenty-three thousand dollars, and 16 percent of households received public assistance. Poverty, however, has increased among families with children: the percentage of families below poverty level was 33 percent citywide, while 39 percent of households with children under eighteen were in poverty, along with 52 percent of single mothers. See U.S. Census Bureau (2012).

29. See Ventura and Bachrach (2000, table 4).

30. The Kensington and Fishtown sections of Greater Kensington lie to the northeast of Center City Philadelphia and are predominantly white. Pennsport and Manayunk are also white and, while gentrifying, have suffered the effect of decades of deindustrialization and still contain some of the more economically struggling white families in the city. The neighborhoods west of Kensington Avenue contain most of Philadelphia's Puerto Ricans, along with a sizable number of poor African Americans. Just to the west, the neighborhoods of North Central and Strawberry Mansion are overwhelmingly black. West Philadelphia offers a number of poor black neighborhoods to study; we chose Mantua and Mill Creek, just north of the University of Pennsylvania, and Kingsessing, which lies southwest of University City. Finally, we incorporated the South Philadelphia neighborhoods of Point Breeze, which is almost all black, and Grays Ferry, which still has white working-class holdouts but is in the process of rapid racial turnover.

31. Of Philadelphia's roughly 567,000 households, just under 45,000 claimed SSI and 42,000 got cash welfare benefits in the prior year, while 90,000 received Food Stamps.

32. These figures are for 2008–10. See U.S. Census Bureau (2012).

33. "Local Area Unemployment Statistics" (2012).

34. See Bishaw and Semega (2008).

35. Shelley (2012).

36. Due to language difficulties (very few of the Hispanic men we encountered spoke English fluently, and neither of us speak Spanish) and limited funds, we chose not to interview Puerto Rican fathers for this study.

37. We targeted neighborhoods that were at least 20 percent poor in 2000.

38. For a description of this method, see Edin and Lein (1997) and Duneier (2011).

39. Two of our interviewers were African American and the rest were Caucasian. We used both men and women as interviewers.

40. See Edin and Kefalas (2005).

41. See Murray (2012).


## CHAPTER ONE. ONE THING LEADS TO ANOTHER

1. All names are pseudonyms, often chosen by the respondent. Street names, addresses, places of employment, and other potentially identifying details have been changed to protect confidentiality, but we have substituted streets, addresses, and employers in the same neighborhoods and with similar characteristics. For ease of reading, we have not shown ellipses or bracketed interpolations in our respondents' quotes. Quotes with ellipses and brackets intact can be viewed on the University of California Press website (www. ucpress.edu/book.php?isbn=9780520274068).

2. The Absalom Jones disciplinary school is a pseudonym.

3. Other qualitative research on teens navigating troubled neighborhoods argues that boys exhibit more risky behavior because their patterns of leisure offer greater exposure to the immediate neighborhood (Clampet-Lundquist et al. 2011) and to older peers (Harding 2009).

4. "Strawberry Mansion Neighborhood" (2011).

5. See Edin and Kefalas (2005). From 2006 to 2010, 86 percent of female teens and 93 percent of their male counterparts reported using contraceptives—condoms are by far the most common—at last sex. In the same period one in five sexually active girls (20 percent) and a third of sexually active boys (34 percent) reported that they used both a condom and a hormonal method of birth control the last time they had sex (Martinez, Copen, and Abma 2011).

6. We know of no survey data that assess the context of parental relationships at conception other than whether the couple is married at the time. But the four-year in-depth qualitative study of a subsample of unmarried Fragile Families survey couples offers some information in this regard (Edin et al. 2007). In wave one of the study, interviewers asked detailed questions about the nature of the relationship prior to the focal child's birth. They devoted much of the fourth-wave interview, which occurred in 2004, to asking parents about the circumstances surrounding the conception of *all* their children, including those conceived with other partners and those occurring before and after the focal

child's. They also queried parents about miscarriages and abortions and the circumstances surrounding these conceptions. Parents who stayed in the study through the fourth wave—70 percent—reported 202 pregnancies. The mothers in the study said that only one in five conceptions was in the context of a casual relationship (where the couple is not clearly "together"), while for fathers, the figure was about one in three (34 percent). Another 17 percent of mothers' conceptions—and 11 percent of fathers'—were within stable relationships, but the couple was struggling. The remaining pregnancies—64 percent (nearly two-thirds) of mothers' and 55 percent of fathers'—occurred in stable relationships. A closer look at the texture of these relationships, revealed through qualitative analysis of these parents' relationship narratives, shows that the nature and quality of these "stable" relationships prior to the couple's *first* conception together are often quite similar to Amin's. In other words, they are neither casual nor serious from the father's point of view. Mothers are more likely to view these relationships as serious than fathers are.

7. "Kensington Neighborhood" (2001).

8. The corner of Hagert and Jasper and the intersection of Emerald are both now occupied by Cavco, a company manufacturing vinyl windows and steel doors; William Beatty's Mills has been converted into spaces for income-qualified artists; and the Weisbrod and Hess Brewery is now the Philadelphia Brewing Company.

9. "Kensington Neighborhood" (2001).

10. The area's Hispanics and Asians who are practicing Catholics typically worship at Visitation of the Blessed Virgin Mary, just across Kensington Avenue in West Kensington. This area has seen its other large parishes close; Saint Edward the Confessor, Saint Bonaventure, and Saint Bonafice closed in 2006.

11. Test scores are available at the U.S. News education website (2012). Kensington High is now divided into several small schools, all of which qualify among the worst schools in the city in on-time graduation rates. See "On-Time Graduation Rate" (2010). Overall, students in the Kensington neighborhood are among the most likely to drop out in the city. See Neild and Balfanz (2006).

12. This is a common pattern in our data; an early unplanned pregnancy is terminated, but then closely followed by a pregnancy taken to term. We do not know for sure why this is so, but our best guess is that this is a reflection of the strong underlying desire to have a child, even when the circumstances are not ideal.

13. See also Roy, Buckmiller, and McDowell (2008).

14. For data on hooking up, especially on college campuses, see Bogle (2008); England, Shafer, and Fogarty (2008); Glenn and Marquardt (2001); Hamilton and Armstrong (2009); and Manning, Giordano, and Longmore (2006).

15. See also Hamer (2001, 94).

16. Other researchers have also noted the use of these terms. One in-depth assessment of their meaning comes from Allen's (2009) ethnography of a mixed-income housing development in Chicago.

17. Hanging out on the stoop, an occasional outing to a bar or a club, a window-shopping trip to a hot venue such as the Gallery in Center City or the popular South Street strip, and fantasizing about shared children are what usually constitute romance. See also Edin and Kefalas (2005).

18. How typical are the men we talked to of other disadvantaged young fathers living in urban areas across the United States? Most surveys tell us little about the relationship contexts of unmarried men at the time a child is conceived. One exception is the Fragile Families and Child Wellbeing Study, a survey of about four thousand unmarried couples who had a child between 1998 and 2000. This survey, nationally representative of births in large cities, asks all unmarried new mothers and fathers—not just low-income couples in high-poverty neighborhoods like ours—how long they had known each other before the birth. The typical young unmarried couple knew each other for less than a year before their first child was conceived. This figure is for mothers giving birth before age twenty-five. For those mothers twenty-five and older, the average is much longer, 2.4 years. Most disadvantaged men, however, bear their first child with a partner who is under twenty-five (Edin and Tach 2011).

Researchers then conducted in-depth intensive interviews with forty-eight of the unmarried couples in the Fragile Families survey about two to three months after their child was born. These researchers asked the new parents a slightly different question: rather than query them about how long they had known each other prior to conception, they asked how long they had been "together." Here, the modal length of courtship prior to a conception was only six or seven months (Edin, Nelson, and Reed 2011). See also Reed (2008). Finally, in-depth interviews with 165 unmarried mothers in eight low-income Philadelphia-area neighborhoods, conducted at about the same time as we were talking with fathers, also put the median length of the relationship at about half a year (Edin and Kefalas 2005). These studies suggest that the rapid pace with which courtship leads to conception and birth for the men in our study is not unusual.

19. See Augustine, Nelson, and Edin (2009); Edin et al. (2007); Reed (2007); and Roy, Buckmiller, and McDowell (2008).

20. See also Edin and Kefalas (2005); Edin et al. (2007); and Augustine, Nelson, and Edin (2009).

21. See also Davis, Gardner, and Gardner (1941, 127).

22. Men and women in these neighborhoods do not always view their relationships in the same light. For example, in in-depth interviews with a sub-sample of Fragile Families couples, both mothers and fathers were queried about the state of their relationships at the time of each conception, and mothers were far less likely (34 versus 20 percent) to characterize them as "casual" (Edin et al. 2007). When Edin and Kefalas (2005) asked low-income unmarried mothers living in these same Philadelphia-area neighborhoods how they would describe their relationships with their children's fathers, they were also less likely to view them as casual than fathers. The large majority of respondents across all these studies, however, did not characterize their relationships at the time of conception as casual but said they were something more.

23. Byron does not say what this illness was, but notes that his father had been sick for several years before his death.

24. Edin and Tach (2011).

25. "Fairhill Neighborhood" (2011).

26. See Harknett and Knab (2007).

27. The Fragile Families study—the survey of nonmarital births to couples living in large cities—offers additional support for the idea that an unmarried couple's relationship is often galvanized by pregnancy. First, the survey reveals a surprisingly high rate of couple cohesion at the time of a typical nonmarital birth—more than 80 percent of mothers (and even a higher percentage of fathers) say they are "romantically involved" with their child's other parent, and eight in ten fathers think there is at least a fifty-fifty chance they'll marry the mother of their child (the mothers usually agree with this prediction). Roughly six in ten couples giving birth outside of marriage cohabit at some point between the time of conception and the child's first birthday—some of these couples live together before conception, but a good number of them enter cohabitation "shotgun," yet arrangements such as these are usually a strong signal that the couple has some desire to stay together and parent their child cooperatively (Bendheim-Thoman Center 2002b).

28. David is referring to his daughters who visit occasionally as well as to Julian.

29. See the Bendheim-Thoman Center for Research on Child Wellbeing (2007).

## CHAPTER TWO. THANK YOU, JESUS

1. The results of a qualitative study of forty-seven young unwed fathers participating in a child-support demonstration project in the early 1990s bear some similarity to our own; however, more of their respondents reacted negatively to the news, perhaps because the sample was exclusively made up of fathers under twenty-five (Achatz and MacAllum 1994). The Fragile Families survey does ask mothers whether the birth was intended, but as we show, happiness and planned pregnancies are hardly synonymous.

But there is some evidence that offers a guide to how typical our fathers' responses might be. The in-depth four-year study of forty-eight unmarried couples from the Fragile Families survey we mentioned in the notes to chapter 1 asked both the child's mother and father to describe the circumstances surrounding each conception they could recall, including those ending in termination or miscarriage. For each new child that was conceived, they asked how the respondent had reacted to the news of the pregnancy. Strikingly, an equal proportion of fathers' conceptions in this study—75 percent—were greeted with a happy response or a somewhat ambivalent but accepting response. Ironically, the mothers said that they reacted to the news of a conception positively only 58 percent of the time (Edin et al. 2007). Both this study and ours have limitations: the in-depth interviews of forty-eight couples did not include fathers who were not romantically involved with the mother at the time of the birth—this probably excluded nearly one in five fathers (83 percent of mothers in the Fragile Families survey claimed romantic involvement when the baby was born)—and uninvolved fathers are presumably the least likely to respond positively.

It may also be true that the recruitment strategies we deployed in Camden and Philadelphia missed those men for whom fatherhood was least salient, though, as we show in chapter 6, our rates of father involvement by child age are only slightly higher than those reported by mothers in the Fragile Families survey and about as high as fathers' reports. Even given these drawbacks, the in-depth study of the forty-eight Fragile Families couples and our study both suggest that a significant proportion of disadvantaged unmarried men might well greet the news of a pregnancy with some level of expectancy.

2. See also Fosse (2010).

3. Men who said they expressed ambivalence were typically very young, had no source of income, were struggling with an alcohol or drug problem, or had relationship "complications." But men with happy responses had these problems too.

4. One might wonder about the retrospective nature of these accounts. These characterizations of pregnancy reaction, however, are nearly identical to those captured by the in-depth qualitative study of forty-eight unmarried fathers in three cities—a subsample of the Fragile Families and Child Wellbeing Study. As noted above, these men were first interviewed, and asked this question, two to three months after their child's birth and report a preponderance of happy responses. See Edin et al. (2007).

5. Edin and Kefalas (2005) find that mothers living in these same neighborhoods agree with these characterizations of pregnancy intentionality, though more men place pregnancies in the "just not thinking" group and fewer men describe their pregnancies as "semiplanned" when compared to women. A similar gender divide was also documented by Edin et al. (2007).

Men's circumstances play some role in the degree to which pregnancies are planned. Typically, men who planned a child were somewhat more likely than those with a semiplanned pregnancy to have been stably housed and employed and to have established a somewhat stronger bond with their partner. Conversely, some of the men who were "just not thinking" about the possibility of conception, or had an accidental pregnancy, were also more ambivalent about the suitability of their circumstances for raising a child. Some were only seasonally employed or feared an imminent layoff or job loss. Others were struggling to overcome drug or alcohol problems or had been relying on drug sales or other criminal activity to get by.

There is some evidence that fathers' pregnancy intentions might affect their fathering behavior. In one analysis using the Early Child Longitudinal Study-Birth Cohort study, men who did not want the pregnancy are less likely to exhibit paternal warmth following the birth, whereas men who wanted the pregnancy sooner than it occurred are more likely to exhibit nurturing behaviors (Bronte-Tinkew et al. 2007).

6. In both our study and in another that assessed men's responses in regard to the degree that a given conception was intended, planned pregnancies were more common among subsequent conceptions with the same partner (Edin et al. 2007).

7. "Oral Contraceptives" (2003).

8. These conceptions are underreported, both in this study and in surveys, either because the fathers did not know about the pregnancy or because the

pregnancy is made less salient in fathers' minds, due to social stigma or some other factor, by the fact that it is not brought to term.

9. Thomas's second child was conceived while he and Laurie were on a one-week hiatus—a fallout over his cheating—around the time when their child, Gina, turned two. Thomas thought nothing of the one-night stand with his neighbor Nikki until nine months later while in jail awaiting trial on a charge of attempted homicide. "I got a letter from Nikki with a picture, and it said, 'This is your son.' That was a bomb. That was not planned at all." That news was also explosive for Laurie, and the beginning of the end of their relationship.

10. In the Fragile Families survey, nearly all unmarried fathers said they were planning on active involvement in their children's lives (Center for Research on Child Wellbeing 2007).

11. As we have shown, in a study of forty-eight fathers with a nonmarital birth in 2000, a subsample of fathers responding to the Fragile Families survey, the rate of "happy or accepting" responses was nearly identical to our own (see Edin et al. 2007). Their female partners' responses, however, were far less favorable (only just over half were "happy or accepting"). We know of no a priori reason why fathers should be subject to more social desirability bias than mothers.

12. Single mothers in these neighborhoods report similar sentiments (Edin and Kefalas 2005).

13. Frazier put the gym up for sale in 2009.

14. Lacey's narrative suggests he was guilty of this crime, a drug-related killing.

15. See Edin and Kefalas (2005).

16. See Colimore (1995b).

17. See Jennings and Lewis (1995).

18. See Rhor (1995a).

19. See John-Hall (1998).

20. See Jennings (1997).

21. See Jennings and Rhor (1996).

22. See Rhor (1995b).

23. See Colimore (1995a).


### CHAPTER THREE. THE STUPID SHIT

1. See the Bendheim-Thoman Center for Research on Child Wellbeing (2007).

2. For many fathers we spoke to, hope for reunion with their children's mothers is a common refrain, even after years of separation and other partners, particularly if their children's mothers are somewhat better off than they are.

3. For a couple-level analysis of breakups among unmarried parents that features the role of infidelity, see Hill (2007).

4. For a review of this literature, see McLanahan and Beck (2010).

5. See Edin and Kefalas (2005).

6. Here, we break with Liebow ([1967] 2003), who claims that the street-corner men he studied base their expectations of family life on the experiences of those around them. Our men, and the women in these neighborhoods (Edin and Kefalas 2005), are clearly far more optimistic about each other and about their future together than the experiences of others in the neighborhood would warrant. This is what social psychologists call "optimism bias." See Armor and Taylor (2002) and Weinstein (1980).

7. For further discussion of how couple tensions may be submerged during pregnancy, see Edin et al. (2007).

8. *Black Men: Obsolete, Single, Dangerous?* is the title of a work of African American literature by Haki Madhubuti (1991).

9. Similar to the period prior to pregnancy, straight talk between couples is rare at this stage, so each must ascribe meaning to the other's actions in absence of real communication—another instance of "don't ask, don't tell."

10. See Edin and Kefalas (2005).

11. See Gibson, Edin, and McLanahan (2005).

12. See Edin and Kefalas (2005).

13. These relationships are not necessarily causal. Waite and Gallagher (2000) compile an impressive array of associations between marriage and a wide array of positive outcomes for both men and women. Sampson, Laub, and Wimer (2006) use a unique data set and innovative methods to demonstrate a causal relationship between marriage and crime. Duncan, England, and Wilkerson (2006) do the same for men's binge drinking and drug use.

14. See Bianchi, Robinson, and Milkie (2006).

15. Paul, a thirty-four-year-old black father of a four-year-old child lives in a prison halfway house and is looking for a job. He believes that today's women seem eager to dispense with men altogether—all they want out of men is their sperm. He bemoans modern times, where women's incursions into the labor market make them more able to survive on their own, a condition he feels they are appallingly eager to capitalize on. "You have a lot of women that just want to have the baby and have no intention of staying with the man." Paul points

to advances in modern technology—sperm banks and test-tube babies—as proof of his assertions. "That is why these sperm banks is popping up everywhere, and these test-tube babies. Women believe that they don't need a man."

16. For a discussion of the impact that this ideology had in working-class men's notions of fatherhood a generation ago, see Townsend (2002).

17. See Furstenberg and Cherlin (1994, 118).

18. See Liebow ([1967] 2003, 89).

19. Hirschi (1969) was not the first to articulate this idea. In 1957, for example, Toby (1957) advanced the idea that youth delinquency could be explained by a low "stake in conformity." Hirschi has since moved away from control theory and points to self-control as a critical mechanism in explaining delinquency and crime. See Gottfredson and Hirschi (1990).

20. Attachment is the emotional element of the bond. Involvement is the level of participation in conventional activities—this is the active element. Beliefs involve worldviews—to what degree does an individual embrace the conventional values and norms? Commitment is the rational part—it involves decisions, not emotions. Hirschi's (1969) theory predicts that when these four types of bonds are strong, men will conform.

21. See Sampson and Laub (1993).

22. Attachment to the child may be strong, but strong attachments are effective because they carry sanctions—the attachment is something of value that one could lose. Because babies or even toddlers aren't aware of how their father behaves when he's out of the house, men have several years' leeway before they can do much to damage this bond—so long as they stay involved.

23. See also Edin and Kefalas (2005) and Gibson, Edin, and McLanahan (2005).

24. Such claims have a long history; the 1960s-era black street-corner men Elliot Liebow studied often said they had "too much dog" in them—they were just too manly—to live up to the norm of fidelity (Liebow [1967] 2003, 78).

25. One might assume that such men use multiple women for material gain. Though a few of our fathers say this, it is relatively rare. Edin and Lein (1997) show that women seldom have the resources to support men other than by offering them shelter and that most reject men who don't contribute, claiming "I can do bad by myself."

26. Convincing a woman to give over her phone number requires considerable game; in the courtship ritual that is endemic to neighborhoods like Boy Boy's West Kensington, women typically withhold their numbers and ask for the man's number instead, so they can assess whether he has the wherewithal to have a phone and whether somebody else—another woman—might answer it.

27. Anderson (1993, 77) has noted this dynamic as well. He writes, "When encountering a girl, the boy usually sees a challenge: he attempts to 'run his game.'" See also Jamie Fader's (forthcoming) ethnography of young men released from a juvenile detention facility. In one couple she followed, his proclivity to "talk to other girls" and record their numbers in his cell phone was a frequent source of conflict. In retaliation, his pregnant girlfriend threatened to move away and not give the baby his last name.

28. See Oppenheimer, Kalmijn, and Lim (1997).

29. Paul explains the pragmatic logic of this key criterion as follows: "The jobs that you are going to get is not going to be that good. So I really think that, say I am making eight dollars an hour, and she just sitting home and doing nothing. If she went out and got a job making eight dollars an hour, now we are looking at sixteen dollars [an] hour, and now we can base what we are going to do on that sixteen dollars instead of just that plain eight dollars."

30. Nathan Fosse's in-depth interviews with African American, low-income men in Boston highlight the special role of sexual mistrust. Few of his men thought a man could trust a woman to be faithful, and they felt that this justified their own infidelity. He writes, "nearly all respondents describe high levels of mistrust, viewing monogamous partners as an exception to the rule. Daily experiences of violence and betrayal lead to the expectation of infidelity in their partners, even as they engage in long-term heterosexual relationships" (2010, 137). Our men often harbor similar suspicions, and this is part of the reason why paternity denials are as high as they are (9 percent).

31. Furstenberg (2001) argues that marriage is a "fading dream" among inner-city residents. While it is true that marriage is becoming less common in this population, our evidence suggests that many still hold on to the dream.

32. On sources of dissolution among unmarried couples, see Tach and Edin (forthcoming); Osborne, Manning, and Smock (2007); and Lichter, Qian, and Mellott (2006). On the importance of economic factors on unmarried couples' transition to marriage, Carlson, McLanahan, and England (2004) found that men's employment encouraged marriage among unmarried parents one year after a child's birth. See also Gibson, Edin, and McLanahan (2005); Gibson-Davis (2007, 2009); Watson and McLanahan (2009); Smock and Manning (1997); and Smock, Manning, and Porter (2005).

33. A closer look at each of the stories we've featured—especially the stories of Amin, Donald, and Bill—suggests that in some cases, blaming their lack of commitment on a woman's flaws, namely her mercenary nature, may be little more than whitewash for their own significant shortcomings. Yet the

perception that women can't be trusted, which is an article of faith in many men's narratives, doesn't have to be true to influence their behavior.

34. See Bzostek, McLanahan, and Carlson (2012).

35. See Jones (2009, chap. 4).

36. See Edin and Kefalas (2005).

## CHAPTER FOUR. WARD CLEAVER

1. Another exception is when they feel that complying with the law and paying official support will put them in a better position to obtain or enforce visitation rights. See also Achatz and MacAllum (1994) and Furstenberg, Sherwood, and Sullivan (1992).

2. For an analysis of this dynamic among divorced couples, see Weiss and Willis (1993).

3. Men don't qualify for many types of government assistance because they don't often have custody of their children. Custodial parents who meet income guidelines are eligible for housing subsidies, short-term cash welfare, a generous Earned Income Tax Credit, and other benefits that lower their living costs or subsidize their incomes. Poor men without custodial children are sometimes eligible for modest short-term cash benefits from welfare, plus in-kind benefits such as food stamps. If they work, they are also eligible for a very small Earned Income Tax Credit.

4. Furstenberg, Sherwood, and Sullivan (1992, 50) discuss how the challenges of forming a new family can interfere with financial support of children from past relationships.

5. Liebow ([1967] 2003); see also Rainwater (1970, 186–87).

6. Even after breakups men often try to maintain these bonds, but the mother often sees little sense in promoting an ongoing tie to a man who is not her child's biological father, especially if a new partner, who also seeks to play daddy, comes along.

7. Rainwater (1970).

8. Mothers sometimes report that they splurge for these extras as well, in part because they are trying to demonstrate to the community at large that they are good parents. See Edin and Kefalas (2005).

9. This dynamic was evident in Rainwater's (1970, 313) study of life in a federal housing project among young men who had births outside of marriage.

10. This abridged sense of financial responsibility, despite lip service to a fifty-fifty ideal, is also discussed by Furstenberg, Sherwood, and Sullivan (1992).

11.  Edin and Kefalas (2005).

12.  See Waller (2002) and Hamer (2001). See also Waller (2010); Jarrett, Roy, and Burton (2002); and Furstenberg, Sherwood, and Sullivan (1992).


## CHAPTER FIVE. *SESAME STREET* MORNINGS

1.  These days the school ranks near the bottom of all the high schools in the entire state (630 out of 639), and only a handful of its students test as proficient in reading, or science, or math. See "Bartram John" (2010).

2.  These data come from the Philadelphia Neighborhood Information System Crime Base (2012).

3.  Brandywine School is a pseudonym.

4.  Ernest says, "My mother has supported me from the time I was born to now. When I was down and out, man, when I was at my lowest point, my mother was there. When I was in jail, there was only one person that would accept my collect calls, my mother. There was only one person that sent me money orders, my mother. You know what I mean? My mother is just tremendous."

5.  Participants in the Parent's Fair Share child-support demonstration used these terms differently (Johnson, Levine, and Doolittle 1999). "Daddy" referred to the expressive aspects of the parental role while "father" referred to the more instrumental aspects.

6.  On the difference between "fathers" and "daddies," see also Furstenberg, Sherwood, and Sullivan (1992).

7.  See Parke (1996).

8.  Waller (2002). This is a clear break from Liebow's famous argument that it is lack of money that drives fathers away from their children (Liebow [1967] 2003). This made sense in Liebow's day when fathering equaled providing; clearly times have changed.

9.  Erikson (1959).

10.  For excellent reviews of the literature that calls for expanding scholarly conceptions of father involvement to include generative components, see Hawkins and Palkovitz (1999) and Snarey (1993, 1997).


## CHAPTER SIX. FIGHT OR FLIGHT

1.  Both of these schools have since closed.

2.  Sampson and Laub (1993).

3. "Bullwork" is a slang term for hard manual labor.

4. Ritchie suspects that Kate had become addicted to drugs and was trying to regain her sobriety during this time.

5. For patterns of visitation among formerly married fathers, see Cheadle, Amato, and King (2010).

6. This is due in part to a sharp falloff in the percentage of fathers who remain in a romantic relationship with the mother (Edin, Tach, and Mincy 2009). For estimates of levels of father involvement over time by union status using both mothers' and fathers' reports, see McClain and DeMaris (2011).

7. See McClain and DeMaris (2011) for figures over time.

8. See Carlson, McLanahan, and Brooks-Gunn (2005); Lerman and Sorensen (2000); Sorensen and Hill (2004); and Yeung et al. (2001). But our black men are somewhat more connected and our white fathers somewhat less connected than mothers' reports in the Fragile Families survey shows, likely because our white fathers are more disadvantaged than the white portion of the Fragile Families and Child Wellbeing sample. See table 6 in the appendix for a comparison of mother's reports in the Fragile Families survey compared to those of the fathers in our study. Unlike the Fragile Families survey, we limited our sample to men whose earnings in the prior year were less than the poverty rate for a family of four.

9. Coley and Morris (2002), McClain and DeMaris (2011), and Mikelson (2008) have all noted the discrepancy in mothers' and fathers' reports of involvement. McClain and DeMaris (2011) estimate that for men with our sample characteristics, the discrepancy ranges from a third of a day to two-thirds of a day per week.

10. A small portion (8 percent) seemed to be hampered not so much by external circumstances but simply by a lack of desire to stay involved.

11. Even fathers' supportiveness during pregnancy exerts a long-term influence on whether fathers remain engaged (Cabrera, Fagan, and Farrie 2008) or stay in a coresidential relationship with their children's mother (Shannon et al. 2009). There is also a long-term link between father residence during early childhood and the quality of the father-child relationship in the fifth grade. Father-child relationship quality is in turn directly linked to children's social adjustment but not to their behavioral problems or peer relationships (Cabrera et al. forthcoming).

12. See Tach, Mincy, and Edin (2010) for data on the falloff in father involvement following the mother forming a new partnership.

13. See Hill (2007) for a discussion of sexual mistrust and infidelity with past partners.

14. Note that Katrina's new man had already lost the connection to his own children from prior relationships. This is not uncommon for low-income, inner-city men who take on the father role for another man's child (Claessens 2007).

15. Ironically, despite men's attempts to reject the old-fashioned package deal, it gets enacted nonetheless because of the critical role their relationship with the mother plays in ensuring they have access to their children.

16. Edin and Kefalas (2005) find that mothers use restraining orders with surprising frequency to keep fathers away. Sometimes this is because the father poses serious risks to her or the child. At other times, though, retaliation is the main motive.

17. One paper utilizing the Fragile Families and Child Wellbeing Study finds that fathers with temperamentally difficult children are less involved than fathers with easier children (Lewin-Bizan 2006).

18. Center for Research on Child Wellbeing (2007). This figure is based on mothers' reports. Fathers' reports put the figure higher, but fewer of them are interviewed.

### CHAPTER SEVEN. TRY, TRY AGAIN

1. Morris (2009).

2. The mother is Marty's age, and the two had used drugs together in the past.

3. The mothers' story has been told elsewhere. See Edin and Kefalas (2005), Stack (1974), Ladner ([1971]1995), and Bell-Kaplan (1997).

4. Tach, Edin, and McLanahan, 2011.

5. David had witnessed all five of his children's births.

6. Jamie Fader's (forthcoming) ethnography of young men in Philadelphia who had been released from a juvenile detention facility included one respondent, Sincere, who said that he longed for a "mini-me, a part of me that's never been bad."

7. Another of Fader's (forthcoming) respondents, James, said the following of fatherhood: "You have to leave your mark on this earth."

8. See Cherlin (2009a).

9. See Carlson and Furstenberg (2006); Meyer, Cancian, and Cook (2005); and Tach, Edin, and McLanahan (2011).

10. See Tach, Edin, and McLanahan (2011). For international comparisons, see Andersson (2002).

11. Lerman and Sorensen (2000) included men who had a nonmarital birth but had then married the mother of that child as well as those who did not marry her (see table 8 in the appendix). Our sampling strategy excluded men currently married to their children's mothers. When we recalculated Lerman and Sorensen's figures to also exclude such men, we still found relatively high rates of involvement. For men in their late twenties and to their midthirties, 53 percent see at least one of their children at least once a week—while nearly two-thirds (65 percent) report visiting one of their nonmarital children at least monthly. And these figures leave out those men who are playing the father role for children who are not their own—quite a common occurrence among men in our sample. In short, while not all fathers are engaged with their children on a regular basis, most are (see table 9 in the appendix).

12. One analysis reports that annual visitation among men whose children were living with never-married mothers shows an increase from thirty-three to forty-nine days between 1987 and 1997. See Huang (2006).

13. See Tach, Edin, and McLanahan (2011).

14. See Tach, Mincy, and Edin (2010).

15. This shared experience makes it especially remarkable that Kelly is referred to only as a "friend."

16. The women in these neighborhoods have a parallel, though not identical, story to tell. For generations women have had to barter their charm and other assets for economic security through marriage. And in past generations women often married up—they married men with better education and higher earnings than theirs. Perhaps this is why women hold out more hope for marriage—they are waiting for the proverbial young guy in the nice car to come around. Meanwhile, there are the easy gets—the men they happen to have children with—who are seldom anything like the Mr. Right they were envisioning.

If our men are correct, and they might not be, the women in their lives are ready to walk away at any moment should the guy with the nice car suddenly appear. Women who do remain "on the market" while simultaneously trying to forge a relationship with their children's dad—what men sometimes refer to as "gaming"—can still claim the virtue of fidelity, but there is a hint of mental cheating here, and men take strong exception to this. Men find it hard to shake the suspicion that they're being gamed, even in the best of their relationships.

1. See Bendheim-Thoman Center (2002a) and Sigle-Rushton and McLanahan (2002a, 2002b). Fathers' response rates are lower than mothers' are, leading to an upward bias in fathers' reports. When only mothers with a partner who was surveyed are considered, the levels of relationship optimism are about the same for men and women.

2. See Giddens (1993).

3. In 2007 *Time* magazine ranked *Leave It to Beaver* as one of the hundred best TV shows of all time. See Poniewozik (2007).

4. Though average levels of father involvement decline as children age, fathers typically stay at one end of the father-involvement continuum or another over time with a given child (Ryan, Kalil, and Ziol-Guest 2008). This analysis does not assess, however, the degree of continuity in a father's behavior across children.

5. See Lerman and Sorensen (2000).

6. See Gans ([1962] 1982) and Liebow ([1967] 2003).

7. See Rainwater (1970, 156) and Liebow ([1967] 2003, 89).

8. Edin and Kefalas (2005).

9. See Wilcox (2010, fig. 19 on p. 48).

10. See Cherlin (1978, 2004). Scholars have extended the deinstitutionalization metaphor to describe other new family forms such as cohabitation. See Nock (1995) and Brown and Manning (2009).

11. See Blankenhorn (1995, 134–35).

12. See Mincy, Garfinkel, and Nepomnyaschy (2005). Nearly seven in ten nonmarital children had a legal father by 2000 and six in seven paternities are established in the hospital when the father voluntarily claims responsibility for the child (ibid.).

13. Mignon Moore's (2011) study of black working-class lesbian couples with children also shows that a power imbalance ensues when one partner gave birth to the children in the household and the other did not. The former demands, and is granted, more decision-making power in the domestic sphere (see chapters 4 and 5).

14. See Martin, Hamilton, and Ventura (2011, 8).

15. Edin and Kefalas (2005) have written about this battle between the sexes from a woman's point of view.

16. For example, the Bradley Amendment prohibits retroactive modifications of child-support orders or forgiveness of arrears even for men whose nonpayment

is due to incarceration or unemployment. Recall that this amendment was part of that late 1980s crackdown on deadbeat dads that occurred after Bill Moyers's *The Vanishing Family* TV special was aired in May 1986. Thus, along with the public outcry and success of the broadcast, there was also targeted congressional action.

17. For an appraisal of how family law has changed in light of the huge changes in family structure and American attitudes toward alternative family forms, see Cherlin (forthcoming).

18. See Griswold (1993) and Mintz and Kellogg (1988).

19. Dimitri and Effland (2005).

20. For an excellent history of low-skilled men's work in Philadelphia, see Licht (1992).

21. Americans now work more hours than anyone else in the industrialized world except for South Koreans. See Fleck (2009, table A-1).

22. Martina Morris and Bruce Western (1999) offer an excellent review of the sources for the increase in earnings inequality in the United States. They argue that shifts in labor supply cannot explain declining pay for non–college workers. On the demand side, they write that "the penalty for not having a college degree has risen dramatically. While some have taken this as evidence of a technology-driven shift in demand for higher skilled workers, workplace studies suggest that the impact of technological change may be polarizing rather than simple upskilling. Demand was clearly restructured during this period, however, through both deindustrialization and the return to market-mediated employment relations. The empirical findings regarding the impact of this economic restructuring on inequality are mixed, but the complexity of the measurement issues here plays a greater role in obscuring the view. National labor market institutions, in particular unions and the minimum wage, have also had an impact. While institutions are among the most contested explanatory factors for labor economists, they enjoy some of the most consistent support in the evidence. All of these dynamics, finally, are subject to the pressures of 'globalization,' as the flows of capital, goods, and people across national boundaries modify the effective supply of and demand for specific kinds of labor, the resulting strength of traditional labor organizations, and the role of the monetary system in national politics."

23. See Graefe and Lichter (2008).

24. See Ellwood and Jencks (2002) and Martin (2005).

25. Greenstone and Looney (2012).

26. Edin and Kefalas (2005) review this literature in chapter 7 of their book and argue that both cultural and structural factors must be considered in any attempt to explain changes in family composition. See also Cherlin (2004).

27. See Murray (2012, chap. 8). For a discussion of why behaviors might be different than espoused norms in the lower class, see Rodman (1963).

28. See Edin and Kefalas (2005, 202).

29. See Ehrenreich (1983).

30. We will not attempt to chronicle the reasons for the rise here—other scholars have already covered this ground. For examples, see Goldin and Katz (2002), Mincer (1962), Neumark and Postlewaite (1998), and Smith and Ward (1985).

31. See Griswold (1993, chap. 11). Wilcox (2004) finds that conservative evangelical Christians and, to a lesser extent, mainline Christians, are especially likely to practice "new fatherhood," when compared with religiously unaffiliated peers.

32. See Bianchi, Robinson, and Milkie (2006). Women also increased their time spent in caring for and interacting with their children—it doubled in this period. But the amount of time American men are spending in households with children has declined rather markedly as well. Some form of selection is clearly at work: presumably, those who find family life the most congenial are engaging with their children perhaps as never before, while those who do not find it appealing leave the family or avoid fatherhood altogether (ibid.).

33. College-educated men's wives brought in a median 26 percent of the household income (Taylor et al. 2010).

34. See Lee and Waite (2005) and Fisher et al. (2007).

35. We can only speculate how these new cultural notions of fatherhood were transmitted across the classes. But it's not hard to imagine how the dads at the bottom of the class distribution came across the new-father ideal. For quite some time now, through favorite family television shows from the *Brady Bunch* (which first aired in 1969) to the *Cosby Show* (debuting in the mid-1980s), new-father images have permeated popular media.

36. See Licht (2012).

37. In the past three decades alone (from 1979 to 2007) employment to population ratios for white male high school dropouts have declined by 10 percent nationwide, and for those who have jobs real wages have fallen by 16 percent (see Autor 2010, fig. 8b and app. fig. 1b).

38. Robert L. Griswold (1993, chap. 11) also points to the therapeutic culture that has arisen around new fatherhood.

39. In terms of child development, "very little about the gender of the parent seems distinctly important" (Lamb 2010, 5).

40. This insight is not ours alone. See Waller (2002) and Hamer (2001).

41. See Sampson and Laub (1993).

42. See Edin and Kefalas (2005).

43. Based on in-depth interviews with a diverse sample of American men, Gerson (1993, 224–25) describes how men deploy the "mother's helper" strategy to avoid the "dirty work" of parenting while embracing the roles of playmate and friend. Cherlin (2009b) uses the similar term "kindly uncle" to describe the role of stepfathers in their stepchildren's lives. Like our portrayal, Liebow ([1967] 2003, 45) also depicts unwed fathers in his 1960s study playing the "favorite uncle" role and taking on little financial responsibility.

44. It seems plausible that the wish to experience fatherhood reduces the desire to prevent unplanned conceptions as men move from one relationship to another (and remember that it is *prevention* that requires intentional behavior) and may thus be a primary force behind multiple partner fertility—a family-go-round that puts children on a dizzying father-go-round that is almost surely deleterious to their well-being. It is certainly true that the ability to accomplish "good fatherhood" through selective, serial parenting is predicated on having children by multiple partners and reduces the cost of having children for fathers as long as they can evade the child support system.

45. See Tach, Edin, and McLanahan (2011).

46. Two studies (Fomby and Cherlin 2007; Osborne and McLanahan 2007) found that the greater the number of transitions that parents had in and out of coresidential unions and, in the second study, romantic relationships of significant duration, the more behavior problems their children displayed. Cavanagh and Huston (2006) showed that more parental transitions lowered children's competency in interacting with peers at school.

47. See Grall (2009, table 4).

48. See Wood, Moore, and Clarkwest (2011).

49. See Berlin (2007).

# REFERENCES

Achatz, Mary, and Crystal MacAllum. 1994. *Young Unwed Fathers: A Report from the Field*. Philadelphia: Public Private Ventures.

Allen, Tennille. 2009. "What About Your Friends? Social Networks in a Mixed-Income Housing Development." PhD diss., Northwestern University.

Anderson, Elijah. 1990. *Streetwise: Race, Class and Change in an Urban Community*. Chicago: University of Chicago Press.

———. 1993. "Sex Codes and Family Life among Poor Inner-City Youths." In Lerman and Ooms 1993, 74–98.

Andersson, Gunnar. 2002. "Children's Experience of Family Disruption and Family Formation: Evidence from 16 FFS Countries." *Demographic Research* 7 (7): 343–64.

Armor, David A., and Shelley E. Taylor. 2002. "When Predictions Fail: The Dilemma of Unrealistic Optimism." In *Heuristics and Biases: The Psychology of Intuitive Judgment*, edited by Thomas Gilovich, Dale Griffin, and Daniel Kahneman, 334–47. Cambridge: Cambridge University Press.

Augustine, Jennifer March, Timothy Nelson, and Kathryn Edin. 2009. "Low-Income Non-custodial Men's Role in Fertility Decisions." *Annals of the American Academy of Political and Social Science* 624 (1): 99–117.

Autor, David. 2010. *The Polarization of Job Opportunities in the U.S. Labor Market: Implications for Employment and Earnings*. Hamilton Project. Washington, DC: Brookings Institution / Cambridge, MA: Center for American Progress, MIT.

"Bartram John: Main School." 2012. LocalSchoolDirectory.com. Accessed October 5. http://www.localschooldirectory.com/public-school/73854/PA.

Belkin, Lisa. 1987. "Moyers Wins a Top Prize in Broadcast Journalism." *New York Times,* March 5.

Bell-Kaplan, Elaine. 1997. *Not Our Kind of Girl: Unraveling the Myths of Black Teenage Motherhood.* Berkeley: University of California Press.

Bendheim-Thoman Center for Research on Child Wellbeing. 2002a. "Is Marriage a Viable Alternative for Fragile Families?" Fragile Families Research Brief 9, Princeton University, NJ / Social Indicators Survey Center, Columbia University, NY.

―――. 2002b. "The Living Arrangements of New Unmarried Mothers." Fragile Families Research Brief Number 7, Princeton University, NJ.

―――. 2007. "Parents' Relationship Status Five Years after a Nonmarital Birth." Fragile Families Research Brief Number 39, Princeton University, NJ.

Bennett, William. 2001. *The Broken Hearth: Reversing the Moral Collapse of the American Family.* New York: Random House.

Berlin, Gordon. 2007. "Rewarding the Work of Individuals: A Counterintuitive Approach to Reducing Poverty and Strengthening Families." *Future of Children* 17 (2): 17–42.

Bianchi, Suzanne M., John P. Robinson, and Melissa A. Milkie. 2006. *Changing Rhythms of American Family Life.* New York: Russell Sage Foundation.

Bishaw, Alemayehu, and Jessica Semega. 2008. *Income, Earnings, and Poverty Data from the 2007 American Community Survey.* U.S. Census Bureau, American Community Survey Reports, ACS-09. Washington, DC: U.S. Government Printing Office.

Blankenhorn, David. 1995. *Fatherless America: Confronting Our Most Urgent Social Problem.* New York: Harper Perennial.

Bogle, Kathleen A. 2008. *Hooking Up: Sex, Dating, and Relationships on Campus.* New York: New York University Press.

Bronte-Tinkew, Jacinta, Suzanne Ryan, Jennifer Carrano, and Kristin A. Moore. 2007. "Resident Fathers' Pregnancy Intentions, Prenatal Behaviors, and Links to Involvement with Infants." *Journal of Marriage and Family* 69 (4): 977–90.

Brown, Susan L., and Wendy D. Manning. 2009. "Family Boundary Ambiguity and the Measurement of Family Structure: The Significance of Cohabitation." *Demography* 46 (1): 85–101.

Bzostek, Sharon, Sara McLanahan, and Marcia J. Carlson. 2012. "Mothers Repartnering after a Nonmarital Birth." *Social Forces* 90 (3): 817–41.

Cabrera, Natasha, Gina A. Cook, Karen F. McFadden, and Robert Bradley. Forthcoming. "Father Residence and Father-Child Relationship

Quality: Peer Relationships and Externalizing Behavioral Problems." Special issue, *Journal of Family Science.*

Cabrera, Natasha, Jay Fagan, and Danielle Farrie. 2008. "Explaining the Long Reach of Father's Prenatal Involvement on Later Paternal Engagement with Children." *Journal of Marriage and Family* 70 (5): 1094–107.

Carlson, Marcia J., and Frank F. Furstenberg Jr. 2006. "The Prevalence and Correlates of Multipartnered Fertility among Urban U.S. Parents." *Journal of Marriage and Family* 68 (3): 718–32.

Carlson, Marcia, Sara S. McLanahan, and Jeanne Brooks-Gunn. 2005. "Unmarried but Not Absent: Fathers' Involvement with Children after a Nonmarital Birth." Working Paper 2005–07-FF, Bendheim-Thoman Center for Research on Child Wellbeing, Princeton University, NJ.

Carlson, Marcia, Sara McLanahan, and Paula England. 2004. "Union Formation in Fragile Families." *Demography* 41 (2): 237–62.

Carmody, John. 1986. "Moyers Scores." *Washington Post,* February 4.

Cavanagh, Shannon E., and Aletha C. Huston. 2006. "Family Instability and Children's Early Problem Behavior." *Social Forces* 85 (1): 551–81.

Cheadle, Jacob E., Paul R. Amato, and Valarie King. 2010. "Patterns of Nonresident Father Contact." *Demography* 47 (1): 206–25.

Cherlin, Andrew J. 1978. "Remarriage as an Incomplete Institution." *American Journal of Sociology* 4 (3): 634–50.

———. 2004. "The Deinstitutionalization of American Marriage." *Journal of Marriage and Family* 66 (4): 848–61.

———. 2009a. *The Marriage-Go-Round: The State of Marriage and Family in America Today.* New York: Knopf.

———. 2009b. *Public and Private Families: An Introduction.* 6th ed. Columbus, OH: McGraw Hill.

———. Forthcoming. "The Growing Diversity of Two-Parent Families: Challenges for Family Law." In *Marriage at the Crossroads,* edited by Elizabeth Scott and Marsha Garrison. New York: Cambridge University Press.

Claessens, Amy. 2007. "Gatekeeper Moms and (Un)Involved Dads: What Happens after a Breakup?" In England and Edin 2009, 204–27.

Clampet-Lundquist, Susan, Jeffrey R. Kling, Kathryn Edin, and Greg J. Duncan. 2011. "Moving Teenagers Out of High Risk Neighborhoods: How Girls Fare Better than Boys." *American Journal of Sociology* 116 (4): 1154–89.

Cohen, Phil. 2012. "The Streets of Camden New Jersey." Accessed October 2. http:// www.dvrbs.com/camden-streets/CamdenNJ-Streets-Westfield Avenue.htm.

Cohen, Richard. 1986. "... And for Government Aid." *Washington Post,* January 26.

Coley, Rebekah Levine, and Jodi E. Morris. 2002. "Comparing Father and Mother Reports of Father Involvement among Low-Income Minority Families." *Journal of Marriage and Family* 64 (4): 982–97.

Colimore, Edward. 1995a. "Camden Teens: We Are Being Cheated Out of Life." *Philadelphia Inquirer,* November 22.

———. 1995b. "Couple's Service Draws More Than Family." *Philadelphia Inquirer,* January 6.

Corry, John. 1986. "CBS Report Examines Black Families." *New York Times,* January 28.

Cosby, Bill. 2004. "Bill Cosby's Address at the NAACP's Gala to Commemorate the 50th Anniversary of Brown v. Board of Education." May 17. American Rhetoric Online Speech Bank. http://www.americanrhetoric. com/speeches/billcosbypoundcakespeech.htm.

Davis, Allison, Burleigh Bradford Gardner, and Mary R. Gardner. 1941. *Deep South: A Social Anthropological Study of Caste and Class.* Chicago: University of Chicago Press.

Dimitri, Carolyn, Anne Effland, and Nielson Conklin. 2005. *The 20th Century Transformation of U.S. Agriculture and Farm Policy.* Electronic Information Bulletin Number 3. Washington, DC: U.S. Department of Agriculture.

Dorwart, Jeffrey. 2001. *Camden County, New Jersey: The Making of a Metropolitan Community, 1626–2000.* New Brunswick NJ: Rutgers University Press.

Duncan, Greg, Paula England, and Bessie Wilkerson. 2006. "Cleaning Up Their Act: The Effects of Marriage and Cohabitation on Licit and Illicit Drug Use." *Demography* 43 (4): 691–710.

Duneier, Mitch. 2011. "How Not to Lie with Ethnography." *Sociological Methodology* 49 (1): 1–11.

Edin, Kathryn, Paula England, Emily Fitzgibbons Shafer, and Joanna Reed. 2007. "Forming Fragile Families: Was the Baby Planned, Unplanned, or In Between?" In England and Edin 2009, 25–54.

Edin, Kathryn, and Maria Kefalas. 2005. *Promises I Can Keep: Why Poor Women Put Motherhood before Marriage.* Berkeley: University of California Press.

Edin, Kathryn, and Laura Lein. 1997. *Making Ends Meet: How Single Mothers Survive Welfare and Low-Wage Work.* New York: Russell Sage Foundation.

Edin, Kathryn, Timothy Nelson, and Joanna Miranda Reed. 2011. "Daddy, Baby; Momma Maybe: Low-Income Urban Fathers and the 'Package Deal' of Family Life." In England and Carlson 2011, 85–107.

Edin, Kathryn, and Laura Tach. 2011. "Becoming a Parent: The Social Contexts of Fertility during Young Adulthood." In *Early Adulthood in a Family Context,* edited by Alan Booth, Susan L. Brown, Nancy S. Landale, Wendy D. Manning, and Susan M. McHale, 185–208. Washington, DC: Urban Institute Press.

Edin, Kathryn, Laura Tach, and Ronald Mincy. 2009. "Claiming Fatherhood: Race and the Dynamics of Paternal Involvement among Unmarried Fathers." *Annals of the American Academy of Political and Social Science* 621 (1): 149–77.

Ehrenreich, Barbara. 1983. *The Hearts of Men: American Dreams and the Flight from Commitment.* Garden City, NY: Anchor/Doubleday.

Ellwood, David T., and Christopher Jencks. 2002. "The Spread of Single-Parent Families in the United States since 1960." Mimeo. Harvard Kennedy School of Government. Malcolm Wiener Inequality and Social Policy Seminar Series. Harvard University, Cambridge, MA. http://www.hks.harvard.edu /inequality/Seminar/Papers/ElwdJnck.pdf.

England, Paula, and Marcia Carlson, eds. 2011. *Social Class and Changing Families in an Unequal America.* Palo Alto: Stanford University Press.

England, Paula, and Kathryn Edin, eds. 2009. *Unmarried Couples with Children.* New York: Russell Sage Foundation.

England, Paula, Emily Fitzgibbon Shafer, and Alison C.K. Fogarty. 2008. "Hooking Up and Forming Romantic Relationships on Today's College Campuses." In *The Gendered Society Reader,* edited by Michael Kimmel and Amy Aronson, 531–47. New York: Oxford University Press.

Erikson, Erik H. 1959. *Identity and the Life Cycle.* New York: International Universities Press.

Fader, Jamie. Forthcoming. *Falling Back: Incarceration and Transitions to Adulthood for Urban Youth.* New Brunswick, NJ: Rutgers University Press.

"Fairhill Neighborhood in Philadelphia, Pennsylvania (PA): 19133, 19134, 19140 Detailed Profile." 2011. Urban Mapping. http://www.city-data.com /neighborhood/Fairhill-Philadelphia-PA.html.

Fisher, Kimberley, Muriel Egerton, Jonathan I. Gershuny, and John P. Robinson. 2007. "Gender Convergence in the American Heritage Time Use Study (AHTUS)." *Social Indicators Research* 82 (1): 1–33.

Fleck, Susan E. 2009. "International Comparisons of Hours Worked: An Assessment of the Statistics." *Monthly Labor Review,* May, 3–31.

Fomby, Paula, and Andrew J. Cherlin. 2007. "Family Instability and Child Well-Being." *American Sociological Review* 72 (2): 181–204.

Fosse, Nathan. 2010. "The Repertoire of Infidelity among Low-Income Men: Doubt, Duty, and Destiny." *Annals of the American Academy of Political and Social Science* 629 (1): 125–43.

Furstenberg, Frank F., Jr. 2001. "The Fading Dream: Prospects for Marriage in the Inner City." In *Problem of the Century: Racial Stratification in the United States,* edited by Elijah Anderson and Douglas Massey, 224–47. New York: Russell Sage Foundation.

Furstenberg, Frank F., Jr., and Andrew Cherlin. 1994. *Divided Families: What Happens to Children When Parents Part.* Cambridge, MA: Harvard University Press.

Furstenberg, Frank F., Jr., Kay E. Sherwood, and Mercer L. Sullivan. 1992. *Caring and Paying: What Fathers and Mothers Say about Child Support.* New York: Manpower Demonstration Research Corporation.

Gans, Herbert. (1962) 1982. *The Urban Villagers: Group and Class in the Lives of Italian Americans.* New York: Free Press.

Gerson, Kathleen. 1993. *No Man's Land: Men's Changing Commitments to Family and Work.* New York: Basic Books.

Gibson, Christina, Kathryn Edin, and Sara McLanahan. 2005. "High Hopes but Even Higher Expectations: A Qualitative and Quantitative Analysis of the Marriage Plans of Unmarried Couples Who Are New Parents." *Journal of Marriage and Family* 67 (5): 1301–12.

Gibson-Davis, Christina M. 2007. "Expectations and the Economic Bar to Marriage among Low-Income Couples." In England and Edin 2009, 84–103.

———. 2009. "Money, Marriage, and Children: Testing the Financial Expectations and Family Formation Theory." *Journal of Marriage and Family* 71 (1): 146–60.

Giddens, Anthony. 1993. *The Transformation of Intimacy: Sexuality, Love, and Eroticism in American Society.* Palo Alto: Stanford University Press.

Gillette, Howard. 2005. *Camden after the Fall: Decline and Renewal in a Post-industrial City.* Philadelphia: University of Pennsylvania Press.

Glenn, Norval, and Elizabeth Marquardt. 2001. "Hooking Up, Hanging Out, and Hoping for Mr. Right: College Women on Dating and Mating Today." New York: Institute for American Values.

Goldin, Claudia, and Lawrence F. Katz. 2002. "The Power of the Pill: Oral Contraceptives and Women's Career and Marriage Decisions." *Journal of Political Economy* 110 (4): 730–70.

Gottfredson, Michael R., and Travis Hirschi. 1990. *A General Theory of Crime.* Palo Alto: Stanford University Press.

Graefe, Deborah Roempke, and Daniel T. Lichter. 2008. "Marriage Patterns among Unwed Mothers: Before and After PRWORA." *Journal of Policy Analysis and Management* 27 (3): 479–97.

Grall, Timothy. 2009. "Custodial Mothers and Fathers and Their Child Support: 2007." *Current Population Reports.* http://www.census.gov/hhes/www/childsupport/chldsu07.pdf.

Greenstone, Michael, and Adam Looney. 2012. "The Marriage Gap: The Impact of Economic and Technological Change on Marriage Rates." Brookings Institution. February 3. http://www.brookings.edu/opinions/2012/0203_jobs_greenstone_looney.aspx.

Griswold, Robert L. 1993. *Fatherhood in America: A History.* New York: Basic Books.

Hamer, Jennifer. 2001. *What It Means to Be Daddy: Fatherhood for Black Men Living Away from Their Children.* New York: Columbia University Press.

Hamilton, Laura, and Elizabeth A. Armstrong. 2009. "Gendered Sexuality in Early Adulthood: Double Binds and Flawed Options." *Gender and Society* 23 (5): 589–616.

Harding, David J. 2009. "Violence, Older Peers, and the Socialization of Adolescent Boys in Disadvantaged Neighborhoods." *American Sociological Review* 74 (3): 445–64.

Harknett, Kristen, and Jean Tansey Knab. 2007. "More Kin, Less Support: Multipartnered Fertility and Kin Support among New Mothers." *Journal of Marriage and Family* 69 (1): 237–53.

Hawkins, Alan J., and Rob Palkovitz. 1999. "Beyond Ticks and Clicks: The Need for More Diverse and Broader Conceptualizations and Measures of Father Involvement." *Journal of Men's Studies* 8 (1): 11–32.

Hill, Heather. 2007. "Steppin' Out: Infidelity and Sexual Jealousy among Unmarried Parents." In England and Edin 2009, 104–32.

Hirschi, Travis. 1969. *Causes of Delinquency.* Berkeley: University of California Press.

Hofferth, Sandra L., Joseph Pleck, Jeffrey L. Stueve, Suzanne Bianchi, and Liana Sayer. 2002. "The Demography of What Fathers Do." In Tamis-LeMonda and Cabrera 2002, 63–90.

Huang, Chien-Chung. 2006. "Child Support Enforcement and Father Involvement for Children in Never-Married Mother Families." *Fathering* 4 (1): 97–111.

Jarrett, Robin L., Kevin M. Roy, and Linda M. Burton. 2002. "Fathers in the 'Hood: Insight from Qualitative Research on Low-Income African-American Men." In Tamis-LeMonda and Cabrera 2002, 211–48.

Jennings, John Way. 1997. "Two Charged in Slaying of Camden Man." *Philadelphia Inquirer*, March 26.

Jennings, John Way, and Larry Lewis. 1995. "As Fire Killed, Suspect Watched, Officials Say." *Philadelphia Inquirer*, March 31.

Jennings, John Way, and Monica Rhor. 1996. "In Camden, 1995 Was Deadly from Beginning to End." *Philadelphia Inquirer*, January 2.

John-Hall, Annette. 1998. "Good Attendance Has Rewards." *Philadelphia Inquirer*, June 13.

Johnson, Earl S., Ann Levine, and Fred C. Doolittle. 1999. *Father's Fair Share: Helping Poor Men Manage Child Support and Fatherhood*. New York: Russell Sage Foundation.

Johnson, Waldo. 2001. "Young Unwed African American Fathers: Indicators of Their Paternal Involvement." In *Forging Links: African American Children Clinical Developmental Perspectives*, edited by Angela M. Neal-Barnett, Josefina M. Contreras, and Kathryn A. Kerns, 147–74. Westport, CT: Praeger.

———. 2002. "Social Work Strategies for Sustaining Paternal Involvement among Unwed Fathers: Insights from Field Research." *Professional Development: The International Journal of Continuing Social Work Education* 5 (1): 70–83.

Jones, Nikki. 2009. *Between Good and Ghetto: African American Girls and Inner-City Violence*. New Brunswick, NJ: Rutgers University Press.

"The Kensington Neighborhood." 2001. *CityData.com*. http://www.city-data.com/neighborhood/Kensington-Philadelphia-PA.html.

Ladner, Joyce. (1971) 1995. *Tomorrow's Tomorrow: The Black Woman*. 2nd ed. Lincoln, NE: University of Nebraska Press.

Lamb, Michael E. 2010. "How Do Fathers Influence Child Development? Let Me Count the Ways." In *The Role of the Father in Child Development*, 5th ed., edited by Michael E. Lamb, 1–26. Hoboken NJ: Wiley and Sons.

Landsberg, Michele. 1986. "Lifelines Being Hauled in as Economy Drowns the Black Poor." *Globe and Mail*, March 1.

Lawrence, Jill. 2007. "Obama's Views Not Always What Some Expect." *USA Today*, July 10.

Lee, Yun-Suk, and Linda J. Waite. 2005. "Husbands' and Wives' Time Spent on Housework: A Comparison of Measures." *Journal of Marriage and Family* 67 (2): 328–36.

Lepkowski, James M., William D. Mosher, Karen E. Davis, Robert M. Groves, and John Van Hoewyk. 2010. "The 2006–2010 National Survey of Family Growth: Sample Design and Analysis of a Continuous Survey. National Center for Health Statistics. Vital Health Stat 2(150)." *Vital and Health*

*Statistics* 2, no. 150. June. Hyattsville, MD. http://www.cdc.gov/nchs/data/series/sr_02/sr02_150.pdf.

Lerman, Robert I., and Theodora J. Ooms, eds. 1993. *Young Unwed Fathers: Changing Roles and Emerging Policies.* Philadelphia: Temple University Press.

Lerman, Robert, and Elaine Sorensen. 2000. "Father Involvement with Their Nonmarital Children: Patterns, Determinants, and Effects on their Earnings." *Marriage and Family Review* 29 (2–3): 137–58.

Lewin-Bizan, Selva. 2006. "Identifying the Associations between Child Temperament and Father Involvement: Theoretical Considerations and Empirical Evidence." Working Paper 921, Woodrow Wilson School of Public and International Affairs, Bendheim-Thoman Center for Research on Child Wellbeing, Princeton University, NJ. http://ideas.repec.org/p/pri/crcwel/921.html.

Licht, Walter. 1992. *Getting Work: Philadelphia, 1840 to 1950.* Cambridge, MA: Harvard University Press.

———. 2012. "Workshop of the World." *Encyclopedia of Greater Philadelphia.* http://philadelphiaencyclopedia.org/wp-content/uploads/2011/10/Workshop-chart.png.

Lichter, Daniel T., Zhenchao Qian, and Leanna M. Mellott. 2006. "Marriage or Dissolution? Union Transitions among Poor Cohabiting Women." *Demography* 43 (2): 223–40.

Liebow, Elliot. (1967) 2003. *Tally's Corner.* 2nd ed. Lanham, MD: Roman and Littlefield.

"Local Area Unemployment Statistics." 2012. Bureau of Labor Statistics, United States Department of Labor. Accessed October 7. http://www.bls.gov/web/metro/laulrgma.htm.

Madhubuti, Haki R. 1991. *Black Men, Obsolete, Single, Dangerous? The Afrikan American Family in Transition.* Chicago: Third World.

Manning, Wendy D., Peggy C. Giordano, and Monica A. Longmore. 2006. "Hooking Up: The Relationship Contexts of 'Nonrelationship' Sex." *Journal of Adolescent Research* 21 (5): 459–83.

Manning, Wendy D., Pamela J. Smock, and Debarun Majumdar. 2004. "The Relative Stability of Cohabiting and Marital Unions for Children." *Population Research and Policy Review* 23 (3): 135–59.

Martin, Joyce A., Brady E. Hamilton, and Paul D. Sutton. 2010. "Births: Final Data for 2008." *National Vital Statistics Reports* 59 (1): http://www.cdc.gov/nchs/data/nvsr/nvsr59/nvsr59_01_tables.pdf.

Martin, Joyce A., Brady E. Hamilton, and Stephanie J. Ventura. 2011. "Births: Final Data for 2009." *National Vital Statistics Reports* 60 (1). Hyattsville, MD: National Center for Health Statistics.

Martin, Steven P. 2005. "Growing Evidence for a 'Divorce Divide'? Education and Marital Dissolution Rates in the U.S. since 1970." Working Papers Series. New York: Russell Sage Foundation. http://www.russellsage.org /research/reports/steve-martin.

Martinez, Gladys, Casey E. Copen, and Joyce C. Abma. 2011. "Teenagers in the United States: Sexual Activity, Contraceptive Use, and Childbearing, 2006–2010 National Survey of Family Growth." *Vital and Health Statistics*. Series 23, no. 31.

McClain, Lauren Rinelli, and Alfred DeMaris. 2011. "A Better Deal for Cohabiting Fathers? Union Status Differences in Father Involvement." Working Paper WP11-17-FF, Bendheim-Thoman Center for Research on Child Wellbeing, Princeton University, NJ.

McLanahan, Sara. 2011. "Family Instability and Complexity after a Nonmarital Birth: Outcomes for Children in Fragile Families." In England and Carlson 2011, 108–33.

McLanahan, Sara, and Audrey N. Beck. 2010. "Parental Relationships in Fragile Families." *Future of Children* 20 (2): 17–38.

Meyer, Daniel R., Maria Cancian, and Steven T. Cook. 2005. "Multiple-Partner Fertility: Incidence and Implications for Child Support Policy. *Social Service Review* 79 (4): 577–601.

Meyerson, Adam. 1989. "One Hundred Conservative Victories: The Reagan Years." *Policy Review*. Hoover Institution, Stanford University. http://www. hoover.org/publications/policy-review/article/6006.

Mikelson, Kelly S. 2008. "He Said, She Said: Comparing Mother and Father Reports of Father Involvement." *Journal of Marriage and Family* 70 (3): 613–24.

Mincer, Jacob. 1962. "Labor Force Participation of Married Women: A Study of Labor Supply." In *Aspects of Labor Economics: A Conference of the Universities–National Bureau Committee for Economic Research,* edited by H. Lewis Gregg, 63–97. Princeton, NJ: Princeton University Press.

Mincy, Ronald, Irwin Garfinkel, and Lenna Nepomnyaschy. 2005. "In-Hospital Paternity Establishment and Father Involvement in Fragile Families." *Journal of Marriage and Family* 67 (3): 611–26.

Mintz, Steven, and Susan Kellogg. 1988. *Domestic Revolutions: A Social History of American Family Life*. New York: Free Press.

Moore, Mignon R. 2011. *Invisible Families: Gay Identities, Relationships, and Motherhood among Black Women*. Berkeley: University of California Press.

Morris, Martina, and Bruce Western. 1999. "Inequality in Earnings at the Close of the Twentieth Century." *Annual Review of Sociology* 25 (1): 623–57.

Morris, Peter. 2009. "Kensington: For Better or for Worse?" *Philadelphia Neighborhoods*. School of Media and Communication, Temple University. May 19. http://sct.temple.edu/blogs/murl/2009/05/19/for-better-or-for-worse/.

Moynihan, Daniel Patrick. 1965. *The Negro Family: The Case for National Action*. Washington, DC: U.S. Department of Labor. http://www.dol.gov/oasam/programs/history/moynchapter2.htm.

Murray, Charles. 2012. *Coming Apart: The State of White America, 1960–2010*. New York: Crown Forum.

Musick, Kelly. 2012. Unpublished calculations. National Survey of Family Growth. Cornell University, Ithaca, NY.

Neild, Ruth, and Robert Balfanz. 2006. *Unfulfilled Promise: The Dimensions and Characteristics of Philadelphia's Dropout Crisis, 2000–2005*. Baltimore: Center for Social Organization of Schools, Johns Hopkins University. http://www.projectuturn.net/unfulfilled_promise.html.

Neumark, David, and Andrew Postlewaite. 1998. "Relative Income Concerns and the Rise in Married Women's Employment." *Journal of Public Economics* 70 (1): 157–83.

Nock, Steven. 1995. "A Comparison of Marriages to Cohabiting Relationships." *Journal of Family Issues* 16 (1): 53–76.

"On-Time Graduation Rate Is Down Slightly." 2010. *The Notebook: An Independent Voice for Parents, Educators, Students, and Friends of Philadelphia Public Schools* 17 (5): http://www.thenotebook.org/april-2010/102392/time-graduation-rate-down-slightly.

Oppenheimer, Valerie K., Matthijs Kalmijn, and Nelson Lim. 1997. "Men's Career Development and Marriage Timing during a Period of Rising Inequality." *Demography* 34 (3): 311–30.

"Oral Contraceptives: Birth Control Pills." 2003. American Pregnancy Association. http://www.americanpregnancy.org/preventingpregnancy/birthcontrolpills.html.

Osborne, Cynthia, Wendy D. Manning, and Pamela J. Smock. 2007. "Married and Cohabiting Parents' Relationship Stability: A Focus on Race and Ethnicity." *Journal of Marriage and Family* 69 (5): 1345–66.

Osborne, Cynthia, and Sara McLanahan. 2007. "Partnership Instability and Child Well-Being." *Journal of Marriage and Family* 69 (4): 1065–83.

Parke, Ross D. 1996. *Fatherhood*. Cambridge, MA: Harvard University Press.

Parke, Ross, and Armin Brott. 1999. *Throwaway Dads: The Myths and Barriers That Keep Men from Being the Fathers They Want to Be*. Boston, MA: Houghton Mifflin Harcourt.

Philadelphia Neighborhood Information System. 2012. Accessed October 2. http://cml.upenn.edu/nis/.

Philadelphia Neighborhood Information System Crime Base. 2012. Accessed October 2. http://cml.upenn.edu/crimebase/.

Poniewozik, James. 2007. "All-Time 100 TV Shows." Time Entertainment. September 6. http://entertainment.time.com/2007/09/06/the-100-best-tv-shows-of-all-time/#how-i-chose-the-list.

Rainwater, Lee. 1970. *Behind Ghetto Walls: Black Families in a Federal Slum*. Cambridge, MA: Harvard University Press.

Raspberry, William. 1986. "An Absence of Context." *Washington Post*, March 5.

Reed, Joanna. 2007. "Anatomy of the Break-Up: How and Why Do Unmarried Couples with Children Break Up?" In England and Edin 2009, 133–56.

———. 2008. "A Closer Look at Unmarried Parenthood: Relationships, Meanings, Trajectories and Gender." PhD diss., Northwestern University.

Rhor, Monica. 1995a. "Creators Hope to Put It in City Hall, to Be Seen by Those with Power to End Violence." *Philadelphia Inquirer*, May 1.

———. 1995b. "From Youngsters, Solemn Vows to Be Drug Free." *Philadelphia Inquirer*, October 25.

Rodman, Hyman. 1963. "The Lower-Class Value Stretch." *Social Forces* 42 (2): 205–15.

Roy, Kevin M., Nicole Buckmiller, and April McDowell. 2008. "Together but Not 'Together': Trajectories of Relationship Suspension for Low-Income Unmarried Parents. *Family Relations* 57 (2): 198–210.

Ryan, Rebecca M., Ariel Kalil, and Kathleen M. Ziol-Guest. 2008. "Longitudinal Patterns of Nonresident Fathers' Involvement: The Role of Resources and Relations." *Journal of Marriage and Family* 70 (4): 962–77.

Sampson, Robert J., and John H. Laub. 1993. *Crime in the Making: Pathways and Turning Points through Life*. Cambridge, MA: Harvard University Press.

Sampson, Robert J., John H. Laub, and Christopher Wimer. 2006. "Does Marriage Reduce Crime? A Counterfactual Approach to Within-Individual Causal Effects." *Criminology* 44 (3): 465–508.

Shannon, Jacqueline D., Natasha J. Cabrera, Catherine Tamis-LeMonda, and Michael E. Lamb. 2009. "Who Stays and Who Leaves? Father

Accessibility across Children's First Five Years." *Parenting: Science and Practice* 9 (1): 78–100.

Shelley, Kevin C. 2012. "Camden's 'Poorest' Label Is No Surprise: Effects on City's Residents 'Devastating.'" September 22. http://www.courierpostonline.com/apps/pbcs.dll/article?AID=2012309220018.

Sigle-Rushton, Wendy, and Sara McLanahan. 2002a. "For Richer or Poorer? Marriage as Poverty Alleviation in the United States." *Population* 57 (3): 509–26.

———. 2002b. "The Living Arrangements of New Unmarried Mothers." *Demography* 39 (3): 415–33.

Smith, James P., and Michael P. Ward. 1985. "Time-Series Growth in the Female Labor Force." *Journal of Labor Economics* 3 (1): S59–90.

Smock, Pamela J., and Wendy D. Manning. 1997. "Cohabiting Partners' Economic Circumstances and Marriage." *Demography* 34 (3): 331–41.

Smock, Pamela J., Wendy D. Manning, and Meredith Porter. 2005. "'Everything's There Except Money': How Money Shapes Decisions to Marry among Cohabitors." *Journal of Marriage and Family* 67 (3): 680–96.

Snarey, John. 1993. *How Fathers Care for the Next Generation: A Four-Decade Study.* Cambridge, MA: Harvard University Press.

———. 1997. "Forward: The Next Generation of Work on Fathering." In *Generative Fathering: Beyond Deficit Perspectives,* edited by Alan J. Hawkins and David Curtis Dollahite, ix–xii. Thousand Oaks, CA: Sage.

Sorensen, Elaine, and Ariel Hill. 2004. "Single Mothers and Their Child Support Receipt: How Well Is Child Support Enforcement Doing?" *Journal of Human Resources* 39 (1): 135–54.

Stack, Carol. 1974. *All Our Kin: Strategies for Survival in a Black Community.* New York: Basic Books.

"Strawberry Mansion Neighborhood in Philadelphia, Pennsylvania (PA): 19121, 19132, 19130 Detailed Profile." 2011. Urban Mapping. http://www.city-data.com/neighborhood/Strawberry-Mansion-Philadelphia-PA.html.

Tach, Laura, and Kathryn Edin. Forthcoming. "Comparing the Sources of Couple Dissolution among Married and Unmarried Parents." *Demography.*

Tach, Laura, Kathryn Edin, and Sara McLanahan. 2011. "Multiple Partners and Multiple-Partner Fertility in Fragile Families." Working Paper WP11-10-FF. Bendheim-Thoman Center for Research on Child Wellbeing, Princeton University, NJ.

Tach, Laura, Ronald Mincy, and Kathryn Edin. 2010. "Parenting as a 'Package Deal': Relationships, Fertility, and Nonresident Father Involvement among Unmarried Parents." *Demography* 47 (1): 181–204.

Tamis-LeMonda, Catherine S., and Natasha Cabrera, eds. 2002. *Handbook of Father Involvement: Multidisciplinary Perspectives.* Mahwah, NJ: Erlbaum.

Taylor, Paul, Richard Fry, D'Vera Cohn, Wendy Wang, Gabriel Velasco, and Daniel Dockterman. 2010. *Women, Men, and the New Economics of Marriage.* Social and Demographic Trends Report. Philadelphia: Pew Research Center.

Toby, Jackson. 1957. "Social Disorganization and Stake in Conformity: Complementary Factors in the Predatory Behavior of Hoodlums." *Journal of Criminal Law, Criminology, and Police Science* 48 (1): 12–17.

Townsend, Nicholas W. 2002. *The Package Deal: Marriage, Work and Fatherhood in Men's Lives.* Philadelphia: Temple University Press.

U.S. Census Bureau. 2012. "American FactFinder." Accessed October 5. http://factfinder2.census.gov.

U.S. News Education. 2012. "The School District of Philadelphia." Accessed October 2. http://www.usnews.com/education/best-high-schools/pennsylvania/districts/the-school-district-of-philadelphia.

Ventura, Stephanie J., and Christine A. Bachrach. 2000. "Nonmarital Childbearing in the United States, 1940–99." *National Vital Statistics Reports* 40 (16). Hyattsville, MD: National Center for Health Statistics.

Waite, Linda J., and Maggie Gallagher. 2000. *The Case for Marriage: Why Married People Are Happier, Healthier, and Better Off Financially.* New York: Doubleday.

Waller, Maureen. 2002. *My Baby's Father: Unmarried Parents and Paternal Responsibility.* Ithaca, NY: Cornell University Press.

———. 2010. "Viewing Low-Income Fathers' Ties to Families through a Cultural Lens: Insights for Research and Policy." *Annals of the American Academy of Political and Social Science* 629 (1): 102–24.

Watson, Tara, and Sara McLanahan. 2009. "Marriage Meets the Joneses: Relative Income, Identity, and Marital Status." NBER Working Paper 14773, National Bureau of Economic Research, Cambridge, MA.

Weinstein, Neil D. 1980. "Unrealistic Optimism about Future Life Events." *Journal of Personality and Social Psychology* 39 (5): 806–20.

Weiss, Yoram, and Robert J. Willis. 1993. "Transfers among Divorced Couples: Evidence and Interpretation." *Journal of Labor Economics* 11 (3): 629–79.

Wilcox, W. Bradford. 2004. *Soft Patriarchs, New Men: How Christianity Shapes Fathers and Husbands.* Chicago: University of Chicago Press.

———. 2010. *When Marriage Disappears: The New Middle America.* Charlottesville, VA: National Marriage Project, University of Virginia.

Will, George F. 1986. "Voting Rights Won't Fix It." *Washington Post,* January 23.

Winkler, Renee. 2007. "Rioting Deepened Camden's Divisions." *Camden Courier-Post,* February 1. http://courierpostonline.com/125anniversary/camden/html.

Wood, Robert G., Quinn Moore, and Andrew Clarkwest. 2011. *The Building Strong Families Program: BSF's Effects on Couples Who Attended Relationships Skills Sessions; A Special Analysis of 15-month Data.* OPRE Report 2011–17, Mathematica Policy Research, Princeton, NJ.

Yeung, W. Jean, John F. Sandberg, Pamela E. Davis-Kean, and Sandra L. Hofferth. 2001. "Children's Time with Fathers in Intact Families." *Journal of Marriage and Family* 63 (1): 136–54.

Young, Alford A., Jr. 2004. *The Minds of Marginalized Black Men: Making Sense of Mobility, Opportunity, and Future Life Chances.* Princeton, NJ: Princeton University Press.

# INDEX

portrayal of in earlier studies, 210; and psychological resources, 174–78, 209; role of intermediaries in, 171–72; and substance abuse, 168, 176, 183, 208–9; among unmarried fathers, 190, 191; and younger children, 191; variations in, 166–67. *See also* child support

*Flintstones, The,* 82

Fragile Families and Child Wellbeing study, 100, 230–31, 246n18, 247n27, 249n4, 250nn10,11, 256n8

Franklin Institute, 152

Freidan, Betty, 220

Furstenberg, Frank, 86

Gans, Herbert, 210

generativity, 153–55, 255n10. *See also* fatherhood

Gibson-Davis, Christina, 80

Giovanni, 171

Girard College, 193, 196

Golden Slipper Summer Camp, 33–34

Goode, Wilson, 38, 131

Great Migration, 9, 46

Green, Andre, 46–50, 53, 60, 64, 69, 170, 172, 203, 212, 221

Griswold, Robert L., 219

Hamer, Jennifer, 129

Hill, 61

Hill, Sonny, 193

Hirschi, Travis, 89, 252n19. *See also* control theory

Hispanics: and birth outside of marriage, 4, 13

Holmes, Marty, 117, 172, 178, 182–86, 190, 191, 200

*Honeymooners, The,* 82

Houtzdale Prison, 21–22

incarceration, 133, 134; fathers' involvement and, 168, 176, 182, 184, 188

Independence Park, 140, 152

infidelity. *See* sexual infidelity

Inner City Missions, 26

Jefferson Hospital, 155

Jenkins, Amin, 19–24, 31, 32, 42, 43–44, 52, 64, 143, 178, 186, 191, 202, 203, 213, 217, 230

J.J., 148

Job Corps, 57, 78, 79, 161

Joe, 142

Johnson, Lyndon, 4

Jones, Byron, 33–37, 41, 43, 44, 51, 62, 217

Jones, Dave, 121–29, 217

Jones, Lacey, 59–60, 110, 111, 112, 115, 118, 172–73, 178, 187, 191, 222

Kefalas, Maria, 24, 63, 81, 101, 211, 218, 219, 221

Kensington High School, 28, 194, 245n11

Kramden, Ralph, 82

*Kramer vs. Kramer,* 180

Ku Klux Klan, 3

LaBelle, Patti, 131

Larry, 141

Laub, John H., 89

Lavelle, 87–89, 102, 145

*Leave It to Beaver,* 109, 110, 206

Lee, 94–95, 96

Lerman, Robert, 190, 191, 200, 210, 231, 258n11

Lewinski, Peter, 139–40, 143, 200

Liebow, Elliot, 86, 115, 210–11, 251n6, 252n24, 255n8

Mallory, Robert ("Bear"), 70–78, 86, 204, 205, 221

marriage: barriers to, 287; cultural redefinition of, 218–19; men's attitudes toward, 36, 90–98, 205, 225, 253n31; men's income and, 94–95; "shotgun," 40, 203; social status and, 95; women's attitudes toward, 219, 258n16. *See also* couple relationship

Mary Mother of Peace Catholic School, 38

men's circumstances and, 56–58, 64; men's reactions to, 46–56, 62–65, 67–69, 73, 132–33, 139, 201, 203, 235, 248n1; planning of, 29, 32, 53–56, 229, 235, 249n5; "semi-planned," 53, 54–55, 62. *See also* contraception; paternity

Purvis, Robert, 38

racial conflict, 11, 12, 21, 25, 38, 39

Rainwater, Lee, 210

Ralph Rizzo Hockey Rink, 121

RCA Victor, 10

Reagan, Ronald, 5

religion, 211

research methods, 6, 7, 242n19; interviewing, 16, 244n39; recruitment of sample, 14–17; sample characteristics, 243nn36,37

Roger, 141

Roman Catholic High School, 39

Rose, Jabir, 110, 111, 112–15, 168

Roxborough High School, 39

Saint Anne Catholic Church, 27

Saint Anne Catholic School, 156

Saint Francis Inn soup kitchen, 26

Salvation Army, 9, 135, 138, 152

Sam, 150

Sampson, Robert J., 89

selective fathering, 191–92, 200, 226, 262n44. *See also* father's involvement

Self, 59, 78–79

serial fathering, 187–89, 200, 209–10, 226, 262n44. *See also* multiple partner fertility

Sesame Place, 152

*Sesame Street*, 140, 143, 152

sexual infidelity, 29, 30, 31, 36, 42, 60, 100–101, 195; men's attitudes toward, 91–93. *See also* women: men's mistrust of

single-parent families, study of, 5

Smalls, Montay, 225

social fatherhood, 169–70, 193–97

Sonny Hill Community Involvement League, 193, 194, 196

Sorensen, Elaine, 190, 191, 200, 210, 231, 258n11

substance abuse, 157–58, 188; father's involvement and, 168, 176, 183, 208–9

suburbanization, 10, 11

Sulzberger Middle School, 34

Tacony Park, 155

*Tally's Corner* (Liebow), 211

Tasker Homes housing project, 21, 22, 42, 182

Tastycake, 160

Taylor, Frederick Winslow, 160

Temple University, 79

Terrell, 57–58

Tony, 143

University City High School, 78

unmarried fathers: lack of research on, 5; public perceptions of, 5, 215; and race, 12, 13, 215; rhetoric about, 1–4

unmarried mothers, 16; importance of children to, 76, 81, 211; men's expectations of, 221; study of, 5. *See also* Edin, Kathryn; Kefalas, Maria

*Urban Villagers* (Gans), 210

*Vanishing Family, The*, 2–4, 241n5, 260n16. *See also* Moyers, Bill

Vaux High School, 193

visitation rights, 157, 214, 215, 254n1

Wake Forest University, 194

Waller, Maureen, 129, 151

Weber, Ritchie, 155–60, 165, 166, 167, 169, 170–71, 172, 173, 174, 175, 177, 180, 209, 228

welfare reform, 5

West Philadelphia High School, 34, 35, 57

whites, 244; and birth outside of marriage, 4, 12–13; population of in Elmwood Park, 38; population of in Kensington, 25; reaction to pregnancy, 229; in study group, 15

Will, George, 3, 204
William (African American father), 54
William (white father), 61
William (white father, Kensington), 97
Williams, David, 41–43, 168, 187, 191, 200, 212
Williams, Ernest, 97–98, 131–39, 144, 146, 151, 152, 205, 207, 208, 223

Williams, Jeff, 83–84, 85, 212
Wilson Park housing project, 42
women: men's attitudes toward, 251n15; men's mistrust of, 28, 50, 83–85, 95, 111–12, 169, 204, 205, 253n30, 258n16
Wyeth, Andrew, 132